OBAMA AND THE BIRACIAL FACTOR

The Battle for a New American Majority

Edited by Andrew J. Jolivette

First published in Great Britain in 2012 by

The Policy Press
University of Bristol
Fourth Floor
Beacon House
Queen's Road
Bristol BS8 1QU
UK

t: +44 (0)117 331 4054
f: +44 (0)117 331 4093
tpp-info@bristol.ac.uk
www.policypress.co.uk

North American office:
The Policy Press
c/o The University of Chicago Press
1427 East 60th Street
Chicago, IL 60637, USA
t: +1 773 702 7700
f: +1 773 702 9756
sales@press.uchicago.edu
www.press.uchicago.edu

British Library Cataloguing in Publication Data
A catalogue record for this book is available from the British Library.

Library of Congress Cataloging-in-Publication Data
A catalog record for this book has been requested.

ISBN 978 1 44730 100 4 paperback
ISBN 978 1 44730 101 1 hardcover

The right of Andrew J. Jolivette to be identified as editor of this work has been
asserted by him in accordance with the Copyright, Designs and Patents Act 1988.

Cover design by The Policy Press.
Front cover: image kindly supplied by www.alamy.com
Printed and bound in Great Britain by Hobbs, Southampton.
The Policy Press uses environmentally responsible print partners.

Dedicated to President Obama's parents,
Stanley Ann Dunham and Barack H. Obama Sr.,
and to the millions of multiracial families battling for a new
American majority

For my grandmothers:
Isabella Americus Hicks and Gertie Lee Fontenot

Contents

About the authors

Darryl G. Barthé, Jr. is currently a Ph.D. candidate at the University of Sussex, writing his doctoral dissertation "In-Between the Color Lines: Community, Race, and Identity in Creole New Orleans, 1896–1958." He also holds a Master's degree in history from the University of New Orleans where he wrote his thesis, "New Orleans' Plasterers' Union Local 93: Afro-Creole Identity, Family and Organized Labor, 1898–1954." Through the history of Local 93, Barthé examined the lingering traces of the tripartite racial division left over from the French and Spanish colonial era, and the complex interplay of racial identification, class, and cultural identity in New Orleans in the early twentieth century.

David L. Brunsma, Professor of Sociology at the University of Missouri-Columbia is the author/editor of six books including: *The Leading Rogue State: The U.S. and Human Rights* (with Judith Blau, Alberto Moncada and Catherine Zimmer) (Paradigm Publishing, 2009); *Beyond Black: Biracial Identity in America* (with Kerry Rockquemore) (Sage, 2001); *The Sociology of Katrina: Perspectives on a Modern Catastrophe* (with David Overfelt and Steven Picou) (Rowman and Littlefield, 2007); *Mixed Messages: Multiracial Identities in the "Color-Blind Era"* (Lynne Rienner Publishers, 2006); *Uniforms in Public Schools: A Decade of Research and Debate* (Scarecrow Education, 2005); *The School Uniform Movement and What it Tells Us about American Education: A Symbolic Crusade* (Scarecrow Education, 2004). Brunsma, former interim director of the Black Studies Program at UMC, received his Ph.D. in sociology from Notre Dame in 1998 and specializes in critical race theory, social psychology, sociology of education, and the sociology of culture.

Robert Keith Collins, Assistant Professor of American Indian Studies at San Francisco State University, holds a BA in anthropology from the University of California, Los Angeles, and a BA in Native American studies from the University of California at Berkeley. Using a person-centered ethnographic approach, his research explores American Indian cultural changes and African and Native American interactions in North, Central, and South America. Collins was co-curator of the Smithsonian's, *IndiVisible: African-Native American Lives in the Americas.*

G. Reginald Daniel is Professor of Sociology at the University of California, Santa Barbara, and an affiliated faculty member in the departments of Black Studies, Latin American and Iberian Studies, and Asian American Studies. A leading expert in multiracial studies and race theory, Daniel is the author of three books: *More Than Black? Multiracial Identity and the New Racial Order* (Temple University Press, 2001); *Racial Thinking in the United States: Uncompleted Independence* (with Paul Spickard) (University of Notre Dame Press, 2004); and *Race and Multiraciality in Brazil and the United States: Converging Paths?* (University of Pennsylvania Press, 2006) In 1997, Daniel provided key testimony before the 105th Congress on Racial Categories on the U.S. Census to the Subcommittee on Government Management, Information, and Technology which led to the inclusion of the "two or more races" option in the 2000 U.S. Census.

Wei Ming Dariotis is Assistant Professor of Asian American Studies, with an emphasis on Asians of Mixed Heritage and Asian Pacific American literature, arts, and culture at San Francisco State University. She is the faculty advisor of the Hapa Club at SFSU and she co-founded the San Francisco Chapter of Hapa Issues Forum, a national organization dedicated to Asians of Mixed Heritage. Dariotis has served as a member of the Advisory Boards of Pacific Fusion TV, iPride, Kearny Street Workshop, and on the Board of the Asian American Theater Company. Recent publications include, "Developing a Kin-Aesthetic: Multiraciality and Kinship in Asian and Native North American Literature," in *Mixed Race Literature*, edited by Jonathan Brennan (Stanford University Press, 2002), and "On Growing up Queer and Hapa" in the *Multiracial Child Resource Book*, edited by Maria P.P. Root and Matt Kelley (Mavin Foundation, 2003).

Andrew J. Jolivette (editor) received his Ph.D. in sociology from the University of California, Santa Cruz. He is Associate Professor and chair of American Indian Studies at San Francisco State University. Jolivette is an affiliated faculty member in Race & Resistance Studies and Educational Leadership at San Francisco State University. He is the author of two books, *Cultural Representation in Native America* (AltaMira Press, 2006) and *Louisiana Creoles: Cultural Recovery and Mixed Race Native American Identity* (Lexington Books, 2007). Jolivette is currently working on a new book, *Indian Blood: Mixed Race Native Gay Men, Transgender Women and HIV*. He is a former Ford Foundation postdoctoral fellow and the editor of a special volume of the *American Indian Culture and Research Journal*, "Indigenous Landscapes Post-

Katrina: Beyond Invisibility and Disaster." He is the board president of, and a national speaker with, the Institute for Democratic Education and Culture-Speak Out, the co-chair of the GLBT Historical Society Board and an IHART Fellow at the Indigenous Wellness Research Institute at the University of Washington in Seattle.

Kathleen Odell Korgen is Professor of Sociology at William Paterson University in Wayne, New Jersey. Her publications on multiracial Americans include *Multiracial Americans and Social Class* (Routledge, 2010) and *From Black to Biracial* (Praeger, 1999). Korgen is also the co-author (with Jonathan M. White) of *The Engaged Sociologist* (Pine Forge, 2011) and co-editor (with Jonathan M. White and Shelley White) of *Sociologists in Action* (Pine Forge, 2011).

Rebecca Chiyoko King-O'Riain is a senior lecturer in the department of Sociology at the National University of Ireland, Maynooth. She has published in *Ethnicities, Sociology Compass, Journal of Asian American Studies* and *Amerasia Journal*. Her most recent book is: *Pure Beauty: Judging Race in Japanese American Beauty Pageants* (University of Minnesota Press, 2006).

Zebulon Vance Miletsky is Assistant Professor of Black Studies at the University of Nebraska at Omaha. Miletsky received his Ph.D. in African American studies with a concentration in African American history from the University of Massachusetts-Amherst. Dr. Miletsky recently completed his dissertation entitled "City of Amalgamation: Race, Marriage, Class, and Color in Boston, 1890–1930." Documenting the high number of interracial marriages in Boston during these years in the face of virulent anti-miscegenation forces and the context of the intense political fight to keep interracial marriage legal, the dissertation explores the black response to this assault on the dignity and lives of African Americans. A scholar-activist specializing in urban history, history of Boston, mixed race and biracial identity, and history of miscegenation/interracial marriage, he has published book reviews in *The Journal of African American History* and *The New England Quarterly*.

Justin Ponder is Assistant Professor of English and Ethnic Studies at the University of Wisconsin-Platteville. His research focuses on exploring how multiracial autobiography can inform the politics and social theory of mixed race studies. He is also the author of several articles on mixed race identity, autobiography, anti-miscegenation laws, film, and theology.

Grace J. Yoo is Professor of Asian American Studies at San Francisco State University. Yoo holds a Ph.D. in sociology from the University of California, San Francisco. She is the author of the *Encyclopedia of Asian American Issues Today* (with Edith Wen-Chu Chen) (Heinemann Educational Books, 2009). Professor Yoo is a leading expert in health disparities in minority ethnic communities and specifically within the Korean American population. She is the author of more than two dozen peer-reviewed essays and oral history projects in the fields of public health, ethnic studies, and social justice.

Acknowledgements

Putting together a collection of essays is never an easy task. It takes patience, continuity, and intellectual relevance. The authors of this collection are owed a huge debt of gratitude for their unique, timely, and evocative essays. Students and general audiences alike will find the writing style to be open, accessible, and eye-opening on many levels. I am extremely grateful to my colleagues in the department of American Indian Studies at San Francisco State University. In particular I would like to thank Gabriela Segovia-McGahan, Joanne Barker, Melissa Nelson, Robert Keith Collins, John-Carlos Perea, Clay Dumont, Phil Klasky, and Kathy Wallace for their support throughout the writing process. Kenneth Monteiro, Dean of the College of Ethnic Studies along with Associate Dean, Laureen Chew also provided support in helping to see this book through to completion. I would like to extend my gratitude to the reviewers and editors whose feedback and comments on the anthology proved crucial in reaching this point. The Policy Press team was amazing from beginning to end. I am particularly grateful to Alison Shaw, Laura Vickers, Kathryn King and Laura Greaves. I owe a huge debt of gratitude and appreciation to Ryan Gates and Tasheka Arceneaux for their superb feedback and assistance with ideas for the design of this book. Their feedback and professional assessment went a long way in producing an amazing final product.

Growing up as a mixed race kid isn't easy. Sometimes it can be quite difficult when you're not really sure where you fit in at school and around other members of your own family. I've been quite fortunate over the years to see my family grow and evolve in their thoughts and acceptance of our multiracial background. They continue to support me in my personal and professional work. It is because of my family— both immediate and extended—that I continue to produce academic and community work. I count among my family many friends and colleagues as well. In many ways if it were not for my students at San Francisco State University I'm not sure that this book would have been completed. Their ideas, discussions, and new takes on seemingly "old" issues often made me think more deeply about the relevance of it. It is inspiring to feel the support of so many and it is also an awesome responsibility to know that people are counting on you to produce socially meaningful work. To the folks at Speak Out, the Institute for Democratic Education and Culture (Felicia Gustin, Jean Caiani, and

Joan Miura), many thanks for your support of this work and all that you do to bring progressive voices to high school and college campuses.

I'd like to thank my parents, Kenneth and Annetta Jolivette who continue to be my best teachers when it comes to politics and social justice. Thanks also to my extended family: Amy Sueyoshi, Mary Rose Fernandez, Tanya Santiago, Mayra Castro, Ron Brown, and to the host of friends with mixed race children—this work is also for them. My sister and my brothers have always been there when I needed support and encouragement to pursue my work. They, along with my aunts and uncles and many cousins, were often in the back of my head as I developed this book because of its multiracial focus. Therefore I would be remiss if I did not thank my sister Makeba Jolivette, my brothers, Eric and Derick Adams, Nathan, Charles, and Kevin Jolivette for always having my back when things seemed too difficult to move forward. I love their children dearly.

To Johnasies McGraw, we have shared eight amazing and magical years together. I hope there will be many more to come. To Haruki Eda, your light came at a time when I needed it most. You taught me to live, laugh, love, and to write again. Thanks to you both for being my inspiration. And to the millions of multiracial families here in the United States and across the world—I hope this book touches on some aspect of your lived experience. It is on your behalf that it is written with love, care, and a sincere hope for a better tomorrow.

Preface

The election of President Barack Obama has set off a chain of reactions from jubilation to rejection. As this book nears its end the nation will soon be preparing for a re-election campaign in 2012. The true test of the efficacy of Obama's new leadership style and the broad based multiracial/interracial coalition that he built will also be tested. Many wonder if Mr. Obama will be able to maintain broad support from independent voters, from Latino/Hispanic voters, from blue collar communities, and even from his liberal base of voters. President Obama has governed, according to some, in the middle. This means that for "liberals" he has been too weak, idealistic, and quick to compromise with Republicans. To conservative opponents he has been too idealistic because of his new policies such as the sweeping overhaul of the healthcare system, the repeal of Don't Ask, Don't Tell military policy, and because of his attempt to end the Bush era tax cuts for the wealthiest Americans. It is difficult, however, to deny that during the first three years of President Obama's term in office that there hasn't been a heightened awareness of his every move, in part because of his ethnic background. This awareness is not just due to the current economic crisis, it is also because he represents at least two firsts. He is not only the first self-identified African American/person of color to be elected President of the United States—but he is also the first biracial person to hold this office. Many political commentators, analysts, and scholars have neglected to provide a more nuanced perspective on the impact of Mr. Obama's mixed racial heritage.

This collection of essays is a response to the many sociological, political, and cultural questions that have yet to be addressed as they relate to the mixed race experience in America and to the election of this nation's first biracial President. The authors of this work seek to not only address race as a factor in the 2008 presidential election, but we each specifically attempt to expose the salience of Mr. Obama's biracial background as a factor in these historic events. Each generation throughout United States' history has left historic moments for proceeding generations. John F. Kennedy's assassination, Martin Luther King's "I Have a Dream" speech, the 9/11 attacks are all examples of moments when U.S. citizens can remember where they were at the precise moment that history was being made. The election of Barack Obama as the 44th President is another such moment. Here in Oakland, California, where I live, shouts of joy could be heard from the street for miles. As I ventured outside my door people were everywhere celebrating the moment and for weeks following November 4 2008 it seemed as though everyone was friendlier, happier, and much more hopeful about the future.

Obama and the Biracial Factor: The Battle for a New American Majority examines both the idealism and the pragmatism that has taken place as a result of our history-making moment. That so many rural, independent, white, middle- and upper-class Americans along with people of color and LGBT activists launched Mr. Obama into White House is no small feat. Many still wonder if, had he not been biracial, would his nomination have even been possible. Yet others contend that it is a sign that we have finally achieved Dr. King's dream of racial equality. It is our hope that readers of this collective work will use these essays as a tool to analyze, interpret, and assess more critically the validity of both of these arguments. Leaders, as the saying goes, are made not born (Vince Lombardi). Barack Obama was made a leader not just through his own ambition and hard work, but ultimately by the power of the people. Time will tell if his goal of a post-Reagan era American majority will be long-lasting. Time will tell what role race, and mixed race specifically, play in his ability to achieve success. For the sake of our nation and for our world let's all hope and work for the best.

Part I

The biracial factor in America

CHAPTER ONE

Obama and the biracial factor: an introduction

Andrew J. Jolivette

Roots of racialization, structuralism, and power in the United States

The United States has a long history of racial, ethnic, and economic competition for resources, political power, and socio-cultural capital. Since first contact with the indigenous peoples in the United States there has been a structural system used through political and military mechanisms to control, define, and articulate a socially constructed racial classification system. While most social scientists have for decades asserted that the notion of race is itself a social construct, most critical race theorists also argue that race remains a salient feature in U.S. society because it is deeply embedded in our social, cultural, political, and legal systems. Race is real because it has actual material consequences on the lives of every person living in the United States. Sociologists Michael Omi and Howard Winant provide a clear definition and theoretical framework for understanding how race and racial projects structure race relations, economic conditions, political arrangements, and access to power.

> We define *racial formation* as the sociohistorical process by which racial categories are created, inhabited, transformed, and destroyed. Our attempt to elaborate a theory of racial formation will proceed in two steps. First, we argue that racial formation is a process of historically situated *projects* in which human bodies and social structures are represented and organized. Next we link racial formation to the evolution of hegemony, the way in which society is organized and ruled. Such an approach, we believe, can facilitate understanding of a whole range of contemporary controversies and dilemmas involving race, including the nature of racism, the relationship of race to other forms of

differences, and the dilemmas of racial identity today. (Omi and Winant, 1994)

Omi and Winant's articulation of racial formation continues to be important to our understanding of group relationships in the United States. One of the most significant changes, though, since the publication of this groundbreaking work is the growth of the multiracial population in the United States and across the world. The other significant shift in racial representation is that a person of color, of mixed ethnic heritage, a black man was elected President of the United States. These changes lead us into asking the question whether the theory of racial formation as asserted by Omi and Winant still remains applicable today? I would argue that not only is this theory still viable, it is perhaps even more salient when we add the notion of what I term *mixed race hegemony* to the concept of racial projects and the practice of neoliberalism so carefully delineated by Omi and Winant in *Racial Formation in the United States*.

Mixed race hegemony, I argue, is the assertion by neoliberals, ethnocentric nationalists, and by some mixed race people themselves that biracial and multiracial individuals and families will lead to the end of a race-conscious and racially-discriminatory society in the United States. In other words ethnic nationalists believe that multiracial people dilute the resources of people of color and strides that have been made as a result of civil rights while neoliberals articulate an ideology of multiraciality as the next logical stage in a "colorblind" or "post-racial" society. On both sides hegemonic ideologies are used to control the way that people of color and whites understand and respond to the growing population that identifies with being of multiple ethnic backgrounds. This discourse includes how President Obama has been represented and how he has had to respond to issues of race differently than any other president in U.S history.

Mixed race hegemony is also rooted in a long history of academic discourse and theorization about the experience of mixed race people and people of color in general (see Daniel, Chapter Two and Barthé, Chapter Four). Sociologist Robert Park argues that race relations are a function of a long historical process where diverse groups are brought together in complex ways, but that these seemingly new formations are a repeat of previous periods in history.

> Looking at race relations in the long historical process, this modern world which seems destined to bring presently all the diverse and distant peoples of the earth together

4

framework that takes into account the nuances of racial and ethnic ascription used to define Mr. Obama and multiracial people in general.

The campaign and election for the 44th President of the United States unlike any other in history has brought the issues of race, ethnicity, and changing population demographics to the forefront of the U.S. political arena. What many have specifically failed to address are the sociological factors that have given rise to the election of the first self-identified (biracial) African American President. This book examines the ways in which President Obama's biracial identity functioned during his bid for the White House as well as during his first three years in office. The United States is at an important cross-road—where the American majority certainly once dominated by a white racial hierarchy—is now potentially beginning to shift. This shift though is not simply because a person of color was elected to the highest office in the country, some say in the world. This shift is also about Mr. Obama's ability to build a critical mass coalition of supporters that was also a first in U.S. history. Since his election we have witnessed a rise in political backlash, attempts to reinvigorate the culture wars, to dismiss President Obama's legitimacy as a citizen, and the deafening slogan "take our country back" from the socialist, foreign-born dictator. This response is about the "battle" to maintain the status quo of more than two centuries of white supremacy. Today the climate of the country is shifting. People are afraid that as more people of color come into political, social, and economic power that they, too, will seek to create a racial hierarchy that excludes a soon-to-be white minority. This fear can be seen in the response of neoliberal whites and ethnocentric nationalist organizations whereby each sees mixed race identity and the new census category (that allows individuals to check two or more races) as a tool to reform U.S. public policy. At stake is everything from federal funding dollars to hate crimes and anti-discrimination tracking systems. In 2012 all states will be required to track the multiracial population by incorporating the two or more races federal census option onto state and local forms. Any entity receiving federal dollars will be required to count multiracial people. This new federal mandate is causing concerns on college and university campuses and employment agencies alike, because many fear it will diminish the numbers of underrepresented groups of color which would lead to the loss of federal funding in some cases. There is in the election of Barack Obama an opportunity to question the fundamental nature of structural inequality and the role that mixed race identity will play in the changing demographics of the country.

In the late 1980s and early 1990s, some sociologists, political scientists, and ethnic studies scholars argued that the United States might turn toward a South African or Brazilian racial model where a majority population of people of color might be governed and controlled by a white racial minority (Daniel, 1992; Winddance-Twine, 1997). Now with the election of President Barack Obama there is a new turn toward discussions of a supposedly "post racial" America which is inspiring new debates about the future of American race relations. *Obama and the Biracial Factor* examines the role that biracial and multiracial identity might play in these emerging debates across America. This book seeks to understand the impact of President Obama's biracial identity on the election campaign of 2008, on Obama's first three years in office, and what his historic election might mean in the current battle for a new American majority.

As we enter this current age of American politics we must ask ourselves how have new debates and the cultural wars over affirmative action, public education, abortion rights, the Supreme Court, immigration, and national security re-emerged in the form of a backlash by conservative and "liberal-minded" Americans who see the potential for a new racialized political majority that is led by people of color, women, white anti-racists, lesbians and gays, and the post-baby boom generation? As the racial and ethnic demographics of the United States move closer to a non-white majority, *Obama and the Biracial Factor* attempts to answer the question: what can we expect in the battle for a new American majority where a more diverse ethnic, racial, gendered, religious, and class-based coalition continues to grow over the next decade?

Since the election in 2008 of Barack Obama to the presidency of the United States there have been a plethora of books, films, and articles about the role of race in the election of the first person of color to the White House. None of these works, though, delves into the intricacies of Mr. Obama's biracial background and what it means, not only in terms of how the President was elected and is now governing, but what multiraciality may mean in the context of a changing U.S. demographic. *Obama and the Biracial Factor* examines the sociological and political relationship between race, power, and public policy in the United States with an emphasis on public discourse and ethnic representation in the 2008 presidential election. This book brings biracial identity and multiraciality to the forefront of our understanding of racial projects during the first three years of President Obama's term in office. The contributors to this book assert the salience of mixed race identity in U.S. policy and in the media and popular culture on the development, implementation, and interpretation of government policy and ethnic relations in the U.S. and globally. *Obama and the Biracial Factor* is the first book to explore the significance of mixed race identity as a key factor in the election of President Obama. As the first work to assert the influence of biracial and multiracial discourse in U.S. policy it offers foundational analysis and theorization of key new concepts such as mixed race hegemony and critical mixed race pedagogy. This timely work offers a nuanced exploration of the ongoing significance of race in the contemporary political context of the United States with international examples of the relevance of Mr. Obama's election on U.S. foreign relations and a shifting American electorate. Demographic issues are explained as they relate to gender, race, class, and religion. *Obama and the Biracial Factor* speaks to a wide array of academic disciplines ranging from political science and public policy to sociology and ethnic studies. Scholars, researchers, undergraduate and graduate students as well as community organizers and general audiences interested in issues of equity, social justice, cross-cultural coalitions and political reform will gain new insights into critical mixed race theory and social class in multiracial contexts and beyond. These new and innovative essays provide a template for rethinking race in a "post-colonial," decolonial, and ever-increasing global context. In articulating new frameworks for thinking about race and multiraciality this work challenges readers to contemplate whether we should strive for a "post-racist" rather than a "post-racial" society. The remainder of this chapter reviews some of the most critical moments of the 2008 election campaign and of Mr. Obama's first term in office, followed by a description of the rest of the chapters in the book.

The Iowa primary: toward a new American majority

On January 3 2008, when then Democratic senator from Illinois, Barack Obama, won the opening Iowa caucus contest among the field of Democratic contenders, many across the country watched in amazement and many wondered how he was able to defeat people with so much more experience. This victory became a watershed moment in the 2008 presidential campaign as Obama proved he was a force to be reckoned with. How did he do it? Many political pundits talked about his enormous grassroots organizing efforts and campaign fundraising, but money alone does not always win campaigns. People have to buy into a message. For the Obama campaign this message was a simple one—hope! However, a subtle aspect of the campaign that was overlooked because of the continuing focus on black–white binary relationships was the way in which Obama himself invoked multiracial discourse and solidarity to build a broad coalition of supporters. He saw what previous Democratic candidates hadn't—the power in speaking to the "opposite" side. As a mixed race man raised by his white grandparents he was likely use to walking between different worlds and seeing points of convergence as strengths. This is not to suggest that being of mixed race is easier or better, rather it suggests a resiliency on the part of mixed race individuals to develop mechanisms to see the world through multiple lenses for their own survival.

Therefore, to answer the question about how Obama won the Iowa caucus, it is important to turn to the words of Barack Obama himself on the night of his historic victory:

> In lines that stretched around schools and churches; in small towns and big cities; you came together as Democrats, Republicans and Independents to stand up and say that we are one nation; we are one people; and our time for change has come. You said the time has come to move beyond the bitterness and pettiness and anger that's consumed Washington; to end the political strategy that's been all about division and instead make it about addition—to build a coalition for change that stretches through Red States and Blue States. Because that's how we'll win in November, and that's how we'll finally meet the challenges that we face as a nation. We are choosing hope over fear. We're choosing unity over division, and sending a powerful message that change is coming to America. (Obama, 2008a)

The key passage here refers to bridging differences and reconciling the opposite sides of one specific identity. In this case the United States is the biracial subject both red and blue, both Republican and Democrat. Much like the biracial Obama there is the need to choose the best instead of the worst about being from what seem like completely opposite identities. The question that mixed race and multiracial Americans have been asking for the past three decades is how to be both or all of their identities at once without sacrificing some aspect of themselves and without being delegitimized. Many have argued that rather than seeing these competing identities as a deficit, mixed race people can embrace these identities and argue for multiple actions and approaches to life as opposed to singular, one-dimensional worldviews. Obama is much more explicit about seeing his own biracial identity as a unique strength and as a form of critical rather than diluted politics. Consider the concluding remarks from the Iowa Caucus speech:

This was the moment when we tore down barriers that
have divided us for too long—when we rallied people of all
parties and ages to a common cause; when we finally gave
Americans who'd never participated in politics a reason to
stand up and to do so. This was the moment when we finally
beat back the politics of fear, and doubt, and cynicism; the
politics where we tear each other down instead of lifting this
country up. This was the moment. Years from now, you'll
look back and you'll say that this was the moment—this was
the place—where America remembered what it means to
hope... Hope—hope—is what led me here today—with a
father from Kenya; a mother from Kansas; and a story that
could only happen in the United States of America. Hope
is the bedrock of this nation; the belief that our destiny
will not be written for us, but by us; by all those men and
women who are not content to settle for the world as it
is; who have the courage to remake the world as it should
be. (Obama, 2008a)

Here the explicit mention of tearing down barriers and the direct
reference to his Kenyan father and white mother from Kansas
demonstrate how Obama was able to center the biracial factor from the
very beginning of his campaign in perhaps subtle, but often engaging
ways. Many argued early on that Mr. Obama was not "black enough"
or that he was perhaps "too black" again here we see a binary instead
of a critical reading of the way in which blackness itself is a diverse set
of identities that cannot be articulated by one person and translated
to all other people of the same background. This victory though still
left many—especially African Americans—doubting whether a person
of color, especially a black man could actually win the Democratic
nomination for President of the United States. This would be an
especially daunting task considering his main rival was a white female
candidate who just happened to be a former first lady married to one
of the most popular Democratic presidents in more than 30 years. The
irony, that President Bill Clinton was once lauded by Nobel and Pulitzer
Prize winning author, Toni Morrison, should not be lost on deaf ears
when we consider the ramifications of Obama versus the Clintons in
2008. In fact according to Morrison, after the infamous Monica Lewinsky
incident President Clinton had all but received his "black card":

African-American men seemed to understand it right away.
Years ago, in the middle of the Whitewater investigation,

one heard the first murmurs: white skin notwithstanding, this is our first black President. Blacker than any actual black person who could ever be elected in our children's lifetime. After all, Clinton displays almost every trope of blackness: single-parent household, born poor, working-class, saxophone-playing, McDonald's-and-junk-food-loving boy from Arkansas. And when virtually all the African-American Clinton appointees began, one by one, to disappear, when the President's body, his privacy, his un-policed sexuality became the focus of the persecution, when he was metaphorically seized and body searched, who could gainsay these black men who knew whereof they spoke? The message was clear "No matter how smart you are, how hard you work, how much coin you earn for us, we will put you in your place or put you out of the place you have somehow, albeit with our permission, achieved. You will be fired from your job, sent away in disgrace, and—who knows?—maybe sentenced and jailed to boot. In short, unless you do as we say (i.e., assimilate at once), your expletives belong to us." (Morrison, 1998)

As critics argued at the time of Morrison's commentary, to equate blackness and black masculinity specifically with promiscuity was in and of itself an act of not only gross generalization, but an act of nihilism and community denigration. Yet some ten years later President Bill Clinton was still there, the symbol of "black savior" in contradistinction to Barack Obama, who despite being born to an actual African/black parent was somehow not a "real" black man because he did not meet the threshold that Americans expect. At the same time because of his "whiteness", his body was a literal transgression to many Americans, both black and white. It is important then to understand the significance of Bill Clinton simultaneously calling out Obama as "just another Jesse Jackson" as an act of both "blackening" and "whitening" the young presidential hopeful.

Bill Clinton, South Carolina, and neoliberal narratives of race

The irony, that Mr. Obama had to not only prove his "blackness" to African Americans but also to white Americans, reveals the ways in which his biracial identity confused black and white America. Following Obama's South Carolina primary victory, former President Clinton thought he could use his popularity with the black community to undermine Barack Obama as another African American candidate that "could not deliver the White House" and therefore could not do anything for African Americans as Clinton had done. Given some of the comments by prominent African Americans like Morrison during the Clinton administration why wouldn't Mr. Clinton believe that his neoliberal narrative of racial paternalism would not be readily accepted by African Americans? This moment proved crucial however, because it not only "established Obama's blackness" with African Americans, it infuriated other long-time Democratic liberals, like Senator Edward Kennedy, who ultimately chose to endorse Obama in part as a result of Clinton's comments.

Since taking office many have argued that President Obama has not done "enough" for people of color. I argue that his approach to race policy is not only intentional but deliberate. Mr. Obama not only during the 2008 campaign but throughout his first two years of office has taken a more "hands-off" approach for two reasons. First, any action seen as a direct benefit to African Americans, Latinos, American Indians, Asian Americans, Arab Americans or LGBT Americans will not only be read as arrogant liberalism and favoritism, but it will weaken his credibility with independent voters. This isn't to say that he does not intend to slowly and institutionally expose racism and white supremacy. In his silence on some issues, he is allowing neoliberal and conservative racism to expose itself. Not unlike other people of color his legitimacy and qualifications for his current job have been thoroughly questioned. Thus the second reason for what seems to be a "hands-off" approach to race is to maintain the diverse new American majority that he built. Mr. Obama understands that "playing the game" involves having a stronger hand and in the end without at least two terms in office he will not be able to have any lasting impact on the status quo. Consider, then, candidate Obama's response to former President Clinton's comments about having the "race-card" played against him by the Obama campaign:

> "So, former President Clinton dismissed my victory in South Carolina as being similar to Jesse Jackson and he is suggesting that somehow I had something to do with it," Obama said laughing, "Ok, well, you better ask him what he meant by that. I have no idea what he meant. These are words that came out of his mouth, not out of mine." (Amos et al, 2008)

Here again, having lived with both working-class white grandparents and having attended Ivy League majority white universities, Obama knew full well that he was up against a very popular former President— and to openly call him a "racist" would have quickly led to his own downfall as a candidate. Instead, Obama (as he is currently doing with the Tea Party and other anti-Obama individuals and groups) allowed Clinton to expose his own deep-seated sense of superiority not only to Obama, but to any African American candidate who would dare to think s/he could do more for "his people" than Clinton himself had done. Clinton in his own words remarked:

> And as the interview concluded, Clinton turned to an associate and said, "I don't think I should take any s—t from anybody on that, do you?"... "No, no, no, that's not what I said," Clinton told a reporter who asked about the radio comments, "You always follow me around and play these little games. And I am not going to play your games today. This is a day about election day, go back and see what the question was and what my answer was. You have mischaracterized it just to get another cheap story to divert the American people from the real urgent issues before us, and I choose not to play your game today."... "I think that they played the race card on me. And we now know, from memos from the campaign and everything that they planned to do it all along," Bill Clinton said in a telephone interview with WHYY's Susan Phillips. "I was stating a fact, and it's still a fact." The former President says the comment was "used out of context and twisted for political purposes by the Obama campaign." Clinton goes on to say that "you have to really go some place to play the race card on me." He lists a number of his accomplishments on behalf of African Americans, inexplicably putting the fact that he has "an office in Harlem" at the top of the list. (Amos et al, 2008)

Two of the former President's comments clearly reveal his neoliberal views of race. He sees himself as a benevolent father when he states, "You have to really go some place to play the race card on me." Then he goes on to list all the "great" things he has done for African Americans including having "an office in Harlem." In his earlier comments he says he shouldn't have to take any "s—t" from anybody apparently because he has done his "good deeds" and unlike an actual African American, or any person of color for that matter, he can go back to "being white" whenever he wants. This would not be the first dust-up over race that Obama would have to navigate, realizing that he had to walk a very thin tightrope. Nowhere did this thin line become more evident than when he had to address comments by his long-time pastor, Jeremiah Wright.

Yes we can: toward a "more perfect" union—New Hampshire and Reverend Wright

Two of the most significant speeches during the 2008 campaign, "Toward a More Perfect Union" also known as the "Rev. Wright" or "Race" speech and the "Yes We Can" post-New Hampshire primary speech elevated Mr. Obama to what some at the time called a "rock star"-like status. Not since Dr. King's "I Have a Dream" speech has there been such a major focus on race relations in this country by a major public figure that captured the attention of so many people. On January 8 2008, following a dramatic victory in Iowa, the Obama campaign (and most political polls) expected a second stinging victory that would secure the Illinois senator's status as party front-runner.

The unexpected result—a nod to Hillary Clinton—while major news because both the polls and the pundits got it wrong, was, looking back, much less significant than the "concession" speech Mr. Obama delivered after this major loss to senator Clinton. This speech, simply now known as "Yes We Can," became the rally cry of a nation of diverse Americans, a symbol of a new type of American majority, where those most often at the margins were placed at the center of the political arena. That Barack Obama believed that this type of coalition was possible is a testament to in part his own biracial background. One of the things many of us from a mixed background learn over time is to move in and out of different spaces. This is because the mixed race person is often not accepted in either of the communities from which they come, so many turn to other ethnic groups where they might "blend in" more. Moving in and out of social, cultural, and political spaces makes it possible, then, to identify more readily with the histories, experiences, and marginal status ascribed to different communities. As the son of an immigrant (another aspect often overlooked in the black–white binary debate), Obama could speak to other immigrants, he could speak to white Americans, black Americans, mixed race Americans.

The "yes we can" narrative seemed to awaken Americans all across the nation who were hearing their voices and the stories of their ancestors echoed for the first time by a candidate for the presidency. Obama became one of "their own" with this speech because his ability to speak to multiple communities in an authentic manner allowed him to become a candidate of the people in much the same way that Robert Kennedy had been in 1968. Time after time marginalized communities throughout U.S. history have been told why they cannot do something, why they should not believe that a better country is possible. These oppressed peoples have experienced a countless number of disappointments and Obama himself was aware that his candidacy presented the potential for yet another disappointing moment. Thus to insulate the new American majority he spoke frequently and directly to this sense of fear and cynicism.

> We have been told we cannot do this by a chorus of cynics who will only grow louder and more dissonant in the weeks to come. We've been asked to pause for a reality check. We've been warned against offering the people of this nation false hope. But in the unlikely story that is America, there has never been anything false about hope. For when we have faced down impossible odds; when we've been told that we're not ready, or that we shouldn't try, or that we can't, generations of Americans have responded with a simple creed that sums up the spirit of a people. Yes we can. (Obama, 2008b)

Speaking to a history of pain and overcoming obstacles allowed Obama to remind his supporters that despite many disappointments people of color, women, and other oppressed people have been able to accomplish many things in U.S. history when people worked together across communities to hold the nation accountable for its transgressions. These stories of triumph alone were not enough. Mr. Obama also demonstrated in this speech the interconnection between these various struggles which allowed people to examine critically what it means to create a grassroots, coalitional approach to social and political organizing. One of the things I discuss with students about the mixed race experience from a critical perspective is that the either/or and right/wrong approaches often taken by Western and other imperial powers does not work for mixed race people. In fact this paradigm does not work for any marginalized group because it requires that someone always "loses" and it suggests that one experience is more valid than another. For example using the word "but" implies an either/or position; so when someone says, "I'm not racist, but they're just different," this person, by using the word "but" is saying that both things cannot be true.

A more basic example of this might be if a friend asks me if I like his/her hair and I say, "Yes, but it would look great if it was short," I am really telling my friend that I don't like his/her hair. Instead, if I were to say, "Yes, and it would look great if it was short," then both things can be true. However when we are talking about much more serious political issues like education, prison incarceration, or health disparities either/or binaries suggest that only those in power can determine the right answer. This is also why people of color and white people, people who are gay and lesbian and heterosexual people, women and men are often unable to understand the experience of the other group because one side is often given more authority, credibility, and institutional power.

Therefore these groups are always already placed in automatic conflict and opposition by placing them as competing forces, where ultimately only one side can "get it right." Obama, as a biracial subject, had to navigate a both/and experience, meaning that, no matter how he is seen racially by society, he is still both black and white and that experience shapes how he lives and sees the world. His ability to translate his own experience as belonging to more than one group speaks to a new experience happening all across this country where individuals live more complicated lives where multiple rather than singular identities have become not only more prevalent, they are also becoming normalized. Obama was clearly aware that he was trying to shift the nation toward a new majority by focusing on both/and unity rather than either/or divisions as they were previously used by both conservatives like Ronald Reagan and neoliberals like Bill Clinton.

> There is something happening when Americans who are young in age and in spirit—who have never before participated in politics—turn out in numbers we've never seen because they know in their hearts that this time must be different. There is something happening when people vote not just for the party they belong to but the hopes they hold in common—that whether we are rich or poor; black or white; Latino or Asian; whether we hail from Iowa or New Hampshire, Nevada or South Carolina, we are ready to take this country in a fundamentally new direction. That is what's happening in America right now. Change is what's happening in America. You can be the new majority who can lead this nation out of a long political darkness—Democrats, Independents and Republicans who are tired of the division and distraction that has clouded

Washington; who know that we can disagree without being disagreeable; who understand that if we mobilize our voices to challenge the money and influence that's stood in our way and challenge ourselves to reach for something better, there's no problem we can't solve—no destiny we cannot fulfill. (Obama, 2008b)

Obama goes on in the next two paragraphs of the speech to begin both of the first sentences with "our new majority" and "our new American majority" to signify that those on the margins could finally believe that they, too, were really Americans. It is no coincidence that during the campaign and after the election of President Obama that countless people of color could be found wearing or flying American flags for the first time in their lives. Beginning with this now historic speech, Obama's campaign and election allowed Americans from diverse and marginalized backgrounds to believe that the United States is also their country, because of the struggles overcome by so many of their ancestors who believe something other than oppression was possible.

It was a creed written into the founding documents that declared the destiny of a nation. Yes we can. It was whispered by slaves and abolitionists as they blazed a trail toward freedom through the darkest of nights. Yes we can. It was sung by immigrants as they struck out from distant shores and pioneers who pushed westward against an unforgiving wilderness. Yes we can. It was the call of workers who organized; women who reached for the ballot; a President who chose the moon as our new frontier; and a King who took us to the mountaintop and pointed the way to the Promised Land. Yes we can to justice and equality. Yes we can to opportunity and prosperity. Yes we can heal this nation. Yes we can repair this world. Yes we can. (Obama, 2008b)

By linking white and black in his closing remarks and including Latino, Asian American, working-class, Democrat, Republican, and independent voters in his earlier remarks, Obama was again invoking the United States as the biracial/multiracial nation, belonging to different regions, ideologies, and histories and yet still being connected. It isn't as easy as it sounds of course and if there is not belief in the possibility of being more than one thing, of being a better, more perfect nation one is left to wonder what the point of all the work is in the end.

That Obama would later be linked to his pastor of 20 years, the Rev. Jeremiah Wright is a reminder that the nation is indeed not perfect, nor is it post-racial. By March of 2008 it had become clear that Barack Obama was now, along with Hillary Clinton, a leading frontrunner for the Democratic presidential nomination. On March 13 2008 a report from "Good Morning America" on ABC showed clips from sermons delivered by Wright who at the time was senior pastor of Trinity United Church of Christ in Chicago. Wright's most "controversial" comments include blaming the United States for the 9/11 attacks and the now infamous video of him saying "God damn America." According to one 2008 ABC report:

> An ABC News review of dozens of Rev. Wright's sermons, offered for sale by the church, found repeated denunciations of the U.S. based on what he described as his reading of the Gospels and the treatment of black Americans. "The government gives them the drugs, builds bigger prisons, passes a three-strike law and then wants us to sing 'God Bless America.' No, no, no, God damn America, that's in the Bible for killing innocent people," he said in a 2003 sermon. "God damn America for treating our citizens as less than human. God damn America for as long as she acts like she is God and she is supreme." In addition to damning America, he told his congregation on the Sunday after Sept. 11, 2001 that the United States had brought on al Qaeda's attacks because of its own terrorism. "We bombed Hiroshima, we bombed Nagasaki, and we nuked far more than the thousands in New York and the Pentagon, and we never batted an eye," Rev. Wright said in a sermon on Sept. 16, 2001. "We have supported state terrorism against the Palestinians and black South Africans, and now we are indignant because the stuff we have done overseas is now brought right back to our own front yards. America's chickens are coming home to roost," he told his congregation. (Ross and El-Buri, 2008)

Many might argue that Wright's comments, depending upon your worldview and experience, were not at all "controversial" but rather they were statements of fact. This is at least true in the case of U.S. bombings in other countries. Political pundits along with Democratic challengers and Republican candidates for the presidency all used the comments to assert that Wright's views were the same views held by Obama. Why else, according to critics, would Obama have remained in such a church for 20 years? We as a nation are still not prepared to hear words like those expressed by Reverend Wright, instead there are ongoing debates about American exceptionalism. Candidate Obama, not unlike President Obama, rather than completely denounce Wright or ignore the reality of some of his comments, decided to deliver what his campaign at the time called "a major speech on race." It was this speech more than any of the others that would be compared to other historic addresses. In his remarks titled, "A More Perfect Union," we again see Obama successfully invoke his biracial heritage to question not just Reverend Wright and his generation, but to question and not ignore the painful past and present reality of individual as well as institutional racism.

> I believe deeply that we cannot solve the challenges of our time unless we solve them together—unless we perfect our union by understanding that we may have different stories, but we hold common hopes; that we may not look the same and we may not have come from the same place, but we all want to move in the same direction—towards a better future for our children and our grandchildren. This belief comes from my unyielding faith in the decency and generosity of the American people. But it also comes from my own American story. I am the son of a black man from Kenya and a white woman from Kansas. I was raised with the help of a white grandfather who survived a Depression to serve in Patton's Army during World War II and a white grandmother who worked on a bomber assembly line at Fort Leavenworth while he was overseas. I've gone to some of the best schools in America and lived in one of the world's poorest nations. I am married to a black American who carries within her the blood of slaves and slave owners—an inheritance we pass on to our two precious daughters. I have brothers, sisters, nieces, nephews, uncles and cousins, of every race and every hue, scattered across three continents, and for as long as I live, I will never forget that in no other country on Earth is my story even possible. It's a story that hasn't made me the most conventional candidate. But it is a story that has seared into my genetic makeup the idea that this nation is more than the sum of its parts—that out of many, we are truly one. (Obama, 2008c)

Perhaps these comments, more than any other delivered by Obama, expressed his sense of connection to multiple worldviews, cultures, and realities. One of the primary contentions of this book is to understand how President Obama's biracial identity contributes to the way that he now governs. There is never really one answer when it comes to identity for people of mixed descent. Many "liberals" have criticized Mr. Obama since taking office for not being stronger on certain issues. What these critics have actually been calling for is another one-sided approach. Whether wrong or right, President Obama has governed true to the way he campaigned. He is trying to actually build a new majority. He, like the nation itself, as a biracial subject is pulled by both sides and he must try to make a new way. In much the same way that candidate Obama told a nation that the "union could be more perfect" the 44th President is still asking for the same thing. However, while this historic speech may have saved his campaign and helped to catapult him into the White House, the fact remains that millions of Americans still don't believe he is a citizen, others still claim he is Muslim. These two claims are important reminders about the work to be done in this country as it relates to issues of oppression and xenophobia.

What's in a name? Barack *Hussein* Obama and anti-Muslim discourse

Shortly after the Reverend Wright controversy in April of 2008 (although the claims had been made earlier) Barack Obama's religious faith was questioned (along with his citizenship status) in ways that the country has not seen since John F. Kennedy was questioned for being a Catholic when he ran for President in 1960. Unlike the 1960s, when there were no computers or 24-hour news cycles, 2008 proved to be a moment when rumors could be turned into "facts." The problem, though, is that most news reporters and political pundits rarely if ever questioned the Islamaphobia present in the question, "Is Obama a Muslim?" Rather than address the inherent discrimination in the question the blogsphere and pundits ran with the sensationalist stories in an effort for ratings rather than take an opportunity to take up serious questions about heighted anti-Arab and anti-Muslim discourse in the U.S. Consider the following comments from blogger Daniel Pipes in April 2008:

> As Barack Obama's candidacy comes under increasing scrutiny, his account of his religious upbringing deserves careful attention for what it tells us about the candidate's

integrity. Obama asserted in December, "I've always been a Christian," and he has adamantly denied ever having been a Muslim. "The only connection I've had to Islam is that my grandfather on my father's side came from that country [Kenya]. But I've never practiced Islam." In February, he claimed: "I have never been a Muslim. … other than my name and the fact that I lived in a populous Muslim country for four years when I was a child [Indonesia, 1967–71] I have very little connection to the Islamic religion.""Always" and "never" leave little room for equivocation. But many biographical facts, culled mainly from the American press, suggest that, when growing up, the Democratic candidate for President both saw himself and was seen as a Muslim. *Obama's Kenyan birth father.* In Islam, religion passes from the father to the child. Barack Hussein Obama, Sr. (1936–1982) was a Muslim who named his boy Barack Hussein Obama, Jr. Only Muslim children are named "Hussein." *Obama's Indonesian family*: His stepfather, Lolo Soetoro, was also a Muslim. In fact, as Obama's half-sister, Maya Soetoro-Ng explained to Jodi Kantor of the *New York Times*: "My whole family was Muslim, and most of the people I knew were Muslim." An Indonesian publication, the *Banjarmasin Post* reports a former classmate, Rony Amir, recalling that "All the relatives of Barry's father were very devout Muslims." (Pipes, 2008)

Pipes, like other "Obama is Muslim" bloggers bases his assessment primarily on the President's name, ancestry, and early childhood. The problem with this discourse is that it first suggests that there is a problem with being Muslim and second that one is "guilty" of being a Muslim by association with other followers of the Islamic faith. Instead Pipes and those who raised similar questions cloaked their Islamaphobia and bigotry by claiming their questions were ultimately about Mr. Obama's integrity and honesty. Not for one minute did Mr. Pipes or others stop to question their own motives about why it mattered so much. In response I can recall thousands of people on the popular social website Facebook changing their last names to "Obama." This act was a reinforcement of the new majority that Mr. Obama was able to build. And while he only subtly (again walking a political tightrope) questioned the Islamaphobia in the questions he was being asked about his faith—he was still able to maintain overwhelming support among Catholics, Jews, and Muslims. Not unlike many biracial people from blended families he has a unique name, upbringing in both Hawai'i and Indonesia, and he has had his identity and "authenticity" called into question. What's in a name? The ability to acknowledge, remember, and make visible one's ancestors and history. There is also the ability to label, oppress, and de-legitimize a person based upon anti-immigrant and Islamaphobic discourse. The strategy of some conservatives and neoliberals using this discourse was missed by most political pundits, however, because they were too focused on just following the controversial story. Underneath all of these questions about his name and religion were alternative motives to get African Americans (primarily Christian in faith) to also question Obama's religion as they had also been asked to question his "blackness." This was not unfamiliar to Obama and will not be unfamiliar to most biracial, mixed race people in the United States. People ask our names and our backgrounds in order to place us in boxes and to either claim or reject us. By ignoring these claims, candidate and now President Obama is saying what a lot of other mixed race people have said for decades—I am who I am, but in the end you will just make me who you want me to be, so why bother asking the question?

You lie: on "post-race" and mixed race representations

The questions about President Obama's name, citizenship, race, and religious faith have not ceased with his inauguration in January 2009. In some cases as anti-Obama groups like the Tea Party have grown, so, too, have the assertions about the legitimacy of his presidency. So for all the claims that he was a post-race race candidate, we have seen over the past two years that, if anything, his election has re-ignited a battle for ideology and control of the "American narrative." One such battle has been waged by a group simply known as, "The Birthers." One of this group's most vociferous proponents Orly Taitz, is arguing that Mr. Obama was born in Kenya and not Hawai'i so is not a naturalized citizen and is therefore an illegitimate president. Ironically, Taitz, a Moldovan American is herself an immigrant who has aspirations for political office. The interesting thing in her case is that while Mr. Obama's mother was a U.S. citizen, neither of Ms. Taitz' parents were born in the United States, nor were they citizens. Like many of the other critics of President Obama, however, it appears that Taitz' disdain is about more than his citizenship status.

Never before has a sitting U.S. President during a speech in the Chamber of Congress been called a liar by a member of the house or the senate. That was until South Carolina Representative Joe Wilson interrupted a speech to both houses of congress by President Obama in September 2009 by shouting, "You Lie!" This situation, while immediately condemned by Democrats and Republicans, along with an apology by Wilson, still leaves an important question: would the same charge have been made if President Obama had two white parents instead of one? Would Mr. Wilson have had the same audacity as Ms. Taitz to question the legitimacy of John McCain (who was actually born in a different country)? These two incidents are important reminders that we are not even close to a post-race nation. Moreover, we should—as mixed race people have been doing for decades—be more concerned with the multiple views, experiences, and communities that have made it possible for this nation to exist. Instead of working toward a post-race, post-identity worldview, we should seek an anti-racist, anti-oppressive, view that acknowledges difference and identity as central components of whom we have been, whom we are now, and what will shape us in the future.

The biracial factor in America

Obama and the Biracial Factor: The Battle for a New American Majority is divided into three parts. The first, "The Biracial Factor in America" examines how race relations in historic and contemporary contexts have been shaped by narratives of biracial and mixed heritage people. There is a specific analysis in this section of President Obama's biracial background and how it contributed to the 2008 campaign and in his first two years in office. In Chapter Two, "Race, Multiraciality, and the Election of Barack Obama: Toward a More Perfect Union?" sociologist G. Reginald Daniel examines Barack Obama's speech, "Toward a More Perfect Union" and uses it as a springboard for looking at the history of African American political candidates in general and Mr. Obama's specific approach to race and politics vis-à-vis multiraciality. In this evocative essay Daniel argues convincingly that Obama fought to be "defined not by race, but by policy positions."

He goes on to examine how whiteness has continued to be re-framed by both conservatives and liberals to call into question once more the significance of race and class as determinants of social and cultural capital.

In Chapter Three, "'A Patchwork Heritage': Multiracial Citation in Barack Obama's *Dreams from My Father,*" Justin Ponder adds to the analysis of multiracial self-representation addressed by G. Reginald Daniel through a close textual analysis of President Obama's autobiography which details his life and his relationship with his father. Ponder carefully examines the claims of mixed race studies scholars who argue about the power of autobiography to reveal important details as they relate to multiracial self-representation. In this essay, Ponder contends that these scholars have forgotten four important aspects as they relate to self-representation: 1) self-representation communicates with others, 2) self-representation requires signs that do not belong to the self, 3) self-representation often relies on stereotypes, and 4) self-representation constructs a racial subject that identifies through stereotypes. Ponder concludes that Obama's autobiography (commissioned to discuss his blackness) was much more about citation than it was about self-representation. In Chapter Four, "Racial Revisionism, Caste Revisited: Whiteness, Blackness and Barack Obama," Darryl Barthé examines the historic and contemporary meanings of the "one drop rule" and how it was utilized by both the media and President Obama's main political rivals during the 2008 campaign. Barthé builds on the work of noted historian George Fredrickson by asserting that the racial caste system, created during the colonial period through Jim Crow segregation, was strategically reinstituted during the 2008 presidential campaign to position Mr. Obama as not only African American (when in fact his African ancestry is first generation and not connected to the African slave trade), but also a "magic negro." Barthé's essay challenges readers to think about the ways in which whiteness is based upon and invested in the maintenance of race, color, and class-based caste hierarchies even with the election of a person of color to the White House.

Beyond black and white identity politics

In the second part of these collected essays, "Beyond Black and White Identity Politics," the authors examine dimensions of Barack Obama's biracial identity and appeal outside the context of black and white polarized politics by inserting an analysis of gender, global representation, and cultural politics. Wei Ming Dariotis and Grace Yoo's essay, "Obama Mamas and Mixed Race: Hoping for 'a More Perfect Union,'" provides unique empirical data about the concerns, motivations, and organizing efforts of mothers who campaigned for President Obama in 2008. This national study addressed four specific aims: 1) to discover the reasons why mothers became supporters of Barack Obama; 2) to identify how mothers involved themselves in the Obama campaign; 3) to gain an understanding how mothers engaged others, including their children, in their support of Obama; and 4) to uncover the concerns of mothers for their children and the hopes they placed in the Obama presidency. Yoo and Dariotis include a diverse sample of women across both age and race who indicated that this was the most that they had ever participated in a presidential campaign.

"The Voices of Mothers" demonstrates that Barack Obama was able to build a strong coalition among a diverse set of population demographics that was indeed shaped by his biracial identity as a unique factor. Rebecca Chiyoko King-O'Riain underscores this in her essay, "Is 'No One as Irish as Barack O'Bama?'" (Chapter Six). King-O'Riain, a senior lecturer in the department of Sociology at the National University of Ireland, Maynooth, uses the popularity of a song produced by the Corrigan Brothers entitled "There's No One as Irish as Barack O'Bama" which received more than 1,000,000 hits on YouTube to ask important questions about how Mr. Obama is perceived racially not only in the U.S. but globally. Her provocative essay attempts to answer the question posed by the Corrigan Brothers' song by arguing that this claim, that Obama is "more Irish" (and white), is a part of the broader phenomena of Obama's flexible racialization. During and since his presidential campaign, debates about what Barack Obama actually "is" racially, King-O'Riain argues, "tell us more about the state of racial thinking in the U.S." She goes on to assert that these debates reveal particular understandings of whiteness and white people's views of "blackness" than it does about any "racial reality that Obama represents as a multiracial man of both Kenyan and Irish ancestry." I would say by extension that people all around the world, from those in Obama, Japan, to those producing Barack Obama beer or naming their children Obama—they are each placing onto Obama whatever identity they see fit precisely because he is mixed race and has cultural connections to Asia (Indonesia specifically), Ireland through his maternal line, Kenya through his paternal line, and to Hawai'i, the state of his birth.

Chapter Seven, "Mixed Race Kin-Aesthetics in the Age of Obama" by Wei Ming Dariotis takes up similar questions as they relate to the politics of self-representation in the arts and during the campaign and presidency of Barack Obama. Dariotis argues that neither Obama nor the mixed heritage artist Li-lan of Chinese and European descent can ever truly be a part of a "post-racial" America because each has lived through and continues to experience both subtle and overt forms of racialization. "Mixed race kin-aesthetics" forces us to consider how family, the public sphere, and ideology intersect to dictate not only how others perceive us, but ultimately how we view ourselves in an increasingly multiracial nation. Dariotis' essay carefully unpacks the nuances of racial signification in her interview with Li-lan about how Mr. Obama's election might shift ideas about race within the context of a changing U.S. population. The final essay of this section, "Mutt

Like Me: Barack Obama and the Mixed Race Experience in Historical Perspective" by Zebulon Vance Miletsky, traces the contested meanings throughout history of terminology for multiracial people and the role that this historical legacy plays in how President Obama is read as African American but still asserts a strategic biracial identity through the use of language, symbols and interactions with the media. Included in Miletsky's analysis are interviews with leading multiracial figures on the influence of multiraciality in U.S. politics with specific analysis of its impact on President Obama's self-identification during and after the 2008 campaign.

The battle for a new American majority

The third and final part of the book takes up the specific challenges of seeing a different racial ideology emerging in the United States and what these challenges might mean for establishing a truly "new" or at least more truly diverse American majority that is represented not just in terms of racial equity, but also based on socioeconomic, cultural, and educational equality. In Chapter Nine, "A Different Kind of Blackness: the Question of Obama's Blackness and Intraracial Variation Among African Americans", Robert Keith Collins asserts that Mr. Obama's biracial identity reopens old conversations about multiracial identity and specifically calls into question ideas about a monolithic "black racial identity." Collins exposes readers to person-centered ethnography in an attempt to demonstrate the complex and diverse variation of identities that exist within what is currently defined as black America. By expanding upon previously-held views of a universal "blackness" Collins is able to provide a basis for rethinking an American majority that is made more diverse, not simply across different racial and ethnic groups, but also from within those groups themselves.

In Chapter Ten, "Avoiding Race or Following the Racial Scripts? Obama and Race in the Recessionary Part of the Colorblind Era," Kathleen Odell Korgen and David L. Brunsma raise consequential questions about the intersections of race, class, and multiracial identity during the current economic crisis facing the United States. Korgen and Brunsma's analysis focuses on the ways in which Obama's upbringing during the "colorblind" or "post-race" era after the Civil Rights movements of the 1950s and 1960s shapes his self-identification on the census as black despite his biracial background. The authors argue that Mr. Obama's lack of emphasis on race embraced by most white Americans who grew up in the era of colorblindness—helps lead to his election and the majority's increased sense of living in a "post-racial" society. They conclude by addressing the ways in which Obama faces a discontented public looking for a scapegoat (particularly racial minorities whom they justly contend are always targeted during economic downturns) and thus he will be less likely to emphasize racial issues. Korgen and Brunsma assert that the fact that Obama made it to the presidency as a black/biracial person is inspiring to many racial minorities (and can open up a sense of possibilities once seen as impossible), but ultimately his racial background combined with a terrible recession and the influence of "colorblind" ideology has led to a lack of direct action on racial issues and has also caused the re-emergence of an emphasis on cultural, rather than structural factors connected to racial inequality.

In the final analysis what *Obama and the Biracial Factor: A Battle for a Bew American Majority* seeks to address is the view that we are in a post-racial, colorblind era where ethnic and racial discourse no longer matter. It is with this goal that the authors raise fundamental questions not only about the continuing significance of race relations in the United States, and the battle for racial and economic equality, but each essay also provides a particular framework for understanding how biracial and mixed race identity played itself out during the 2008 campaign and in the two years that have followed.

In the Conclusion, "Barack Obama and the Rise to Power: Emmett Till Revisited," I explore the symbolic connections between President Obama and 14-year-old Emmett Till who was murdered in 1955 for "whistling at a white woman" while visiting family in Mississippi. I argue that Till and Obama are seen as northerners (both from Chicago) who had the audacity to break the social mores, "values," and unspoken rules of a white supremacist racial order. In 1955 the most important symbol of whiteness that needed to be protected was the white female body. In 2008 that symbol had become the White House. In the 1950s African Americans and other marginalized groups were organizing for equal representation, they were working for change. That more than 55 years have passed since the murder of Till (which many argue was a catalyst for the rapid growth of the Civil Rights Movement) and people of color, women, queer communities, and other marginalized people are still organizing should be an important reminder that ideology is often more potent than law or policy. Indeed Mr. Obama's election to the White House as the 44th President of the United States is significant, an idea that no one would have ever believed 55 years ago, perhaps not even five years ago. And yet, he too, even held up as a symbol of that racial "bridge" between different worlds—like so many of biracial children and families—cannot escape the reality that who were are, who our ancestors are matters in consequential ways. This chapter also provides a framework for critical mixed race pedagogy and explores the efficacy of this approach within national and international contexts of movements for equity and social justice. In the end I argue that if President Obama truly wants to build a new American majority then he will work to shift ideologies and not just policies. He will work to remember those multiple ancestries, struggles, and identities that helped to elevate him to the highest office in the world.

Note

[1] "Latino" is widely used in the U.S. to refer to Latin Americans who reside in the U.S., while "Latin American" typically refers to populations in the Latin America region.

References

Ali, S 2003, *Mixed-Race, Post-Race: Gender, New Ethnicities, and Cultural Practices* Oxford: Berg.

Amos, S, Klein, R and Miller, S 2008, 'Bill Clinton: Obama Played 'Race Card on Me' from ABC News. January 5 2011 (http://blogs.abcnews.com/politicalradar/2008/04/bill-clinton-ob.html).

Back, L and Solomos, J 2000, *Theories of Race and Racism: A Reader.* London: Routledge.

Daniel, G 1992, 'Passers and Pluralists: Subverting the Racial Divide' in *Racially Mixed People in America* edited by Maria PP Root, Thousand Oaks: Sage.

Morrisson, T 1998, 'Clinton as First Black President' in the *New Yorker*, January 5 2011 (http://ontology.buffalo.edu/smith/clinton/morrison.html).

Obama, B 2008a, 'Iowa Caucus Night' speech, January 5.

Obama, B 2008b, 'New Hampshire Concession Speech', January 5 (www.culturekitchen.com/liza/blog/text_barack_obamas_speech_in_new_hampshire).

Obama, B 2008c, 'A More Perfect Union' from the *Huffington Post*, January 5 2011 (www.huffingtonpost.com/2008/03/18/obama-race-speech-read-th_n_92077.html).

Omi, M and Winant, H 1994, *Racial Formation in the United States: From the 1960s to the 1990s.* London: Routledge.

Pipes, D 2008, 'Barack Obama's Muslim Childhood', January 5 2011 (www.danielpipes.org/5544/barack-obamas-muslim-childhood).

Ross, B and El-Buri, R 2008, 'Obama's Pastor: God Damn America, U.S. to Blame for 9/11' from ABC News, January 5 2011 (http://abcnews. go.com/Blotter/DemocraticDebate/story?id=4443788&page=1).

Stonequist, E 1937, *The Marginal Man: A Study in Personality and Culture*, New York: Russell and Russell.

Winddance-Twine, F 1997, *Racism in a Racial Democracy: The Maintenance of White Supremacy in Brazil,* New Jersey: Rutgers.

CHAPTER TWO

Race, multiraciality, and the election of Barack Obama: toward a more perfect union?[1]

G. Reginald Daniel

The rule of hypodescent: some theoretical considerations

The rule of hypodescent is a social code that designates racial group membership of the first-generation offspring of unions between European Americans and Americans of color exclusively based on their background of color. Successive generations of individuals who have European American ancestry combined with a background of color, however, have more flexibility in terms of self-identification (Daniel, 2002, 2012; Lee and Bean, 2011; Root, 1998).[2] The one-drop rule of hypodescent designates as black everyone with any African American ancestry ("one drop of blood") and precludes any choice in self-identification (Davis, 1991).

The dominant European Americans began enforcing rules of hypodescent in the late 1600s as part of anti-miscegenation legislation aimed at prohibiting interracial intimacy, particularly racial intermarriage, as well as defining multiracial offspring as black in attempt to preserve so-called white racial "purity" and white racial privilege. Hypodescent conveniently exempted white landowners (particularly slaveholders) from the legal obligation of passing on inheritance and other benefits of paternity to their multiracial offspring. Most of these progeny originated in coercive sexual relations involving extended concubinage or rape of indentured or slave women of African descent (Davis, 1991; Spickard, 1989).

Colonial codes varied in terms of the ancestral quanta defining blackness. The one-drop rule gained currency as the informal or "commonsense" (Omi and Winant, 1994, p. 106) definition between the seventeenth and nineteenth centuries. It did not become a normative part of the legal apparatus in the United States until the early twentieth century (circa 1915) (Davis, 1991). The rule has supported legal and informal barriers not only to interracial intimacy and racial self-identification but also racial equality in most aspects of social life. At the turn of the twentieth century, this culminated in Jim Crow segregation.

Those proscriptions were officially dismantled beginning in the mid-1950s and culminated in the 1964 Civil Rights Act, the 1965 Voting Rights Act, the 1968 Fair Housing Act, and the 1967 *Loving v. Virginia* decision, which removed the last laws prohibiting interracial marriage. The United States has repudiated notions of racial "purity"that supported the ideology of white supremacy. Rules of hypodescent have been removed from the statutes of all states. Yet according to Lipsitz, European Americans maintain a "possessive investment in whiteness" (Lipsitz, 1998, p. 2), which continues to uphold identities, privileges, and exclusivity that are grounded in hypodescent (Daniel, 2002). This leads to gross inequities along racial lines in terms of education, employment, housing, transportation, etc. These outcomes are not merely the byproducts of benign neglect. They are the accumulation of the purposeful designs of European Americans that assign people of different racial groups to different social spaces (Lipsitz, 2011). Yet the rule of hypodescent has had some unintended consequences for people of color, particularly African Americans. By drawing boundaries that excluded black people from having contact as equals with white people, hypodescent also forged and legitimated group identities that became the basis for mass mobilization against racial inequality. Consequently black people hold on tenaciously to the one-drop rule (Daniel, 2002).

The rule has become what Bourdieu defines as the "doxa" (Bourdieu, 1977, p. 159), that is to say, the sphere of sacred, sacrosanct, or unquestioned social concepts or dogmas that have acquired the force of nature. It is the linchpin of U.S. constructions of whiteness as well as monoracial thinking and its associated advantages that accrue to European Americans as well as groups of color ("monoracial privilege") (Nadal, 2011, p. 43). This mindset is itself reflective of a broader monological paradigm premised on an "either/or" mentality that seeks to erase complexity, multiplicity, and ambiguity (Daniel, 2002; Wilber, 1997). Singularity is the norm in terms of the construction of all categories of difference including race, gender, sexuality, and a host of others, as well as one's stance on critical social issues relating to morality and politics (Colker, 1996; Daniel, 2012).

More specifically, the rule of hypodescent has suppressed a multiracial identity through macroaggressions involving institutions that structure the attitudes and behavior of actors in the political and cultural economy. Johnston and Nadal argue that it has also sustained microaggressions in the sphere of interpersonal relations, where individuals are the perpetrators (Johnston and Nadal, 2010). Whether intentional or unintentional, these discriminatory patterns uphold what they refer to as "monoracism" (Johnston and Nadal, 2010, p. 127). Accordingly, most individuals in the United States never question the one-drop rule's logic, and thus reinforce, if only unwittingly, blackness and whiteness as if they were objective phenomena, as well as mutually exclusive, if not hierarchical categories of experience, with an independent existence of their own (Daniel, 2002).

This chapter seeks to explore several questions: first, to what extent has the U.S. become more willing to bend or break the one-drop rule, as indicated by the election to the nation's highest office the first African-descent American, who is also the multiracial offspring of an African father and European American mother? In other words, to what extent does the election of Obama indicate a decrease in the rigid enforcement of the one-drop rule as the primary factor determining the social location of African-descent Americans? Finally, to what extent is Obama's election emblematic of increasing inclusiveness of African-descent Americans as equals more generally in U.S. society?

Black and more than black: toward a more perfect union

On March 18 2008, at the National Constitution Center in Philadelphia, Pennsylvania, presidential candidate Barack Obama (then-Senator, D-IL) delivered a speech entitled "A More Perfect Union." It will be remembered as one of the nation's most persuasive pieces of oratory on U.S. race relations. Since announcing his candidacy, Obama sought to maintain a "race-neutral" campaign. He was forced to address racial concerns in response to the controversy surrounding Reverend Jeremiah Wright, the pastor of his church in Chicago, Trinity United Church of Christ. In several sermons, Wright made what were perceived to be inflammatory remarks about U.S. race relations and foreign policy (Ross and El-Buri, 2008).

Obama's 30-minute speech was unlike anything one customarily hears from politicians. It was more analogous to a thoughtful history and sociology lesson. Obama made several references to the topic of multiraciality. As previously, he mentioned his interracial parentage, and also pointed out that some commentators questioned whether he is either "too black" or "not black enough." He stated that Michelle Obama is the descendant of slave owners and slaves, a heritage that has been passed on to their two daughters; and finally, Obama acknowledged his large international family which includes individuals scattered across several continents (Obama, 2008). Obama also offered some context for Wright's remarks. He discussed white racism, white privilege, racial inequality, and provided a remarkably nuanced framing of "black anger" and "white resentment" (Obama, 2008).

Obama acknowledged these phenomena as expressions of the racial and class strife that has marred the egalitarian principles set forth in the nation's founding documents. Accordingly, the title and sentiment of his speech were taken from the U.S. Constitution and, by extension, the Bill of Rights, and Declaration of Independence. The speech also called to mind Dr. Martin Luther King, Jr.'s "I Have a Dream" speech at the August 28 1963 March on Washington.[3] King called upon the nation to live out the true meaning of its founding documents and judge individuals by the content of their character rather than by the color of their skin. Obama demonstrated "the transformative ability of oratory to infuse familiar ideas with new meanings" (Carson, 2009).

Obama's Philadelphia address, like his other speeches and writing, was a masterful example of what Frank calls the "rhetoric of consilience" (Frank and McPhail, 2005, p. 571). Accordingly, "understanding results through translation, mediation, and an embrace of different languages, values, and traditions" (Frank and McPhail, 2005, p. 578). Obama juxtaposes the trials and tribulations of non-black people, including white people, with those of black people, but without equating them (Shafer, 2008). He conceptualizes a space where racial groups may share common principles and the "transcendent value" of equity and justice (Frank and McPhail, 2005).[4]

There can be no doubt about the persuasiveness of Obama's dedication to the "transcendent value" of equity and justice. Yet some black public figures, particularly individuals seeking elective office, studiously avoid or minimize the topic of race in order to appeal to a larger white constituency (Sinclair-Chapman and Price, 2008). Steele refers to this tactic as "bargaining" (Steele, 2004, p. 73). Bargaining seeks to disarm race for white people by extending them racial redemption from the injustices inflicted on black people. Bargaining, however, trusts that white people will reciprocate by not holding the bargainers' race against them given the magnanimity of the original gesture. On the other hand, "challenging" (Steele 2004, p. 73), often embodied in the civil rights tradition of leadership, confronts white people with the injustices perpetuated against black people. An expectation is that white people take some ownership of corrective and compensatory measures, legal and otherwise, to help eliminate racial inequality.

Although Obama conveyed respect for the civil rights tradition of leadership, he sought to differentiate himself from it. He provided a compassionate explanation for Reverend Wright's comments without justifying them, and denounced them without rejecting the minister himself (Obama, 2008). Obama eventually severed ties with Wright and his church by virtue of additional controversial assertions he made in an interview on "Bill Moyers Journal" and in speeches at the NAACP in Detroit and National Press Club in Washington, D.C (Neumeister, 2010; Johnson, 2008). Obama also distanced himself from civil rights activists Reverends Jesse Jackson and Al Sharpton.[5] The delicate task of bargaining, apart from Obama's intense campaign schedule, may explain why he declined to appear at Tavis Smiley's "State of the Black Union" symposium in New Orleans in February 2008 (Mitchell, 2008)[6] and the Lorraine Motel in Memphis on the anniversary of Dr. Martin Luther King Jr.'s assassination in April 2008 (MacGillis, 2008).

Obama's skillful deployment of bargaining and consilience is integrally connected to his experience as the son of a white mother from Kansas, the heartland of the United States, and a black father from Kenya, the African homeland of humanity (Obama, 2004a). This has imbued his consciousness with a broader vision and wider-ranging sympathies in forming an identity. Obama stated, "I am rooted in the African American community. But I'm not defined by it. I am comfortable in my racial identity. But that's not all I am" (CBS, *60 Minutes*, 2007). He also stated, "I learned to slip back and forth between my black and white worlds, understanding that each possessed its own language and customs and structures of meaning, convinced that with a bit of translation on my part the two worlds would eventually cohere" (Obama, 2004a, p. 82).

The immediacy of Obama's interracial parentage, along with his transnational experience and rearing outside the continental United States, in Hawaii and Indonesia, by his white mother and her relatives, along with his Indonesian stepfather, enhances his image as the physical embodiment of the principles of inclusiveness and equity. Yet Obama has never said that he *identifies* as multiracial. This was underscored when he checked only the "Black, African American, or Negro" box, rather than multiple boxes, on his 2010 census form (Roberts and Baker 2010). Moreover, to the disappointment, if not chagrin, of MAVIN, one of the nation's multiracial advocacy groups, Obama cautioned about a multiracial identity in conversation with organization representatives who were hoping to capitalize on his multiraciality as part of their documentary film "Chasing Day Break" (Elam 2011). In the media Obama is generally referred to as black or African American, rarely as multiracial or biracial (Obama, 2004a). For all his hybridity, Obama's identity is situated in the black community and extends outward from that location.

This differs from a multiracial identity, which manifests itself "betwixt and between" (Turner, 1969, p. 97) the boundaries of traditional U.S. racial groups. It extends outward from this liminal location depending upon individuals' orientation toward the groups that compose their background (Daniel, 2002). Despite myriad differences in multiracial backgrounds, experiences, and identities, the shared racial liminality based on identification with more than one racial background becomes an integral, fundamental part of the self-conception of multiracial-identified individuals, and a defining component of the multiracial experience (Cornell and Hartmann, 1998). This identity interrogates the "either/or" thinking that underpins U.S. racial formation and seeks to shift to a "both/neither" mentality (Daniel, 2002).

Since the late 1960s, growing numbers of individuals have embraced a multiracial identity. This is related to the dismantling of Jim Crow segregation and implementation of civil rights legislation during the 1950s and 1960s. More specifically, it is attributable to the landmark 1967 decision in *Loving v. Virginia*, which overturned statutes in the remaining sixteen states prohibiting racial intermarriage. Previously, the racial state regarded interracial intimacy as a private rather than public matter. This was part of the state's tactic of deflecting attention away from the contradictions between its espousal of freedom and justice and the empirical realities of Jim Crow segregation, including anti-miscegenation statutes. In so doing, the state constrained the role interracial intimacy could play in transforming the U.S. political and social order (Lubin, 2005; Moran, 2007).

Civil rights activists wanted to breach the divide between the public and private spheres in terms of interracial intimacy. This became a testing ground for both the general public and the racial state, particularly in terms of black and white relations. Interracial intimacy operated at the center of an important debate about the relationship of private matters to the public sphere of civil rights activism. Many activists wanted interracial intimacy to be considered a public matter and a key component of civil rights discourse that could be deployed symbolically to promote equality and social justice. They endeavored to achieve this primarily through popular culture, but also through litigation, thereby exposing the racism rampant in a nation busy trumpeting itself to the rest of the world as the arsenal of democracy (Lubin, 2005; Moran, 2007).

Nevertheless, the *Loving v. Virginia* decision did not derive from the Civil Rights Movement itself, although the changing racial climate engendered by the movement paved the way. It originated in a lawsuit filed by an interracial couple, Richard Loving, who was European American, and his wife Mildred Jeter, who was an African-descent American. They took their case to the Supreme Court, which ruled anti-miscegenation laws unconstitutional. In 1961, when Obama was born, 21 states still maintained anti-miscegenation statutes, the majority of white people disapproved of racial intermarriage (96 per cent according to survey research), and individuals who dared cross the racial divide were considered deviants (Altman and Klinkner, 2006; Rockquemore and Brunsma, 2002). Furthermore, Obama grew up in an era when a multiracial identity was not an option. Yet this identity is more common among the offspring of interracial marriages, including black–white individuals, born in the post-civil rights era. Many individuals display more traditional single-racial identities. Increasing numbers exhibit a multiracial consciousness based on identification with more than one racial background (Binning et al, 2009; Korgen, 1998; Renn, 2004; Rockquemore and Brunsma, 2002; Rockquemore et al, 2009; Wallace, 2001; Wardle, 1987).

Beginning in the late 1970s, this consciousness was reflected in a movement which, among other things, sought to change standards in official racial-data collection that required individuals to identify with only one racial background. By the 2000 census, this movement succeeded in making it possible for individuals to embrace a multiracial identity by checking more than one box in the census race question (DaCosta, 2007; Daniel, 2002; Williams, 2008). This has led many scholars to argue that the one-drop rule has less impact on identity formation of multiracial individuals of partial African descent. Others argue the rule remains an important factor in shaping identities through external imposition as well as self-ascription (Khanna, 2010; Rockquemore and Brunsma, 2002).

Race and whiteness: the politics of inclusion

Questions of racial identity aside, Barack Obama sought to be defined not by race, but policy positions (e.g., jobs, health care, and education, etc.). Yet the media have been replete with references to his candidacy and election as a milestone in the nation's racial history. Indeed, the long struggle for civil rights and racial justice contributed to advances that made possible Obama's nomination and eventual election. That said, Obama's biography stands outside of the most poisonous aspects of the historic black experience—particularly slavery, Jim Crow segregation, and the emergence of urban ghettos. Moreover, Obama's ability to draw on his racial whiteness has enhanced his appeal. He frequently reminded us of his white mother and grandparents who raised him, as well as his white uncle, a World War II veteran. The image of Obama's white relatives sitting in support of him at the 2008 Democratic National Convention is one of the more remarkable moments underscoring his historic significance (Dedman, 2008).

This affirmative connection to whiteness was stressed in African American educator, activist, political commentator, and Democratic Party affiliate Donna Brazile's appeal to white people who might not vote for Obama simply because he is an African-descent American rather than because they disagreed with his political platform. Brazile strategically emphasized that the Harvard-educated Obama is "biracial" and "spent nine months in the womb of a white woman. He was raised for the first eighteen to twenty-one years by his white grandparents. He ain't spent no time in living rooms like I spent my childhood" (*Life at the Edge of the World*, 2008).

African American reporter Ed Gordon stated that "if ever there was an African American man who had that entree to those folks [white voters], it would be Barack Obama. He's half-white, he's Ivy League. He's all the things that white America considers safe" (MSNBC, 2008). Even more dramatic is the testimony of a white canvasser when she was recruiting voters for Obama. She succeeded in getting many ambivalent white people to acknowledge that their hesitation to vote for Obama could be attributable to their racism. Some individuals changed their opinion after she stated, "You know, Barack's mom looked a lot like me. I wish that you would take a closer look at this man and try to see deeper than just his skin color" (SuzeNYC, 2008).

Similarly, Vice President-elect, then-Senator Joseph Biden (D-DE), said Barack Obama is "the first sort of mainstream African American who is articulate and bright and clean and a nice-looking guy. I mean, that's a story-book, man" (Gregory, 2007). Senate Democratic leader Harry Reid stated in a private conversation that Barack Obama should seek—and could win—the White House because he is a "light skinned African-American... with no Negro dialect, unless he wanted to have one" (Heilemann and Halperin, 2010, p. 37). Senators Biden and Reid later apologized for the unintended insensitivity and racist implications of these comments (Associated Press, 2010b).

These statements are harsh reminders that whiteness, either explicitly or implicitly in all its code words, is still the norm against which all else is measured in terms of value in the post-civil rights era. Although the number of black people holding public office has increased dramatically over the years, Hochschild and Weaver point out that darker-skinned individuals are underrepresented compared to their lighter counterparts (Hochschild and Weaver, 2007). Other research indicates that darker-skinned individuals have more punitive relationships with law enforcement as well as with the criminal justice system in terms of sentencing and time served (Price and Gyimah-Brempong, 2006; Viglione et al, forthcoming).

Survey research indicates that educational attainment, occupational opportunities, and family income among black people increases considerably with lighter skin.[7] Researchers do not attribute these advantages to intergenerational benefits passed on to lighter-skinned individuals because of their families' higher educational and socioeconomic status. This stems from the history of previous preferential treatment of individuals who more closely approximate white people in terms of physical appearance or perceived ancestry. Instead, Hughes and Hertel have concluded that skin color operates as a "diffuse status characteristic" (Hughes and Hertel, 1990, p. 1116) although other physical features (e.g., hair texture, eye color, and nose and lip shape) are also important. European Americans, even if only unconsciously, often privilege individuals of color who more closely approximate them in terms of physical appearance or perceived ancestry, believing that they are making impartial decisions based on competence or other criteria.

Keith, Herring and other scholars, by contrast, hold that white people may consciously express a preference for individuals of color who more closely approximate them in terms of physical appearance or perceived ancestry, as well as assumed behavioral and attitudinal characteristics (Keith and Herring, 1991).[8] Indeed, Livingston and Pearce note that apart from "impeccable credentials, demonstrated competence, and tireless diligence, having a non-threatening, disarming appearance—physical, psychological, or behavioral traits that attenuate perceptions of threat by the dominant group"—has been shown to be a plus, if not a necessity, for successful black leaders, and particularly men (Livingston and Pearce, 2009).

Moreover, this has been effective in obscuring the selective nature of integration, in which a few individuals of color—particularly more socioeconomically advantaged individuals—have been allowed to gain access to wealth, power, privilege, and prestige, provided that they do not challenge the racial status quo. This development indicates that the post-civil rights racial order has largely shifted away from white domination. Yet the latter is not absent. Racial differences still serve as the basis of perpetuating social inequalities, notwithstanding the belief that civil rights and other initiatives eradicated ascribed markers such as race. Social inequities are now said to be largely attributable to other factors, class and culture, which are subject to change through effects of merit and achievement. Compensatory measures such as affirmative action are now considered part of a racial spoils system that at worst is a form of "reverse racism" against white people. Even support for the concept of multiculturalism is often believed to intensify and prolong the fixation on race and racial categories, which supposedly impedes the national project of unifying individuals as Americans. These social forces deflect attention away from the fact that the black masses are retained disproportionately in the secondary labor force and among the ranks of the underemployed and unemployed. Pervasive formal exclusion and coercion (or inegalitarian pluralism) (Figure 2.1g) have been replaced with more informal dynamics, which are increasingly juxtaposed with patterns of selective inclusion (or inegalitarian integration) (Figure 2.1b).[9]

The increase in patterns of inegalitarian integration does not preclude the existence of more egalitarian, if considerably less pervasive, patterns of integration based on equality (Figure 2.1a). However, it follows that integration (inclusiveness) would be deeply marked by more inegalitarian dynamics given that the larger social order is still underpinned by racial hierarchy. Drawing on the work of Gramsci, Omi and Winant (1994) encapsulate the selective nature of this form of integration (or assimilation) with the term "hegemony," which creates the illusion of equality while effectively allowing dominant groups to maintain power, control, and hierarchy (Gramsci,1971, p. 263).

This growth of white hegemony, particularly in terms of African-descent Americans, has been accompanied by a decrease in the rigid ascription of the one-drop rule as the primary factor determining their social location. Correspondingly, skin color and other phenotypical features, as well as perceived ancestry, working in combination with attitudinal, behavioral, and socioeconomic attributes has increased as a form of "racial capital" (Daniel, 2002, p. 155; Hunter, 2011, p. 142). One is struck by the number of African American "firsts" in the post-civil rights era who display comparatively more European ancestry in terms of physical appearance. Consider, for example, Thurgood Marshall, the first black Supreme Court Justice (1967); Edward W. Brooke, the first black senator to be elected since Reconstruction (1966); Patricia Harris, the first black woman cabinet member (1976) and ambassador (1965–7); David Dinkins, the first black elected mayor of New York (1990); L. Douglas Wilder, the first black elected governor (1990);

General Colin Powell, the first black Chairman of the Joint Chiefs of Staff (1989–93) and Secretary of State (2001–5), Vanessa Williams, the first black Miss America (1983); Halle Berry, the first black woman to receive an Academy Award for best actress (2002), to mention only a few.

Figure 2.1: Pluralist and integrationist dynamics

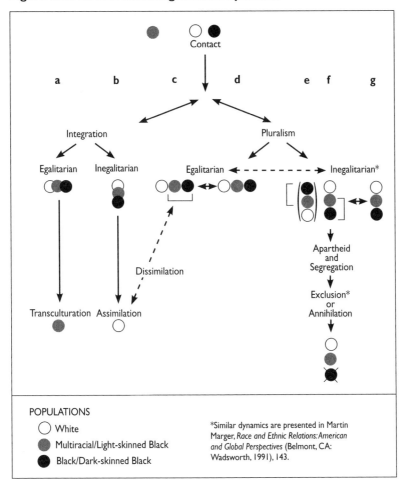

Black, white, and multiracial: a more perfect union

It is impossible to understate Barack Obama's significance as the first African-descent American elected to the nation's highest office. It demonstrates the considerable gains some black people have made since the 1960s. Obama's election has transformed the very aesthetic of the nation's political landscape and instilled a sense of pride and optimism among many black people (Dedman, 2008). If, however, Obama has significance for black people, he has special meaning for the growing population of multiracial-identified individuals (Stuckey, 2008). The 2000 census was the first in U.S. history that allowed individuals to mark more than one race. Multiracial people totaled 7 million, or 2.4 percent of the population (Jones, 2005). The 2010 census data indicate that multiracial people totaled 9 million people, or 2.9 percent of the population. Although multiracial people are still a fraction of the total population, these data indicate a growth rate of about 32 percent since 2000 (Humes et al, 2011).

Obama does not identify as multiracial. Yet his public success, loving extended interracial family, and presentation of himself as an African American who is comfortable acknowledging his multiracial background and experience, indicates how much things have changed since he was born (Dedman, 2008). During his first news conference as President-elect, Obama conveyed this comfort with the throwaway response of "mutts like me," when asked by reporters what types of puppies he would consider getting for his daughters (Fram, 2008). This was a more personalized reference to Obama's own multiraciality than the typically more oblique reference to this phenomenon by mentioning his parents.[10]

Moreover, the increased public attention to ancestry and racial composition are directly attributable to Obama's open discussion of his own multiraciality (Dedman, 2008). For example, Lynne Cheney, in doing research for *Blue Skies, No Fences*, a memoir about growing up in Wyoming, discovered that Obama and then-Vice President Dick Cheney share a seventeenth-century European American male ancestor, which makes them eighth cousins (Associated Press, 2007). Billionaire financier Warren Buffett and Obama are seventh cousins, three times removed. Obama and the newly-elected Republican senator from Massachusetts, Scott Brown, are tenth cousins. Actor Brad Pitt and Obama are ninth cousins. Sarah Palin and Barack Obama are tenth cousins. The President is also tenth cousin (once removed) with Rush Limbaugh. Obama's other distant cousins include former President George W. Bush and his father, George H. W. Bush, Gerald Ford, Lyndon Johnson, Harry S. Truman, James Madison, British Prime Minister Sir Winston Churchill, and Civil War General Robert E. Lee (Johnson, 2010; Jones, 2009; Lavoie, 2008; Rose 2010).

Recently, former professional African American boxer Muhammad Ali visited Ennis, Ireland to celebrate his Irish ancestry. A plaque was unveiled in the city to honor Ali's ancestors, particularly the ancestors and descendants of his great-grandfather, Abe Grady, who immigrated to the United States in the 1860s and married an African American woman (Pogatchnik, 2009). Also, it has been reported that some of Senator John McCain's white male ancestors not only owned slaves but also fathered children with slave women. These individuals have living descendants as do many others who were enslaved on the McCain plantation (Blackmon, 2008). Michelle Obama not only has Native American ancestry, but also her maternal third-great-grandfather was European American (Smolenyak, 2009). This finding not only provides a direct link between Michelle Obama's slave ancestors' journey from servitude and her seat in the Office of the First lady, but her great grandfather also offers another example of the nation's longstanding history of multiraciality (Smolenyak, 2009).

Anyone familiar with U.S. history would not be startled by these revelations. Yet they provide an opportunity not only for increased openness and honesty in discussing multiraciality as an integral part of the nation's history—which has been obscured by several centuries of racism—but also for the United States to embrace itself as a more complex and interconnected racial terrain (Dedman, 2008). A requisite component of this conversation involves acknowledging that the multiracial phenomenon in the United States originated in relationships that were largely consummated more through coercion and violence, as was most likely the case with Michelle Obama's ancestors, than mutual consent and peaceful means, as in the case of Barack Obama's parents.

Indeed, Obama's interracial parentage made it possible for a wide range of individuals to feel comfortable with him. He may be too white for some black people and too black for some white people. Yet individuals have displayed varying responses in terms of how he is viewed racially. Data on these attitudes were collected for Mark Williams by Zogby International in a November 2006 internet poll of 2,155 people. Individuals were told Obama's parents' background, and then were asked to identify Obama's race. Obama was identified as black by 66 percent of African Americans, 9 percent of Latina/o people, 8 percent of white people, and 8 percent of Asian Americans. He was designated with multiracial identifiers by 88 percent of Latina/o people, 80 per cent of white people, 77 percent of Asian Americans, and 34 per cent of African Americans (Williams, 2006).[11]

Obama's multiraciality was instrumental in building an impressive voter coalition. According to election polls, this included 95 per cent of black people and a 2–1 advantage among all other racial groups, including Latina/o people, Asian Americans, and others. Obama carried every age group other than those 65 and older (Mercurio, 2008). Young people of all racial groups born roughly between 1982 and 2003—the "millennial generation" (Winograd and Hais, 2008)—have been among Obama's most ardent supporters. According to figures from the 2008 Current Population Survey, slightly more than half of all "millennials"—56 percent—are European American. The remaining 44 percent are Latina/o (20 percent), African American (15 percent), Asian American (5 percent), multiracial (3 percent), and Native American (1 percent), with a significantly larger share of black and multiracial individuals than previous generations. This population is the most racially diverse cohort in U.S. history and has been exposed to a comparatively more racially diverse society than any previous generations (Tseng, 2008).

That said, Senator McCain led Obama by twelve points among white voters. However, this is hardly the anticipated "Bradley effect"[12] in which white people, who oppose a black politician, mislead pollsters about the candidate for whom they will vote in order to appear racially unbiased (Mercurio, 2008). Obama won decisively in the electoral vote (Obama: 365, McCain: 173). The popular vote was considerably closer (Obama: 66,882,230, McCain: 58,343,671) with Obama winning 53 percent and McCain 46 percent (CNN, 2008). Yet pre-election polls were generally accurate in reflecting voters' preference for Obama as President. The recent economic crisis supplanted Iraq as the dominant campaign issue (MacAskill, 2008). A candidate's perceived ability to handle this turmoil, along with widespread dissatisfaction with the Bush administration, was a deciding factor in the election. These sentiments, apart from questions of race, gave Obama an edge over McCain despite the latter's strength in national security (Feldman, 2008).

Barack Obama is an iconic figure who embodies and at the same time seeks to transcend race and speak to the nation's common destiny (Steele, 2004). He has strategically sought to navigate the treacherous waters of the U.S. racial divide and transform it into a metaphoric bridge that redefines the nation's civic culture and social contract in more inclusive terms (Dedman, 2008). Yet, the Obama phenomenon and its espoused race-neutrality appeals to abstractions and ideals that all too easily obscure or ignore the empirical reality of the historical and contemporary inequities engendered by what Mills refers to as the nation's "racial contract" (Mills, 1997, p. 130).[13] Mills describes the racial contract as an ideological predisposition that informs the beliefs white people have developed about themselves and racialized "others," and the behaviors in which they have engaged as a result of those beliefs. Unlike the social contract idealized in Western philosophy and politics, the racial contract reveals the inequitable ideological presuppositions, policies, and material conditions that have sustained the U.S. racial order for the past five hundred years and continue to underpin contemporary race relations.

Indeed, Obama's presidential campaign and ascent to the nation's highest office has engendered a sea of white anxiety and in the extreme, white rage, whether implicitly or explicitly expressed in racial terms. For example, the foiled plot by white supremacists to assassinate Obama, along with other phenomena during the 2008 election—an Obama monkey doll, Obama waffles that parody Aunt Jemima at the Christian Right Voter Summit, and an effigy of Obama hanging from trees at the University of Kentucky and George Fox University in Oregon—is hardly emblematic of the post-racial society his election supposedly augurs (Associated Press, 2008a; Huckabee, 2008; Stan, 2008). Admittedly these phenomena are reflective of extremist, fringe elements. Yet since the November 4 election, authorities have noticed increased hate group membership, as well as more threatening writings, internet postings, and other activity directed at Obama than with any previous President-elect (Sullivan, 2008).

So-called "birthers" claimed Obama is ineligible to be President because there is supposedly no proof he was born in the United States. Yet Hawaii's health director said in 2008 and 2009 that she had seen and verified Obama's original vital records. Notices in two Honolulu newspapers were published within days of his birth at Kapiolani Maternity and Gynecological Hospital in Honolulu. At Obama's request, state officials eventually made an exception to a 2001 policy that prohibited anyone from obtaining a photocopy of an original birth certificate. They usually release computer-generated versions (Niesse, 2011).

The white racial hysteria that has swept the U.S. since Obama's election is illustrative of the lack of civility endemic to U.S. society, particularly the political arena. It is embodied, for example, in various aspects of the Tea Party Movement and similar developments. Much of these sentiments, however, are framed in supposedly race-neutral protests assailing big government and corporate taxation (Ostroy, 2010). Indeed, a key motivation of the Tea Party's agenda has been an adamant fear of and contempt for Obama with the goal of making certain he is not reelected (Dolan 2010; Burghart and Zeskind 2010; Ostroy 2010). Notwithstanding Obama's keynote address at the 2004 Democratic National Convention, in which he stated there is only one America (Obama, 2004a), the 2008 national conventions provided striking portraits of what were clearly two Americas. The Republican convention was largely a sea of white faces; the Democratic convention was noticeably more diverse (Healy, 2008).

If Obama's election illustrates the gains some African Americans have made since the 1960s, black people overall have higher rates of unemployment, poverty, and incarceration, fewer years of education, shorter life expectancy, and overall less wealth and quality of life. These social indicators were exacerbated by the "Great Recession" from 2007 to 2009, which disproportionately affected black people and Latina/o people in terms of unemployment and foreclosures (Kochhar et al, 2011). The caveats of Obama's race-neutrality in this regard were apparent at the prime time news conference to mark his first 100 days in office as President. A Black Entertainment Television (BET) reporter asked Obama whether targeted programs might be needed to address situations like the depression-level unemployment of black and Latino men in New York City. The President avoided endorsing race-based remedies as a means of dealing with this issue, indicating rather, that the overall success of his "Stimulus Program" will be the rising tide "that will lift all boats" (Daniels, 2009; Ford, 2009).

Similarly, Obama's plan for universal programs such as his American Jobs Act presented on September 8 2011 at a rare joint session of Congress would have measurable benefits for African Americans. Yet criticism of the race-neutral approach has been voiced by Representative Maxine Waters (D-CA) of the Congressional Black Caucus who expressed concern about Obama's persistent refusal to implement initiatives that address the depression level unemployment among African Americans. The legitimacy of addressing the particularistic concern of African Americans is not in question. However, any notion that Obama would specifically target those concerns is based on misplaced expectations (York, 2011).

Obama's race-neutral stance was also previously reflected in his response to Representative Joe Wilson's (R-SC) unprecedented outburst during the President's September 10 2009 speech to Congress in which the congressman shouted "You lie." The shout followed Obama's comment that undocumented immigrants would be ineligible for federal subsidies to buy health insurance. Former President Carter voiced the concerns shared by many Democrats that Wilson's comments, and a considerable amount of opposition to or animosity expressed toward President Obama, is attributable to racial factors, despite the nation's considerable progress toward achieving greater racial equality (Koppelman, 2009; Stein, 2009). Obama acknowledged that individuals may variously view him and his policies through the prism of race. Yet he does not believe Wilson's criticism was racially motivated, but rather, based on differences with his politics or policy (IMDb, 2009). Indeed, beginning with his election campaign, Obama and his advisers have studiously avoided engaging in racial concerns, much less making allegations of racism against Obama, in part as a means of silencing any charges from opponents that he is "playing the race card" (Koppelman, 2009; Stein, 2009). As has been the tradition in other presidential campaigns, Obama's team has typically deployed surrogates to mediate contentious discussions dealing with racial issues (Sinclair-Chapman and Price, 2008).

If Wilson's comment was in any way racially motivated, it need not be indicative of explicit or dominative racism that is more easily verified. It could be reflective of a diffuse and largely unconscious racial animus that can unwittingly lead to a lack of deference and lapse in protocol displayed toward an individual, or negative perceptions about their competence and merit, which are nevertheless thought to be racially impartial. Caruso, Mead, and Balcetis found that individuals tend to view members of their own political party more positively than members of a competing political group, which in turn influences their perceptions of a biracial candidate's skin tone. In three studies, participants rated the representativeness of photographs of a hypothetical (Study 1) or real (Obama: Studies 2 and 3) biracial candidate. The participants were unaware that several of the photographs had been altered to make the candidate's skin tone either lighter or darker than it was in the original photograph. Participants whose partisanship matched that of the candidate they were evaluating consistently rated the lightened photographs as more representative of the candidate than the darkened photographs. Participants whose partisanship did not match that of the candidate showed the opposite pattern. For evaluations of Obama, the extent to which individuals rated lightened photographs as representative of him was positively correlated with their stated voting intentions and reported voting behavior in the 2008 presidential election. This effect persisted when controlling for political ideology and racial attitudes (Caruso et al, 2009).

Even the best-intentioned efforts to eliminate racial inequality will be continually thwarted as long as the nation refuses to confront and eradicate the pathologies of white racism and privilege, however subtle these phenomena may be. Steinhorn and Diggs-Brown argue that this will require a willingness to take collective responsibility for the necessary "social engineering, constant vigilance, government authority, official attention to racial behavior" (Steinhorn and Diggs-Brown, 1999, pp. 222–3) in the pursuit of greater equity in the nation's political, educational, and socioeconomic spheres. These efforts must be accompanied by a more honest assessment of the factors that keep white people in an advantaged position, and communities of color in a disadvantaged one, not to mention a more accurate rendering of the historical, political, social, and cultural forces that put them there in the first place. And, this must be achieved without internalizing any sense of "white guilt" by European Americans and "victimization" by people of color (Steele, 1990). This transformation will necessitate programmatic initiatives in the media and educational system to disabuse the nation of the illusions and falsehoods spawned by four centuries of racism. These initiatives should include a conceptualization of multiraciality as part of the nation's history and should project a national consciousness that views racial backgrounds and identities on a continuum, as being relative rather than absolute, complementary rather than antithetical, with none being superior or inferior to the other.

While multiraciality is a flagship for this alternative consciousness, it should not be viewed as the solution, in and of itself, to racism and racial inequality. Indeed, the impulses behind and implications of the celebration of multiraciality can themselves be mixed, if you will. For example, national racial and cultural identities in Latin America have been officially articulated as hybrid, multiracial, and egalitarian (Figure 2.1a). Yet, they have been hypocritically multiracial ideologies based on what Bonilla-Silva refers to as "colorblind racism" (Bonilla-Silva, 2006, p. 25). This has become a means of erasing racial distinctions and deliberately obscuring subtle hegemonies while deflecting public attention and policy away from tackling continuing racial inequities (Figure 2.1b).

That said, multiraciality, when based on egalitarian premises (e.g., "critical multiraciality"), has the potential to serve not only as an "intellectual weapon" and "theoretical wedge" (Zack, 1994, p. 99) in the pursuit of "colorblind antiracism," but also as a vehicle to interrogate the essentialized conceptualization of biological race and racial categories. This posits a post-racist, if not post-racial, social order where racial distinctions would no longer determine, or at least have considerably less significance in determining, individuals' social location in terms of wealth, power, privilege, and prestige. These distinctions and corresponding identities may serve as the basis for more porous collective subjectivities, which could facilitate building other issue-based coalitions that embrace and racial and ethnic group differences, while working toward an inclusive politics that recognizes the complexity of various types of oppression and how each feeds on the others in order to thrive. This kind of politics would create a constructive and beneficial relationship between the different groups, one marked by mutual respect, interdependence, a balance of power, and a shared commitment to one's community, nation, and the larger human community (and ultimately a more encompassing "human" identity). This would be a necessary component of a genuinely post-racial society (Smith and King, 2009; Iweala, 2008).[14]

Critical multiraciality could further this objective by opening up a long-overdue conversation about humanity's genetic comity, as well as shared ancestral and cultural connections, which have been ignored, obscured, and erased by several hundred years of Eurocentric thought. Indeed, given that humans first evolved in eastern Africa millennia ago, everyone shares this universal heritage that has been bequeathed to the modern world. This also means that everyone in the United States is in some sense an African-descent American, apart from those individuals who are also descendants of the West African Diaspora associated with the Atlantic slave trade from the sixteenth to the nineteenth century.

Between 90,000 and 180,000 years ago, populations from an earlier African Diaspora spread throughout Africa, Asia, Europe, and the Pacific; perhaps as early as 30,000 years ago, but at least as recently as 15,000 years ago, they migrated to the Americas. As they adapted to various environments they evolved into geographical populations displaying differences in various bodily features. Some of the externally visible features—skin color, hair, and facial morphology—are commonly referred to as "racial traits." Although all humans share 99.9 percent of their genes, these physical differences reflect 0.1 percent of some of the differences in genetic information that are transmitted through one's ancestors. So there are populations that, taken as aggregates, exhibit higher incidences of particular genetic and physical traits than do other populations, taken as aggregates.

Nevertheless, the boundaries delineating populations have always been eroded by contact—through migration, trade, and war. This phenomenon was shaped by new ideologies and practices that accompanied European colonial expansion beginning in the sixteenth century. Indeed, the Americas have been the site of unprecedented combinations of indigenous peoples, Africans, and Europeans, and immigrants from across the globe. Yet, racial blending has existed from time immemorial. Therefore, although we recognize certain genetic markers and physical traits as delineating population aggregates as different from one another, in fact, a "multiracial" lineage is the norm rather than the exception, regardless of one's identity. If you trace back 20 generations each individual has 1,048,576 ancestors (Olson, 2006). If we trace back further, the number of ancestors, as well as the myriad possibilities in terms of their "racial" composition, is staggering. This should awaken everyone to the fact that they share the gray liminal space between the extremes of black and white. Moreover, it would serve as a critical part of the foundation upon which to create the more perfect union that has eluded the United States throughout its history.

Notes

[1] An earlier version of this chapter appeared in *The Black Scholar*, vol. 39, no. 1 (Fall/Winter 2009), pp. 51–9.

[2] U.S. attitudes toward the offspring of unions between African Americans and other groups of color (e.g. Native Americans) have varied. More often than not, these individuals have been subject to the one-drop rule.

[3] Some critics such as Houston Baker found Obama's speech less appealing. He stated, "Sen. Obama's 'Race' speech at the National Constitution Center, draped in American flags, was reminiscent of the Parthenon concluding scene of Robert Altman's *Nashville*: a bizarre moment of mimicry, aping Martin Luther King, Jr., while even further distancing himself from the real, economic, religious and political issues so courageously articulated by King from a Birmingham jail. In brief, Obama's speech was a pandering disaster that threw, once again, his pastor under the bus" (Salon, 2008).

[4] Some have argued that this prevents Obama from talking a strong position on some critical issues. For example, they believe that many individuals view bipartisanship as a means of transcending their own prior political identities. For Obama, they argue, it means participating in all political identities, but not being deeply committed to any side except his own (Dowd, 2011).

[5] Sharpton stated that he strategically avoided public appearances with Obama during the election campaign because opponents might use it to discredit him. However, Sharpton has been to the White House at least eight times since Obama took office. Some consider this a cynical ploy by Obama to use Sharpton as a foil to Jackson, embracing what he considers the lesser of two evils (Samuels and Adler, 2010).

[6] Obama asked that his wife Michelle be allowed to speak on his behalf.

[7] Similar trends have been documented among other groups of color (Rondilla and Spickard, 2005; Telles and Murguia, 1990).

[8] Many individuals of color internalize similar biases when judging individuals in their own racial group and other groups of color (Hall, 2003).

[9] Black people and other communities of color also continue to maintain a strong positive sense of identity and differentiation as a collective subjectivity in the form of egalitarian pluralism (Figure 2.1d).

[10] Some individuals viewed this statement as a rearticulation of previous pathological images of multiracials as genetically inferior and as social misfits (Graham, 2008).

[11] Most respondents designated Obama with multiracial identifiers. Small percentages responded with "white," "none of the above," and "not sure." Black people upheld the one-drop rule.

[12] This trend is named after Democratic candidate Tom Bradley, a former black mayor of Los Angeles, who lost the 1982 California gubernatorial election after leading in the polls. Exit polls indicated Bradley leading by a wide margin, and indeed he thought there would be an early election night. However, he lost to Republican candidate George Deukmejian. Subsequently, other black candidates who were comfortably ahead in polls lost or narrowly won the elections. For example, in the 1989 Virginia gubernatorial race, Democrat L. Douglas Wilder, who is African American, won by less than half of 1 percent over Republican candidate Marshall Coleman, a European American. However pre-election exit polls showed Wilder on average with a comfortable 9 percent lead over Coleman. Other elections that have been cited as possible indications of the Bradley effect include the 1983 and 1989 mayoral elections, respectively, in Chicago and New York City (Associated Press, 2008b).

[13] Cornel West reflected this perspective in a recent interview: "Symbolically, black man breaks through makes you want to breakdance…because the hopes that were generated and the call for change, and then we end up with this recycled neo-liberalism. There's no fundamental change at all" (McNally, 2009).

[14] Notwithstanding the lack of consensus on the term "post-racial," MSNBC's Chris Matthews perhaps encapsulated the most common perception of its meaning in his comments about Obama's State of the Union address on January 27 2010. Matthews stated that he "forgot" Obama was black. In other words, it was noteworthy to Matthews that a black president was addressing a room of mostly European Americans and how the issue of race was noticeably absent as compared to the time when he was growing up when racial divisions were pervasive and ever-present (Associated Press, 2010a).

References

Altman, M and Klinkner, PA. (2006) 'Measuring the difference between white voting and polling on interracial marriage,' *Du Bois Review*, vol. 3, no. 2, pp. 299–315.

Associated Press. (2007) 'Lynne Cheney:VP, Obama are eighth cousins,' *MSNBC*, 17 October (www.msnbc.msn.com/id/21340764).

Associated Press. (2008a) 'Monkey doll named for Obama called racist,' *MSNBC*, 14 June (www.msnbc.msn.com/id/25163827).

Associated Press. (2008b) 'What Bradley effect? No hidden bias seen in '08,' *MSNBC*, 7 November (www.msnbc.msn.com/id/27589729/from/ET).

Associated Press. (2010a). 'Chris Matthews on Obama: "I forgot he was black,"' *San Francisco Chronicle*, January 28 (www.sfgate.com/cgi-bin/article.cgi?file=/n/a/2010/01/28/entertainment/e073429S30.DTL).

Associated Press. (2010b) 'Reid: Sorry for "Negro" remark about Obama: Top Democrat says he used "poor choice of words" during 2008 campaign,' *MSNBC*, January 9 (www.msnbc.msn.com/id/34783136/ns/politics-capitol_hill).

Binning, KR, Unzueta, MM, Yuen, JH and Molina, LE. (2009) 'The interpretation of multiracial status and its relation to social engagement and psychological well-being,' *Journal of Social Issues*, vol. 65, no. 1, pp. 35–49.

Blackmon, DA. (2008) 'Two families named McCain: Candidate's kin share a history with descendants of slaves,' *Wall Street Journal*, 17 October (http://online.wsj.com/article/SB122419511761942501.html).

Bonilla-Silva, E. (2006) *Racism without racists: Color-blind racism and the persistence of racial inequality in the United States*, Lanham, MD: Rowman and Littlefield.

Bordieu, P. (1977) *Outline of a theory of practice*, Trans. Richard Nice, New York: Cambridge University Press.

Carson, Clayborne. (2009) 'King, Obama, and the great American dialogue: what would Martin Luther King Jr.—had he been alive today—have thought of our latest President's oratory?,' *American Heritage People*, 25 May (www.americanheritage.com/articles/web/20090525-President-Civil-Rights-Martin-Luther-King-Jr-Barack-Obama-Speech-I-Have-A-Dream.shtml).

Caruso, EM., Mead, Nicole L. and Balcetis, E. (2009) 'Political partisanship influences perception of biracial candidates' skin tone,' *PNAS*, vol. 106, no. 48, pp. 20168–73 (www.pnas.org_cgi_doi_10.1073_pnas.0905362106).

CBS. (2007) 'Candidate Obama's sense of urgency,' *60 Minutes*, CBS (11 February).

CNN. (2008) Election Center 2008, President Full Results (www.cnn.com/ELECTION/2008/results/president/).

Colker, R. (1996) *Hybrid: Bisexuals, multiracials, and other misfits under American law*, New York: New York University Press.

Cornell, S and Hartmann, D. (1998) *Ethnicity and race: making identities in a changing world*, Thousand Oaks, CA: Pine Forge Press.

DaCosta, KM. (2007) *Making multiracials: State, family, and market in the redrawing of the color line*, Palo Alto, CA: Stanford University Press.

Daniel, GR. (2002) *More than black?: Multiracial identity and the new racial order*, Philadelphia, PA: Temple University Press.

Daniel, GR .(2012) *Machado de assis: Multiracial identity and the Brazilian novelist*, University Park, PA: Pennsylvania State University Press.

Daniel, GR. (2006). *Race and multiraciality in Brazil and the United States: Converging paths?*, Pennsylvania State University Press, University Park.

Daniels, R. (2009) *The state of black progress in America* (www.zcommunications.org/zspace/commentaries/3861).

Davis, FJ. (1991) *Who is black? One nation's definition*, University Park, PA: Pennsylvania State University Press.

Dedman, Bill. (2008) 'Historians write 1st draft on Obama victory,' *MSNBC*, 5 November (www.msnbc.msn.com/id/27539416/from/ET).

Dowd, M. (2011) 'Why is he bi? (sigh),' *New York Times*, 25 June (www.nytimes.com/2011/06/26/opinion/sunday/26dowd.html?_r=3&partner=rssnyt&emc=rss).

Elam, M. (2011). *The souls of mixed folk: Race, politics, and aesthetics in the new millennium*, Stanford University Press, CA., Stanford California.

Feldman, S. (2008) 'Why Obama won,' *CBS News*, 5 November (www.cbsnews.com/stories/2008/11/05/politics/main4572555.shtml).

Ford, G. (2009) 'Obama preserves entrenched power, sidesteps racial disparities,' *Black Agenda Report: The journal of African-American Thought and Action*, 6 May (www.blackagendareport.com/?q=content/obama-preserves-entrenched-power-sidesteps-racial-disparities).

Fram, A. (2008) '"Mutts like me" shows Obama's racial comfort,' *MSNBC*, 8 November (www.msnbc.msn.com/id/27606637/).

Frank, DA and McPhail, ML. (2005) 'Barack Obama's address to the 2004 Democratic National Convention: Trauma, compromise, consilience, and the (im)possibility of racial reconciliation,' *Rhetoric and Public Affairs*, vol. 8, no. 4, pp. 571–94.

Graham, S. (2008) 'Dogs are mutts; people are multiracial,' 21 November (www.projectrace.com/fromthedirector/archive/112108_obama_mutt_multiracial.php).

Gramsci, A. (1971) *Selections from the prison notebooks*, Quentin Hoare and G.Nowell Smith (eds), New York: International.

Gregory, D. (2007) 'Sen. Biden apologizes for remarks on Obama,' *MSNBC*, January 31 (www.msnbc.msn.com/id/16911044/).

Hall, R. (ed.) (2003) *Discrimination among oppressed populations*, Lewiston, NY: Edwin Mellen Press.

Healy, P. (2008) 'Two conventions with no shortage of contrasts,' *New York Times*, 3 September (www.nytimes.com/2008/09/04/us/politics/04compare.html).

Heilemann, J and Halperin, M. (2010) *Game change: Obama and the Clintons, McCain and Palin, and the race of a lifetime*, New York: Harper.

Hochschild, JL and Weaver, V. (2007) 'The skin color paradox and the American racial order,' *Social Forces* 86, no. 2, pp. 643–70.

Huckabee, C. (2008) 'U. of Kentucky apologizes after Obama effigy is found on its campus,' *Chronicle of Higher Education*, 29 October (chronicle.com/news/article/5415/u-of-kentucky-apologizes-after-obama-effigy-is-found-on-its-campus).

Hughes, M and Hertel, BR. (1990) 'The significance of color remains: A study of life chances, mate selection, and ethnic consciousness among black Americans, *Social Forces* vol. 68, no. 4, pp. 1105–20.

Humes, KR. Jones, NA and Ramirez, RR. (2011) 'Overview of race and Hispanic origin: 2010,' 2010 census briefs. Washington, D.C.: U.S. Census Bureau, March (www.census.gov/prod/cen2010/briefs/c2010br-02.pdf).

Hunter, M. (2011) 'Buying racial capital: Skin-bleaching and cosmetic surgery,' *The Journal of Pan African Studies* vol. 4, no. 4 (June), pp. 142–61.

IMDb. (2009) 'Obama: heated debate is on role of government,' 18 September (www.imdb.com/video/hulu/vi930415129/).

Iweala, U. (2008) 'Racism in "post-racial" America: Silence about race in the presidential campaign underscores the problem,' *Los Angeles Times*, January 23 (http://articles.latimes.com/2008/jan/23/opinion/oe-iweala23).

Johnson, G. (2010) 'President Obama, Scott Brown related, genealogists say,' *Huffington Post*, January 29 (www.huffingtonpost.com/2010/01/29/president-obama-scott-bro_n_441754.html).

Johnson, LA. (2008) 'Obama candidacy raises old questions about what is black,' *Pittsburgh Post-Gazette*, 8 March (www.post-gazette.com/pg/08129/879988–176.stm).

Johnston, MP and Nadal, KL. (2010) 'Multiracial microagressions: Exposing monoracism,'" In *Microaggressions and marginality: manifestation, dynamics, and impact,* ed DW Sue, Hoboken, NJ: John Wiley and Sons, Inc., pp. 123–44.

Jones, KW. (2009) 'Obama and Buffett: six degrees of Barack includes billionaire, Angelina Jolie Beau,', *National Ledger*, 16 December (www. nationalledger.com/artman/publish/article_272629527.shtml).

Jones, NA. (2005) 'We the people of more than one race in the United States,' Census 2000 Special Reports, CENSR-22. Washington, D.C.: U.S. Census Bureau, April 2005 (www.census.gov/prod/2005pubs/ censr-22.pdf).

Kantor, J. (2009) 'In First Lady's roots, a complex path from slavery,' 7 October, *New York Times* (www.nytimes.com/2009/10/08/us/ politics/08genealogy.html?_r=1).

Keith, V and Herring, C. (1991) 'Skin tone and sratification in the black community,' *American Journal of Sociology*, vol. 97, no. 3, pp. 760–78.

Khanna, N. (2010) '"If you're half black, you're just black": reflected appraisals and the persistence of the one-drop rule,' *The Sociological Quarterly*, vol. 51, pp. 96–121.

Kochhar, Fry, R and Taylor, P. (2011) 'Wealth gaps rise to record highs between whites, blacks and hispanics,' Washington, DC: Pew Research Center.

Koppelman, A. (2009) 'Carter: Animosity towards Obama based mostly on race. *Salon.com*, 15 September (www.salon.com/politics/ war_room/2009/09/15/carter_race/index.html?source=newsletter).

Korgen, KO. (1998) *From black to biracial: Transforming racial identity among Americans*, Westport, CT: Praeger.

Lavoie, D. (2008) 'Barack Obama and Brad Pitt are cousins, Hillary Clinton and Angelina Jolie are also cousins, study says,' *Huffington Post*, 25 March (www.huffingtonpost.com/2008/03/25/barack-obama- and-brad-pit_n_93356.html).

Lee, J and Bean, FA. (2011) *The diversity paradox: Immigration and the colorline in the 21st century*, New York: Russell Sage Foundation.

Life at the Edge of the World. (2008) '*Donna Brazile isn't going to the back of the bus,' 31* October (http://lestyoubejudged.wordpress. com/2008/10/31/vote-for-the-issues-donna-brazile-isnt-going-to- the-back-of-the-bus/).

Lipsitz, G. (1998) *The possessive investment in whiteness: How white people profit from identity politics*, Philadelphia, PA: Temple University Press.

Lipsitz, G. (2011) *How racism takes place,* Philadelphia, PA: Temple University Press.

Livingston, RW and Pearce, NA. (2009) 'Teddy-bear effect: Does having a baby-face benefit black chief executive officers?,' *Psychological Science*, vol. 20, no. 10, pp. 1229–36.

Lubin, A. (2005) *Romance and rights: The politics of interracial intimacy, 1945–1954,* Jackson, MS: University Press of Mississippi.

MacAskill, E. (2008) 'U.S. election: Buffett joins Obama to solve economic crisis,' *Guardian*, 29 July (www.guardian.co.uk/world/2008/jul/29/barackobama.uselections2008).

MacGillis, A. (2008) 'Obama recalls a fuller history,' 4 April, *Washington Post.com* (http://blog.washingtonpost.com/the-trail/2008/04/04/obama_recalls_a_fuller_history.html).

McNally, T. (2009) 'Always controversial Cornel West disses Obama, survives cancer and almost spent his life in prison,' *Alternet*, 18 December (www.alternet.org/rights/144569/always_controversial_cornel_west_disses_obama%2C_survives_cancer_and_almost_spent_his_life_in_prison?page=entire).

Martin M. (1994), *Race and ethnic relations: American and global perspectives,* Belmont, CA: Wadsworth Publishers, Belmont, CA.

Mercurio, J. (2008) 'The final surprise: Obama's key groups,' *MSNBC*, 5 November (www.msnbc.msn.com/id/27557327/).

Mills CW. (1997) *The racial contract*, Ithaca, NY: Cornell University Press.

Mitchell, M. (2008) 'Discussions across the racial divide,' *Chicago Sun-Times*, 14 February (http://blogs.suntimes.com/mitchell/2008/02/sen_barack_obamas_letter_to_ta_1.html)

Moran, RF. (2007) *Loving* and the legacy of unintended consequences, *Wisconsin Law Review*, vol. 2, pp. 241–81.

MSNBC. (2008) 'How much will Obama's race matter,' *Decision 08*, 21 September (www.mefeedia.com/entry/how-much-will-obamas-race-matter/11664714*)*.

Nadal, KL. (2011) 'Microaggressions and the multiracial experience,' *International Journal of Humanities and Social Science* vol.1, no. 7 (June), pp. 36–44

Neumeister, L. (2010) 'Rev. Wright: 'Obama threw me under the bus' President's former pastor complains he is being ignored by the White House.' 18 May, *MSNBC* (www.msnbc.msn.com/id/37208439/ns/politics-white_house/).

Niesse, M. (2011) 'Hawaii Government Hands over Obama's Birth Records,' *Huffington Post*, 27 April (www.huffingtonpost.com/huff-wires/20110427/us-obama-birth-hawaii/).

Obama, B. (2004a) *Dreams from my father: A story of race and inheritance,* New York: Three Rivers Press.

Obama, B. (2004b) 'Democratic national convention keynote address,' *American Rhetoric Online Speech Bank* (www.americanrhetoric.com/speeches/convention2004/barackobama2004dnc.htm).

Obama, B. (2008) 'A more perfect union,' *Black Scholar*, vol. 38, no. 1, pp. 17–23.

Olson, S. (2006) *Mapping human history: Discovering the past through our genes*, New York: Houghton Mifflin.

Omi, M and Winant, H. (1994) *Racial formation: From the 1980s to the 1990s* (2nd edn), New York: Routledge.

Ostroy, A. (2010) 'The Tea Party movement isn't about racism? Read this…,' *Huffington Post* 15 April (www.huffingtonpost.com/andy-ostroy/the-tea-party-movement-is_b_538750.html).

Pogatchnik, S. (2009) 'Boxing legend Ali traces roots to Irish town Ali the Irishman: Fans cheer icon as he finds Irish roots in great-granddad's hometown,' 1 September (http://abcnews.go.com/International/wireStory?id=8460201).

Price, GN and Gyimah-Brempong, K. (2006) 'Black, dark, disadvantaged: Crime, punishment, and skin hue in Mississippi,' *The Murc Digest* 2, no. 2 (April), pp. 2–3.

Renn, KA. (2004) *Mixed race students in college: The ecology of race, identity, and community on campus*, Albany, NY: State University of New York Press.

Rockquemore, KA and Brunsma, DL. (2002) *Beyond black: Biracial identity in America*, Thousand Oaks, CA:.Sage.

Rockquemore, KA, Brunsma, D L and Delgado, D J. (2009) 'Racing to theory or retheorizing race? Understanding the struggle to build a multiracial identity theory,' *Journal of Social Issues*, vol. 65, no. 1, pp. 13–34.

Roberts, S. and Baker, P. (2010), 'Asked to declare his race, Obama checks "black"', *New York Times*, 2 April (www.nytimes.com/2010/04/03/us/politics/03census.html).

Rondilla, JL and Spickard (eds.) (2005) *Is lighter better? Skin-tone discrimination among Asian Americans*, New York: Routledge.

Root, M PP. (1998) 'Experiences and processes affecting racial identity development: Preliminary results from the biracial sibling project,' In *Cultural Diversity and Mental Health,* vol. 4, no. 3, ppp. 237-247.

Rose, A. (2010), 'Obama and Palin related? Website claims president also has ties to Limbaugh, Bush Family,' *Huffington Post*, 13 September (www.huffingtonpost.com/2010/10/13/obama-and-palin-related-w_n_760689.html).

Ross, B and el-Buri, R. (2008) 'Obama's pastor: God damn america, U.S. to blame for 9/11. *ABC News*,' 13 March (http://abcnews.go.com/Blotter/story?id=4443788).

Russell, KY, Wilson, M and Hall, R. (1992) *The color complex: The politics of skin color among African Americans*, New York: Harcourt Brace Jovanovich.

Salon. (2008) 'What should Obama do about Rev. Jeremiah Wright?,' 29 April (www.salon.com/news/opinion/feature/2008/04/29/obama_wright/index1.html).

Samuels, A and Adler, J. (2010) 'The reinvention of the Rev. Al Sharpton,' *Newsweek*, 25 July (www.newsweek.com/2010/07/25/the-reinvention-of-the-reverend.html).

Shafer, J. (2008) 'How Obama does that thing he does: a professor of rhetoric cracks the candidate's code,' *Slate*, 14 February (www.slate.com/id/2184480/).

Sinclair-Chapman, V and Price, M. (2008) 'Black politics, the 2008 election, and the (im)possibility of race transcendence,' *Political Science and Politics* 41, no. 4, pp. 739–45.

Smith, RM and King, DS. (2009), 'Barack Obama and the future of American racial politics,' *Du Bois Review*, 6, no. 1: 25–35.

Smolenyak, M. (2009) 'Michelle Obama's roots,' *Megan TV*, August (www.honoringourancestors.com/megan-tv.html).

Spickard, PR. (1989) *Mixed blood: Intermarriage and ethnic identity in twentieth-century America,* Madison, WI: University of Wisconsin Press.

Stan, A. (2008) 'Christian right voter summit sells racist "Obama waffles,"' *Alternet*, 15 September (www.alternet.org/election08/98908/christian_right_voter_summit_sells_racist_'obama_waffles'/)

Steele, S. (1990), *The content of our character: Aa new vision of race in America*, New York: St. Martin's Press, New York.

Steele, S. (2004) *Bound man: Why we are excited about Obama and why he can't win*, New York: Free Press.

Stein, J. (2009) 'Obama, racism, and Jimmy Carter: Nearly 30 years ago, Carter team kept quiet on race and Reagan campaign,' *MSNBC*, 17 September (www.msnbc.msn.com/id/32895021/ns/politics-cq_politics/).

Steinhorn, L and Diggs-Brown, B. (1999) *By the color of our skin: The illusion of integration and the reality of race*, New York: Dutton.

Stuckey, M. (2008) 'Multiracial Americans surge in number, voice: Obama candidacy focuses new attention on their quest for understanding,' *MSNBC*, 28 May (www.msnbc.msn.com/id/24542138/).

Sullivan, E. (2008) 'Obama faces more personal threats than other presidents-elect. *Huffington Post*,' 14 November (www.huffingtonpost.com/2008/11/14/obama-faces-more-personal_n_144005.html?page=3).

SuzeNYC. (2008) 'How we are getting racists to vote for Obama,' *Daily Kos*, 4 November (www.dailykos.com/story/2008/11/5/11149/2882/55/652861).

Swarns, R L and Kantor, J. (2009) 'In first lady's roots, a complex path from slavery,' 7 October, *New York Times* (www.nytimes.com/2009/10/08/us/politics/08genealogy.html?_r=1)

Telles, EE and Murguia, E. (1990) 'Phenotypic discrimination and income differences among Mexican Americans,' *Social Science Quarterly* vol. 7, no. 4, pp. 682–96.

Tseng, T. (2008) 'Millennials: Key to post-ethnic America?,' *New Geography*, 30 July (www.newgeography.com/content/00137-millennials-key-post-ethnic-america).

Turner, VW. (1969) *The ritual process: Structure and anti-structure*, New York: Cornell University Press.

Viglione, J H, L and DeFina, R. (forthcoming) 'The impact of light skin on prison time for black female offenders,' *The Social Science Journal*.

York, B. (2011), 'Black caucus: tired of making excuses for Obama,' 17 August, *Washington Examiner*," (http://campaign2012.washingtonexaminer.com/blogs/beltway-confidential/black-caucus-tired-making-excuses-obama).

Wade, T. Jl, Romano, M J and Blue, L. (2004) 'The effect of African American skin color on hiring preferences,' *Journal of Applied Social Psychology* vol. 34, no. 12, pp. 2550–58.

Wallace, KR. (2001) Relative/outside: The art and politics of identity among mixed heritage students, Westport, CT: Greenwood. CT

Wardle, F. (1987) 'Are you sensitive to interracial children's special identity needs,' *Young Children*, vol. 42, no. 2 (January), pp. 53–59.

Wilber, K. (1997) 'An integral theory of consciousness,' *Journal of Consciousness Studies*, vol. 4, no. 1 (February), pp. 71–92.

Williams, KR. (2008) *Mark one or more: Civil rights in multiracial America (the politics of race and ethnicity)*, Ann Arbor, MI: University of Michigan Press.

Winograd, M and Hais, MD. (2008) *Millennial makeover: MySpace, YouTube, and the future of American politics*, Piscataway, NJ. Rutgers: University Press.

Zack, N. (1994) *Race and mixed race*, Philadelphia: Temple University Press.

CHAPTER THREE

"A patchwork heritage": multiracial citation in Barack Obama's *Dreams from My Father*

Justin Ponder

On January 20 2009, just moments after being sworn in as America's first black President, Barack Obama rose to the platform and gave his inaugural address. According to rhetoric scholar James Mackin (2009), the speech's defining characteristic was Obama's use of citation to connect himself with tradition. Americans were unfamiliar with a President that looked like him, so he cited familiar discourses. He directly quoted from the constitution, *Swing Time*, the Bible, Thomas Paine, Reagan's 1981 inaugural speech, contemporary statistics, historical events, natural disasters, and world conflicts, but the most notable allusion occurs when he references the crowd. Obama addresses all within range of his voice and claims that they have gathered because they "have chosen hope over fear, unity of purpose over conflict and discord." While poetic, the statement is not exactly accurate. Most of the shivering supporters assembled on the national mall that morning not because they had chosen hope, but because they had elected him. They had not simply chosen unity of purpose, but had voted for him over John McCain whose campaign, during its final days, increasingly evoked racial fears, conflicts, and discords. Preying on American xenophobia, some McCain supporters suggested that Obama was a secret Muslim extremist waiting to usurp the White House before revealing his anti-American intentions. Republican party rally speakers cited his middle name, "Hussein," coyly associating him with the Iraqi tyrant, and photos circulated of Obama wearing a robe and turban, presumably the garb of an Islamic fundamentalist. This campaign of fear, conflict, and discord reached a peak when the National Republican Trust Fund aired commercials that claimed Obama was "too radical; too risky," because, for 20 years, he "followed a preacher of hate." The commercial itself cited a 2003 sermon at Trinity United Church of Christ in Chicago in which Obama's pastor, Reverend Jeremiah Wright

Jr., referred to the nation as the "U.S. of K.K.K.A." and proclaimed, "Not 'God bless America!' God damn America!"

Airing these commercials just days before the election, the Trust Fund sought to stir up the same controversy that rose after the Wright sermon originally aired. On March 13 2008, *Good Morning America* broke the story and first broadcasted the sermon. Soon after, media outlets of all kinds cited excerpts from Wright's sermon until Obama had to respond. He had defied the odds and performed well on a platform of racial unity, but fears that Obama shared Wright's beliefs threatened to incite racial disunities. Determined that he must do something, Obama stayed up writing well into the night of 17 March. The next morning at the National Constitution Center in Philadelphia, he navigated the choppy waters of American racial discourse by employing his characteristic rhetorical strategy, citation. He cited critics who deemed him both "too black" and "not black enough": white citizens who called his candidacy "an exercise in affirmative action," and black citizens who "denigrate both the greatness and the goodness of our nation" (Obama, 2008). Citing historical events and contemporary issues, he constructed the image of an American society divided between black and white before strategically positioning himself in the middle of that discourse as "the son of a black man from Kenya and a white woman from Kansas."

Only after evoking his personal life in this way did Obama address his relationship with the controversial pastor. In the speech, he navigates this controversial topic by once again citing his background, claiming, "I can no more disown him than I can my white grandmother." He references Wright's "incendiary language" that has the potential to "widen the racial divide" but also his grandmother's use of "racial or ethnic stereotypes." Obama neutralizes the racially offensive statements of his black preacher by placing them alongside those of his white grandmother. Doing so, he provokes listeners to compare Wright's statements excerpted from a single sermon to those of common conversations had in the kitchens across white America. At the same time, citing his reverend alongside his grandmother, Obama also references his experiences in multiracial communities. He evokes his experience as the son of a black father figure and the grandson of a white woman. Referencing his familiarity with both sides of the color line, Obama also suggests the ways in which he straddles it, citing the divisive language of both camps to imply how he can bring unity.

Obama's "Race" speech also suggests that Obama is particularly qualified for ushering in an age of racial harmony because of his multiracial identity. According to Jeff Zeleny (2008), the major thread of the speech was Obama's citation of the country's monoracial divides alongside his multiracial background. Obama most clearly references this background when he directly quotes from his autobiography. He reads a passage from *Dreams from My Father* that describes the first time he heard one of Wright's sermons. The sermon entitled "The Audacity of Hope," which would become the title of his second book, caused Obama to imagine "the stories of ordinary black people merging with the stories of David and Goliath, Moses and Pharaoh, the Christians in the lion's den, Ezekiel's field of dry bones." In this passage, Obama cites a sermon where Wright cites the Bible. Doing so, Obama links Wright's provocative comments with a Biblical tradition, suggesting that his reverend's statements are not any more divisive than those made by Judeo-Christian prophets. This is where Obama's "Race" speech most strategically quells the racial controversy that surrounded him. He acknowledges the racial divisions in the United States, but abstracts them into a millennia old struggle between the oppressed and the powerful, citing the struggle of Jews against their gentile oppressors, Christians against their Roman persecutors, and prophets against the valleys of bones.

Obama's "Race" speech was arguably the most important one of his 2008 campaign. When the Wright controversy threatened to undermine his presidential chances, Obama navigated racial discourse with a speech that hinged upon citation. The most pivotal citation in this most pivotal speech is one that forms a cluster of citations from a Wright sermon to the Bible to the Judeo-Christian tradition. It is important to note that this most effective cluster of citations occurs in Obama's "Race" speech when he cites *Dreams from My Father*. If this speech was fundamental to Obama's campaign and, as Zeleny claims, Obama's autobiography was fundamental to that speech, one must also consider the ways in which autobiography is fundamental to Obama's navigation of racial discourse.

Long before the publication of this multiracial man's autobiography, scholars in mixed race studies claimed that multiracial autobiography could change American thinking. They argued that racial discourse stereotypes racially mixed people, and multiracial people can combat those stereotypes with self-representation. Many of these scholars further claim no self-representation can undermine stereotypes better than autobiography. They argue that through autobiographies multiracial people can represent and understand themselves in ways that are free of the stereotypes created by others.

Scholars in mixed race studies make many claims about the potential of multiracial autobiography, but Obama's multiracial autobiography, *Dreams from My Father*, complicates those claims. Many in this academic discipline argue that autobiography unleashes the power of self-representation, but the most striking thing about Obama's autobiography is how little it represents himself. Theorists claim autobiography is the place where multiracial people create themselves on their own terms, but the autobiographical subject of *Dreams* constructs himself on the terms of others. Scholars argue that these texts challenge stereotypes, but throughout his text, Obama represents himself through stereotypes. Ultimately, scholars in mixed race studies argue that multiracial autobiographies foreground the virtues of self-representation, but Obama's *Dreams from My Father* exemplifies the virtues of citation.

Self-representation

According to the *Oxford English Dictionary*, in 1850 C. Hugh Holman defined "stereotype" as the "commonly-held and oversimplified mental pictures or judgments of a person, a race, an issue, a kind of art, or anything" (Sollors, 1997, p. 229). In 1922, Walter Lippman used "stereotype" to denote an oversimplified and perhaps antidemocratic representation of ethnic groups (Sollors, 1997, p. 229). Three years later, literary scholar, Alain Locke racialized the term in *The New Negro* (1986) when he linked the ills suffered by the African American to "the unjust stereotypes of his oppressors" (Sollors, 1997, p. 229). Ever since, those in the humanities have used the term "racial stereotypes" to refer to flat, formulaic characters that make a race seem monolithic. Now, stereotypes are seen not simply as unoriginal but fundamentally racist.

Likewise, scholars in mixed race studies fear the dangers of multiracial stereotypes. In her analysis of the creation and denial of mixed race Americans, Cynthia L. Nakashima claims that religion, science, sociology, and popular culture have all conspired to construct a "negative mythology" about multiracial people as biological, mental, emotional, moral, and sexual degenerates (1992, p. 177). American literature has suggested that people of "mixed blood" and those known as "Amerasians," "mestizos," and "mulattos" are abominable, owners of conflicting bloodlines that doom them to deviant lives and early deaths. Given the prevalence of multiracial stereotypes constructed by monoracials, Nakashima claims that "multiracial people have been defined completely by others" (1992, p. 174). She determines that these damaging images limit what others believe racially mixed people can be and even cause racially mixed people to internalize "the images of themselves as torn and confused and as fitting in nowhere" (p. 174).

To stop this internalization, many scholars in mixed race studies insist that stereotypes must end. In "Multicultural Identity and the Death of Stereotypes," Philip Tajitsu Nash argues that centuries of misrepresentations have taken their toll on multiracial people. He claims many monoracial minorities have created their own images to counter stereotypes created by whites. African, Latina, Native, and Asian Americans have all created their own bodies of literature with positive representations to challenge racist ones. Nash argues, however, that multiracial people have not had the same luxury. Because stereotypes have outweighed self-representation, mixed race people must, he claims, begin to "stand up to them" (1992, p. 330). He calls upon scholars to redefine racially mixed people more accurately by identifying, challenging, and overcoming damaging representations (1992, p. 331). Ultimately, Nash concludes, "Stereotypes must die so that our whole selves can live" (1992, p. 332).

When faced with negative stereotypes, scholars in mixed race studies have followed this thinking, seeking to kill them with positive self-representations. In her introduction to *Mixed: An Anthology of Short Fiction on the Multiracial Experience*, editor Chandra Prasad speculates that multiracial literature will help readers "explore a new, hybridized world" (2006, p. 9). If reductive stereotypes oversimplify racial discourse, multiracial self-representation can provoke readers "to ask sticky questions; to refuse easy answers" (2006, p. 9). Because American discourse frequently denigrates mixed race identities and insists upon monoracial ones, Prasad claims works by mixed race writers can "blur boundaries—or better yet, expose how illusory most boundaries are in the first place" (2006, p. 9).

Seeking to tap this literary potential, many multiracial writers have published autobiographies. Historian Paul R. Spickard claims that the most significant part of mixed race studies has been the "boom" in multiracial autobiography (2002, p. 77). From May-Lee Chai's *Hapa Girl* to Patricia Penn Hilden's *When Nickels Were Indians: An Urban Mixed-Blood Story* to James McBride's *The Color of Water: A Black Man's Tribute to His White Mother*, mixed race autobiographers have challenged stereotypes by telling their own stories. Many American novels have depicted racially mixed people as a problem, but multiracial autobiographers have shown that one can be, as Spickard claims, "unproblematically mixed" (2002, p. 82). With stereotypes of treacherous crossbloods, devious mestizos, sickly hapas, and tragic mulattos, Americans have caricatured multiracial people as hopelessly incoherent, but autobiographers fashion "a coherent ethnic narrative for themselves" (2002, p. 93).

Because autobiography depicts lived experience, many scholars in mixed race studies argue that it can get to the truth of multiracial subjectivity better than any other genre. This is the guiding principle of SanSan Kwan and Kenneth Speirs' *Mixing It Up*. They claim stereotypes have represented mixed race people as "tragic, pathological, or threatening," and autobiographers can combat those negative images with positive self-representations (2004, p. 3). They claim autobiographies can undermine racial assumptions better than scholarly articles because "the individual life offers the best response to both historical and contemporary erasures and misrecognitions of multiraciality" (2004, p. 1). According to them, mixed race studies too often tries "to define and to fix" a racially mixed identity it "cannot fully apprehend," but mixed race literature can comprehend "that which is necessarily unclassifiable" (2004, p. 4). Kwan and Speirs conclude that, unlike the essentializing theories of mixed race studies, personal and problematic autobiographies provide a more accurate picture of multiracial subjectivity.

With this potential for accuracy, many in mixed race studies seek to both deconstruct stereotypes and reconstruct themselves through autobiography. In "Against Erasure," Carole DeSouza claims her inarticulateness as a fledgling writer stemmed from her inarticulateness as a racial subject. Haunted by the "What are you?" question and plagued by feelings of inauthenticity, this mixed race author concludes that her development as a writer hinges on her development as a multiracial person (2004, p. 181). To form her narrative, she has to overcome stereotypes. To find "the multiracial voice," she must fight misrepresentation (2004, p. 183). The stereotype of the confused multiracial person precedes her, but DeSouza claims, "Unlike the tragic mulatta imprisoned by what has been written of her, I am the multiracial who writes herself" (2004, p. 204).

With such claims, the above theorists articulate the general consensus in mixed race studies: monoracial people stereotype multiracial people, these stereotypes damage mixed race people, multiracial people can rewrite themselves, racially mixed people find their voice through autobiography, and with self-writing, the multiracial author sees herself more accurately.

The limits of self-representation

Many insist that mixed race autobiography corrects misrepresentations, but they fail to recognize the genre's limitations. Establishing such a clear dichotomy between self-representation and stereotypes, they overlook four major points about self-representation: 1) self-representation communicates with others, 2) self-representation requires signs that do not belong to the self, 3) self-representation often relies on stereotypes, and 4) self-representation constructs a racial subject that identifies through stereotypes. For a fuller understanding of stereotype, autobiography, mixed race studies, and Obama's autobiography, one must further examine each of these points.

First, some claim that self-representation provides multiracial autobiographers the chance to create themselves, but self-representation is designed to communicate to others. Some suggest autobiographies provide writers the freedom to present themselves, their voice, identity, and accurate self, but this freedom is restricted by the fact that autobiographies require publishers. The autobiographer who wishes to represent herself requires an industry full of others to do so, and this business has limited the kinds of mixed race autobiographies it sells. According to multiracial autobiographer Rebecca Walker, since the late 1990s a certain kind of multiracial narrative has emerged that "fits our ethos of triumph over great odds" (2006, p. 14). After years of surveying different types of mixed race autobiographies, American readers have gravitated towards a certain kind, one that "reaffirms our hopeful belief that our country really is a place everyone can call home" (2006, p. 14). As readers have favored a certain type of racially mixed writing, so have publishers. Rather than exploring fragmentation, psychic struggle, and complexity, the autobiographies that make it onto bookshelves emphasize the multiracial's "self-discovery" and have "uplifting and transcendent" endings (2006, p. 14). Walker claims the autobiography market has reconstructed a kind of multiracial counter-stereotype. If the tragic mulatto was "fragmented and heartbreaking," the multiracial autobiographer must be whole and heartwarming (2006, p. 14). If the mixedblood was doomed to a life of confusion, the racially mixed autobiographer must emphasize "cultural cohesion" (2006, p. 14). With this analysis of the autobiography industry, Walker suggests that multiracial self-representation is really the self-representation that others permit.

The subgenre of multiracial autobiography is not unique in this regard. While this market is motivated by particular material conditions, an "other" always influences the representation of any self. Judith Butler claims this much in her examination of scenes of address. Whether in autobiography, psychoanalysis, or ethical encounters, whenever one is asked to give an account of herself, she does so on behalf of others. Autobiographies do not occur in a vacuum. They are inextricably tied to addressees. According to Butler, regardless of the fantasies of self-possession that autobiography provides, "one can tell an autobiography only to an other" (2005, p. 32). Some claim that life writing gives writers a chance to present themselves on their own terms, but Butler insists that "one can reference an 'I' only in relation to a 'you': without the 'you,' my own story becomes impossible" (2005, p. 32). Giving an account of oneself, writing a memoir, or publishing an autobiography, the self wishes to be heard, read, or published by others. These forms of self-representation are for others, and, therefore, one represents herself on the terms of others.

Likewise, Obama's self-representation is for others. He admits this much in the introduction to his autobiography, *Dreams from My Father*, when he states he did not set out to write the book. After he became president of the *Harvard Law Review*, a flurry of publishers contacted him. Waving advances, opportunities to write exclusively for a year, and the means to print millions of copies, these publishers provided the material conditions that made his self-representation possible. Obama suggests that he abhorred the idea of self-representation, clinging to his "stubborn desire to protect [himself] from scrutiny" (2004, p. xvi). Even after he signed a deal, he still had the "impulse to abandon the entire project," still did not want to represent himself (2004, p. xvi). Others gave Obama the idea to represent himself, and once he signed a contract, they financially, contractually, and legally compelled him to represent himself. Although his autobiography bears his name, this self-representation is started, made possible, and compelled by others.

Because this autobiography is for others, Obama's self-representation is on the terms of others. He recalls that publishers solicited him for his story as the *Harvard Law Review*'s first black President (2004, p. xiii). Obama has a white mother, but he suggests that publishers were less interested in his multiracial background than in his status as "a black first." Publishers sought an autobiography that would feed "America's hunger for any optimistic sign from the racial front—a morsel of proof that, after all, some progress been made," and the autobiography of the law journal's first black President can do that better than its first half-white President (2004, p. xiii). Before he writes a single word, publishers encourage him to write a certain kind of autobiography, and Obama consents. In the introduction, he tells readers that they will not read about his love of basketball, his relationship with his wife, or even the dreams from his white mother, but his search for "a workable meaning for his life as a black American" (2004, p. xvi). He qualifies the autobiography that will follow as an account not of himself, but of his blackness, per the requests of publishers, readers, and even American society. Before a single word of the narrative begins, this multiracial autobiographer reveals the extent to which his self-representation is for others.

Second, scholars who extol the self-creation of autobiographies overlook the extent to which the autobiographer must cite signs that do not belong to the self. Because she wants to be comprehensible by others, the autobiographer uses diction, punctuation, syntax, etc. which others can comprehend. To present her "unique" self, she cannot use a language unique to her. She cannot create her own words, lexicon, or grammar. If she did, she would be unintelligible. Her autobiography would cease to be an autobiography. It would be gibberish. Because an autobiography must be communicated, it must conform to rules that do not belong to the autobiographer. In this regard, no autobiography is truly unique. Each must employ intersubjective discourse that dispossesses the individual subject. According to Jacques Derrida, self-representation dispossesses the self through citation. He claims that citationality is a fundamental feature of all discourses, because each sign that a subject uses can only communicate to others if it "can be *cited*" by others (1988, p. 12). Audiences can understand autobiographers because addressers write with words that their addressees can understand. To communicate, every autobiography must be full of signs that constitute a "citational graft" between language users (1988, p. 12). If this is the case, the self-representation that belongs to the self becomes meaningless rambling. "Self"-representations that make meaning are those that cite others and dispossess the autobiographical self.

To communicate to a wide range of readers, Obama employs this kind of citation in his autobiography. Commissioned to write an autobiography about his blackness, the autobiographical subject approximates blackness by citing black autobiographies. As a child living with his white mother in Djakarta, he desires to learn the meaning of his blackness, but without access to his black father, this proves difficult. Miles from even another black person, his mother oversees a crash course on African American culture. Recalling this education, Obama cites numerous texts: "books on the civil rights movement, the recordings of Mahalia Jackson, the speeches of Dr. King" (2004, p. 51). When he returns to Hawaii and attends an all-white school, he wants to understand what blackness means all the more. To do this, he goes to the library and reads about his father's tribe. Referencing the event, Obama cites books in which he learns that Luo raise cattle, live in mud huts, and traditionally wear leather thongs (2004, p. 64). As he matures into a young man, his desire to learn how to be black grows. Dissatisfied with citing his blackness simply from books, he seeks out black people, but even they cite texts beyond themselves. The only black man he knows on Waikiki is a poet who cites his work alongside that of Langston Hughes and Richard Wright (2004, p. 76). Seeking more black texts, Obama states, "TV, movies, the radio; those were the places to start" (2004, p. 78). Black pop culture provides him "an arcade of images from which you could cop a walk, a talk, a step, a style" (2004, p. 78). Media help him gauge his deficiencies and potentialities: "I couldn't croon like Marvin Gaye, but I could learn to dance all the *Soul Train* steps. I couldn't pack a gun like Shaft or Superfly, but I could sure enough curse like Richard Pryor" (2004, p. 78). And through hours in front of the television or within earshot of the radio, the young Obama positions himself closer and closer to a black identity by citing black representations. Spending hours poring over Baldwin, Ellison, Hughes, Wright, and Du Bois, he shuts himself in his room away from his white grandparents where he "wrestle[s] with words" that may yield something fundamental to his identity (2004, p. 85). Recalling his education with these black texts, Obama recollects, "Only Malcolm X's autobiography seemed to offer something different" (2004, p. 86). Through the mere pages of a book, Obama finds the possibility of "self-creation" (2004, p. 86). In "the blunt poetry" of Malcolm's words, Obama sees the potential to forge a new self "through sheer force of will" (2004, p. 86). Life may offer Obama confusion, but an autobiography offers the promise of "uncompromising order," martial discipline, even cohesion (2004, p. 86). *The Autobiography of Malcolm X* provides the promise of a stable "I." Likewise, the autobiographical subject of *Dreams from My Father* becomes most stable when citing such a text. Like Malcolm, however, he reveals a self indebted to others. Obama's autobiographical "character" comes from citing other characters, and the blunt poetry of his words is simply a recombination of words that do not belong to him. The cohesion that autobiography offers arises less through "sheer force of will" than from the ability to wrestle the words of others so tightly that they seem to belong to the self. Obama's autobiographical subject achieves "self-creation" by citing Malcolm X's "self-creation" which cites Elijah Muhammad's "self-creation," which cites Wallace Fard Muhammad's. *Dreams from My Father* is an autobiography attributed to Obama, but the autobiographical subject in that text continually attributes its subjectivity to other autobiographies. Any self represented in this autobiography is achieved by citing others.

Third, those who claim that self-representation can counter stereotypes overlook the extent to which self-representation relies on stereotypes to communicate to others. According to post-colonial theorist Homi Bhabha, stereotypes are among the most communicative signs. They convey vast amounts of meaning with a single word, phrase, or image, because they articulate clusters of citations. For example, stereotypes of black men communicate so effectively because they swiftly articulate centuries of psychological, scientific, and religious discourses into racist images. They combine innumerable discourses and neatly package them into a single sign that discursive subjects never have to unpack. Stereotypes are a "major discursive strategy" and communicate perhaps more effectively than any other sign (Bhabha, 1994, p. 66). Precisely because stereotypes cite so well, Bhabha concludes that it is unlikely that any discourse can break entirely free from them.

In *Dreams from My Father*, Obama quickly realizes the extent to which people cannot break free from stereotypical discourses when he realizes that white people understand black people through stereotypes. He reaches this realization when he and his mother see *Black Orpheus*, a film about black Brazilians during Carnaval. As she sits riveted by "the depiction of childlike blacks," he discovers that this woman, progressive enough to marry a black man in 1960, still only knew black people as "a reflection of the simple fantasies that had been forbidden to a white middle-class girl from Kansas" (2004, p. 124). He writes that the woman who initiated his education in blackness did not embrace black people as much as the stereotypes of their "warm, sensual, exotic, different" lives (2004, p. 124). This insight leads Obama to claim that "emotions between the races could never be pure" because "the other race would always remain just that: menacing, alien, and apart" (2004, p. 124). Obama concludes that, whether steeped in fear or love, white people understand black people through stereotypes.

Conversely, Obama's comes to realize the extent to which black people understand white people through stereotypes. His black best friend, Ray constantly talks about "*white folks* this or *white folks* that" (2004, p. 81). In Ray's thinking, "white" become shorthand for bigot and cannot become much more (2004, p. 81). The narrator notes that even this black man who has white teachers, friends, and girlfriends fears that white people had a "particular brand of arrogance, an obtuseness" that kept them from knowing that "they were being cruel" (2004, p. 80). Ray is able to cross the racial divide to impress, befriend, and woo white people only when he replaces the stereotypes of cruel white people with stereotypes of naïve white people easily fooled by "the score" of a smooth-talking black man (2004, p. 81). Obama concludes that, whether steeped in fear or friendship, black people understand white people through stereotypes.

Fourth, many establish a dichotomy between stereotypes and self-representation, but fail to admit the extent to which racial subjects come to understand themselves through stereotypes. Some scholars imply autobiography is free from the corrupting influence of the other's mythology, but Stuart Hall argues that self-representation is made from the scraps of stereotypes. He claims, "Who I am—the 'real' me—[is] formed in relation to a whole set of other narratives" (1996, p. 115). He claims that the discursive subject achieves "realness" in relationship to "false" discourses, and the autobiographical subject emerges in relationship to innumerable narratives that exceed and precede her. If the "I" wishes to represent herself, she must cite stereotypes, even ones she seeks to defy.

Likewise, in *Dreams from My Father*, Obama admits the extent to which he knows himself through stereotypes. As a young adult in Hawaii, he seeks sustained connections with the black community and finds them on basketball courts. What he learns there, however, is not the "real" blackness, but "a caricature of black male adolescence" (2004, p. 79). He learns how to perform this stereotypical blackness among black people, but soon feels like he is trapped in a "bad-assed nigger pose" (2004, p. 82). At the same time, however, he seeks to blend in at his predominantly white school. Among white peers and superiors, he learns not the real meaning of his whiteness, but a way to talk "game" (2004, p. 83). He discovers how to perform a stereotype of whiteness among white people but feels like he is trapped, as his best friend claims, kissing "white ass" (2004, p. 83). Among black or white people, the narrator performs stereotypes to fit in, but when he earns the acceptance of either group, he feels like a fraud, writing, "I had no idea who my own self was" (2004, p. 82).

Obama soon realizes, however, the extent to which all racial subjects understand themselves through stereotypes. During a trip to Kenya that demystifies his African identity, Obama meets Dr. Rukia Odero who understands his disappointment, stating that "young black Americans tend to romanticize Africa so" (2004, p. 433). African Americans expected to find all the answers in Africa, but she recalls how "Africans expected to find all the answers in America. Harlem. Chicago. Langston Hughes and James Baldwin" (2004, p. 433). With this statement, she suggests that while African Americans understood themselves through stereotypes of Africa, Africans understood themselves through stereotypes of black America. She goes further to argue that white people also understand themselves through stereotypes, claiming, "The Germans, the English…they all claim Athens and Rome as their own, when, in fact, their ancestors helped destroy classical culture" (2004, p. 434). White people learn about the grandeur of the Renaissance but not the "misery of European peasants," the glory of colonial expansion but not how brutally "Europeans treated their own" (2004, p. 434).

Placing this discussion as the penultimate scene of his autobiography, the moment in which self-discovery usually occurs in such texts, Obama suggests that there is no self to discover. By placing this discussion at the climax stage where most autobiographers most clearly represent themselves, this text suggests that there is no self-representation for himself, black, white, or multiracial people outside of the stereotypes they cite.

Citing stereotypes

Scholars in mixed race studies claim multiracial autobiographers self-identify by rejecting stereotypes, but the multiracial autobiographer of *Dreams from My Father* self-identifies by citing them. Scholars suggest that mixed race people must either contradict or conform to stereotypes, but the narrator of *Dreams from My Father* cites them in subversive ways. According to Bhabha, stereotypes can only effectively label a racial group if they are repeated. For example, stereotypes repeatedly cite "the *same old* stories of the Negro's animality, the Coolie's inscrutability or the stupidity of the Irish" (1994, p. 77). On the other hand, because they are repeated, each telling of these stories becomes different and new. To continue gratifying and terrifying discursive subjects, each telling has to evolve from context to context, making the Negro grow more animalistic, the Coolie more inscrutable, and the Irish more stupid.

This repetition oppressively stereotypes groups, but it also makes subversion possible. According to Butler, the subject cannot undermine stereotypes by trying to stop them because the repetitive character of stereotypes ensures that they will not end. At the same time, however, the subject can undermine stereotypes by repeating them parodically (Butler 1999, p. 185). Butler claims drag kings and queens cite gender stereotypes, but this "parodic repetition" of gender stereotypes exposes the illusion of all gender identity (1999, p. 187). The subversive subject of the drag show does not defy stereotypes with self-representation; the female subject does not defy stereotypes of women with her own, more accurate self-representations of womanhood. Nor does she simply repeat gender stereotypes in ways that keep them oppressively intact. Instead, she repeats stereotypes with a difference, which reveals the extent to which no accurate self-representation of womanhood exists outside of stereotypes. By parodically citing stereotypes, the subject exposes the stereotypical character of all identities. Not self-representation but "self-parodying, self-criticism," and self-stereotyping can reveal the "fundamentally phantasmatic status" of all identities (1999, p. 187).

Similarly, the autobiographical subject of *Dreams from My Father* draws racial identities into question by repeating stereotypes with a difference. For example, he repeats stereotypical blackness to blend in with black people. During his youth, he grows proficient at the caricature of black male adolescence, and the black men on Hawaii's basketball courts seem to accept him. However, when he suggests that the blackness they perform may be nothing more than a pose, Ray responds, "Speak for your own self" (2004, p. 82). Obama calls this the "trump card" that black people use to distance themselves from him (2004, p. 82). He may perform stereotypical blackness, but his whiteness always reminds them that he is "different" (2004, p. 82). On the other hand, by citing stereotypical blackness despite his whiteness, Obama provokes black readers to consider how unreal all blackness is. After Obama questions their group identity, Ray soon confesses that "you couldn't be sure that everything you had assumed to be an expression of your black unfettered self—the humor, the song, the behind-the-back pass—had been freely chosen by you" (2004, p. 85). All these features once distinguished their group from white people, but he explores the extent to which black self-representation does not belong to black people. "Real" black people cite a stereotype of blackness, but when a multiracial cites this same stereotype, he repeats it with a difference that causes Ray to consider the phantasmatic status of black identity.

Conversely, Obama repeats stereotypical whiteness to blend in with white people. By simply mimicking their "language and customs and structures of meaning," he becomes one of them (2004, p. 82). By changing diction, posture, and intonation, he earns the favor of white teachers and classmates (2004, p. 82). Nevertheless, they do not forget his difference. Friends randomly declare how much they like Stevie Wonder, and strangers ask him if he plays basketball (2004, p. 82). No matter how well he performs stereotypical whiteness, his blackness always keeps a distance between him and "real" white people. By repeating stereotypes of whiteness, however, he also forces them to consider how unreal all whiteness is. For example, after endless games of basketball, he and a white assistant coach befriend each other well enough that the coach forgets Obama's blackness. The coach gets so comfortable with him that when they lose to a team of black men, the coach forgets Obama's blackness and mutters that they "shouldn't have lost to a bunch of niggers" (2004, p. 80). Obama swiftly reasserts his blackness, and with a fury that surprises even him, tells the coach to shut up. The white man replies that "there are black people, and there are niggers" (2004, p. 80). Obama has performed stereotypical whiteness long enough for the coach to shatter the stereotypes of blackness and differentiate "black people" from "niggers," but he has not yet shattered the stereotypes of whiteness. Obama incites such a consideration when he retorts, "There are white folks, and then there are ignorant motherfuckers like you" (2004, p. 81). Doing so, he challenges the coach to consider the extent to which whiteness is also stereotyped, that there is a difference between "white folks" and "ignorant motherfuckers." This instance provokes the coach to reconsider his racial assumptions. All the features of whiteness he thought differentiated him and Obama from black people, all the things that he thought they used for self-representation actually hinged on being "ignorant" towards black people. The "real" white players on the Hawaiian courts cite a stereotype of oblivious whiteness, but when a multiracial person cites this same stereotype, he repeats it with a difference that causes the coach to consider the phantasmatic status of white identity.

Perhaps the best way to reveal that phantasmatic status of identity is with phantasmatic self-identifications. Butler claims autobiography suggests a "coherent autobiographer," and the addressees of autobiography expect "the seamlessness of the story" (2005, p. 64). As noted, the autobiographical subject can subvert stereotypes by repeating them with a difference in articulate self-representations. At the same time, however, Butler suggests that the best way to subvert stereotypes might be through inarticulate self-representations. This potential occurs through "moments of interruption, stoppage," and "open-endedness" (2005, p. 64). Through open-ended narratives, the autobiographer risks being misunderstood, misrepresented, or stereotyped by others, but if the autobiographer seeks to control her self-representation, she may inspire resistance from her addressers. In short, Butler claims the more autobiographers try to control their texts, the less addressees yield that control. On the other hand, the autobiographical subject that does not micromanage her self-representation inspires addressees to give more self-representation back to the autobiographer, trying harder to understand her on her terms, how she represents herself, and how she defies stereotypes. If this is the case, the subject may best subvert stereotypes with indeterminate self-representation.

Multiracial autobiographies have a long tradition of subverting stereotypes with indeterminate self-representation. Walker claims that most of the multiracial autobiographies that make it onto bookshelves feature uplifting and transcendent moments of self-identification. Before this trend, however, multiracial autobiographers often used literary techniques to obscure their self-identifications. In his introduction to *Mixed Race Literature*, Jonathan Brennan claims that many of these texts did not seek to reveal multiracial people as they truly were, and, therefore, they should not be read "as *true* books of mixed identity, but as literary works employing literary strategies such as metaphor and myth-making, as true *books* of mixed identity" (2002, p. 8). Brennan claims that because "mixed writers are not adequately served by fixed identities," their autobiographies often feature narrators who struggle "to survive in liminal spaces between races" by blurring their identities (2002, p. 24).

Likewise, the narrator of *Dreams from My Father* obscures his racial identity. In his inaugural address, Obama cites racial divisions that cite the Wright controversy that cites his "Race" speech which itself cites *Dreams from My Father*, and that autobiography ends by citing a scene of racial unity at Wright's church. *Dreams from My Father* concludes with a wedding that brings together the disparate characters from different racial backgrounds who have appeared throughout the text. Through a parade of signifiers, the narrator racially identifies characters but does not racially self-identify. Instead, he ends this autobiography with the image of him standing between his black brother and white mother. Flanking himself in this final, lasting image, the narrator represents himself indeterminately. Racially representing himself by citing the racial identities of his relatives, he provokes readers to ask, "What is the racial identity of a man with a black brother and a white mother?"

This autobiographical subject similarly provokes readers of his identity in his "Race" speech. In one of the most blatant statements of self-identification Obama has ever made, one of the few moments in which Obama states, "I am…," he declares not, "I am black," "I am white," or "I am multiracial." Instead, he states, "I am the son of a black man from Kenya and a white woman from Kansas." The autobiographical subject behind this statement never says what race he is in and of himself. His racial identity cites others, and this indeterminate "self"-representation permits others to define him on their terms. In "Do Multiracial Subjects Really Challenge Race?" Steven Masami Ropp claims multiracial self-identifications do not challenge racial assumptions because people quickly fit those self-identifications back into "the existing logic of conventional racial meanings" (Ropp, 2004, p. 264). He claims multiracial people who self-identify multiracially, monoracially, or even racelessly just lead "to a reinscription of race albeit in more sophisticated hybrid and multiplied forms" (Ropp, 2004, p. 264). In the final scene of *Dreams from My Father*, however, the autobiographical subject resists reinscription by failing to self-identify at all. He suggests racial logic, but does so by citing relatives. He does not declare his identity but dares readers to label him according to their own logic of racial meanings.

And many have. The publishers of this autobiography received their story about the first black president of the *Harvard Law Review*, and Americans received their proof of progress with the first black President of the United States. Nevertheless, throughout his autobiography, his "Race" speech, and his discursive life, President Obama has complicated this identity. He has not challenged racial stereotypes by articulately countering them but by repeating them with a difference. He has not challenged racial assumptions through self-representation but by citing others. Whether in *Dreams from My Father*, his "Race" speech, or his inaugural address, Obama's autobiography has best challenged racial assumptions not by articulately self-identifying but by indeterminately citing relatives. Commissioned by others to write his black life, Obama claims that his autobiography is "a boy's search for his father, and through that search a workable meaning for his life as a black American" (2004, p. xvi). Throughout that search for the absent father, however, the mother remains. Throughout that search for a workable meaning for his life as a black American, the autobiographical subject keeps citing his life as the son of a white person. *Dreams from My Father* is haunted by the white mother. Whether he cites her in his inaugural address, "Race" speech, or *Dreams from My Father*, his autobiography extends beyond the black identity of his self-representation or others' stereotypes. Others may easily represent him as entirely African American, but by citing his white mother, Obama's autobiography makes that a complicated thing to do.

David A. Hollinger claims that because "Obama has never offered himself as the candidate of a particular ethnoracial group," he challenges American assumptions more than previous black candidates (2008, p. 1033). He claims that while Obama is celebrated as the first African American President, his autobiography renders his "whiteness hard to miss" (2008, p. 1034). This indeterminacy has caused, Hollinger argues, Americans to not only question Obama's blackness but their own racial identities. Hollinger argues that Obama's indeterminate self-representation goes beyond challenging notions of racial identity to challenge concepts of all identity by presenting "a compelling invitation to explore the limits of blackness especially, but also of whiteness, and of all color-coded devices for dealing with inequality in the United States" (2008, p. 1037). Whether or not Americans accept this invitation has yet to be seen, but Obama has extended it best not by articulately representing himself as much as indeterminately citing others.

Conclusion

As Obama addressed the shivering crowds gathered that January morning, he stated, "We know that our patchwork heritage is a strength, not a weakness." This statement draws attention to Obama's own extraordinary patchwork heritage. While a poetic image, patchwork is also a theoretical model for autobiography. Autobiographers have sought to undo multiracial stereotypes with seamless self-representation. In suggesting that autobiography corrects stereotypes, they overlook the extent to which autobiography shares stitches with the stereotypes it seeks to contradict. The autobiographical subject of *Dreams from My Father* knows himself according to the stitches he shares with others who are stitched to others who are stitched to others. If autobiography offers coherent self-creation, it also sews together incongruent scraps and is all the more beautiful for it. There is no self-representation any more than there is any patchwork made from a single piece of fabric. The fabric does not completely belong to the self nor does it completely belong to others. A single seam can ruin any piece of fabric except patchwork, and patchwork is ruined if it has too few seams. Patchwork is only beautiful if it perpetually invites more scraps to be sewn upon it. Too many seek to hem their autobiographies, hoping in vain to keep others from stitching onto their self-creation. The best autobiographies, however, are those that allow indeterminacy, that permit frayed edges where others can stitch on their own scraps. Permitting others to darn upon his patchwork, the autobiographer risks losing ownership over his patchwork, but, as Obama claims, this is a strength, not a weakness.

References
Bhabha, H. (1994) *The Location of Culture*. London: Routledge.

Brennan, J. (2002) "Introduction." *Mixed Race Literature*. Ed. J. Brennan, Stanford, CA: Stanford University Press.

Butler, J. (1999), *Gender Trouble: Feminism and the Subversion of Identity*,. New York: Routledge.

Butler, J. (2005) *Giving an Account of Oneself*, New York: Fordham University Press.

Chai, M. (2007) *Hapa Girl: A Memoir*, Philadelphia, PA: Temple University Press.

Derrida, J. (1988) *Limited Inc*, Evanston, IL: Northwestern University Press.

DeSouza, C. (2004) "Against Erasure: The Multiracial Voice in Cherrie Moraga's *Loving in the War Years.*" *Mixing It Up: Multiracial Subjects.* Eds. Kwan, SanSan and Kenneth Speirs, Austin, TX: University of Texas Press.

Hall, S. (1996) "Minimal Selves." *Black British Cultural Studies: A Reader.* Eds.

Houston A. Baker, Jr., Manthia Diawara, and Ruth H. Lindeborg, Chicago: University of Chicago Press.

Hilden, PP. (1995) *When Nickels Were Indians: An Urban Mixed-Blood Story,* Washington: Smithsonian Institution.

Hollinger, DA. (2008) "Obama, the Instability of Color Lines, and the Promise of a Postethnic Future." *Callaloo*, 31.4: 1033–7.

Kwan, S and Speirs, K. (2004) "Introduction." *Mixing It Up: Multiracial Subjects.* Eds. Kwan, SanSan and Kenneth Speirs, Austin, TX: University of Texas Press.

Locke, A. (ed) (1986) *The New Negro: An Interpretation,* Salem, N.H.: Ayer.

Mackin, J. (2009) "Inaugural Speech Focuses on Tradition".

4 March, *NewWave* (http://tulane.edu/news/newwave/012309_inaugural_address.cfm)

McBride, J. (1996) *The Color of Water: A Black Man's Tribute to His White Mother,* New York: Riverhead Books.

Nakashima, CL. (1992) "An Invisible Monster: The Creation and Denial of Mixed Race People in America." *Racially Mixed People in America.* Ed. Maria P.P. Root, Newbury Park: Sage.

Nash, PT. (1992) "Multicultural Identity and the Death of Stereotypes." *Racially Mixed People in America.* Ed. Maria P.P. Root, Newbury Park: Sage.

Obama, B. (2004), *Dreams From My Father: A Story of Race and Inheritance.* New York: Three Rivers Press

Obama, B. (2008), "Race Speech, Transcript." (www.nytimes.com/2008/03/18/us/politics/18text-obama.html).

Obama, B. (2009) "Barack Obama's Inaugural Address, Transcript." *New York Times*, January 20 (www.nytimes.com/2009/01/20/us/politics/20text-obama.html?pagewanted=3&_r=1).

Prasad, C. (2006) "Foreword." *Mixed: An Anthology of Short Fiction on the Multiracial Experience.* Ed. Chandra Prasad, New York: W.W. Norton.

Ropp, SM. (2004) "Do Multiracial Subjects Really Challenge Race?: Mixed Race Asians in the United States and the Caribbean." *"Mixed Race" Studies: A Reader.* Ed. and Intro. Jayne O. Ifekwunigwe, London: Routledge.

Sollors, W. (1997) *Neither Black Nor White Yet Both: Thematic Explorations of Interracial Literature,* Cambridge, MA: Harvard University Press.

Spickard, P. (2002) "The Subject is Mixed Race: The Boom in Biracial Biography." *Rethinking Mixed Race.* Eds. David Parker and Miri Song, London: Pluto Press.

Walker, R. (2006) "Introduction." *Mixed: An Anthology of Short Fiction on the Multiracial Experience.* Ed. Chandra Prasad, New York: W.W. Norton.

Zeleny, J. (2008) "Obama Urges U.S. to Grapple With Race Issue." *The New York Times.* 19 March, *New York Times* (www.nytimes. com/2008/03/19/us/politics/19obama.html?ref=politics).

CHAPTER FOUR

Racial revisionism, caste revisited: whiteness, blackness, and Barack Obama

Darryl G. Barthé, Jr.

In 1903, W.E.B. Du Bois observed that the problem of the twentieth century was the problem of the "color line." At the turn of the twentieth century, racial divides were being chiseled through the American working class. These divides were codified in laws demanding racial segregation and led to an era referred to by Rayford Logan as the "nadir of American race relations." Historians argue over when that era came to a close, but the vast majority agrees that it is over. Yet, is it possible that over the course of the last 100 years, or so, the United States has progressed through its darkest racial hour to the "post-racial" promised land envisioned by the Reverend Doctor Martin Luther King, Jr. where people are judged not by the color of their skin but the content of their character?

Millions of Americans passionately wished for that to be the case when the Democratic Party certified Barack Hussein Obama as the official party candidate for President. His was an American story for a new America where King's vision had manifested itself in the first non-white President of the United States. He was from humble beginnings, raised in a single-parent household by his mother. His name was Arabic and he identified himself as African American. When Obama won the White House on November 4 2008, his victory was hailed, by some, as the definitive end of Du Bois' "color line" problem.

While perceptions of race in the United States have certainly changed over the last century, it is hard to understand Obama's presidency as proof of a new "post-racial" America. In the immediate aftermath of his election, crimes of racial hatred were reported all over the United States directly linked to Obama's victory. In Standish, Maine, not exactly a hotbed of racial intolerance (or multicultural diversity), a local store even sponsored an informal "dead pool" wherein people were asked to wager on the date of Obama's assassination (Harnden, 2008).

Further complicating the "post-racial America" narrative is the circumstances of Barack Obama's parentage. Given that Obama's father was an immigrant from Kenya and his mother was white and from the American mid-west, it would seem that his self-identification as African American would be absolutely appropriate. Yet, Obama's self-identification was assaulted from all sides. Many asked that, if African American was synonymous with "black," then why should Obama be considered African American when he was only "half-black?" If African Americans have a claim to him, then, some argued, white Americans have an equal claim. Why should he be considered the first "black" President when he was "half-white?" Indeed, why could he not be considered "white" if he were just as much a child of his mother's as he was his father's?

These questions point to a new and different "color line" problem. This problem is rooted in a "racial revisionism" which serves primarily to obscure the realities of racism through a redefining of terms. There have always been Americans of mixed African and European ancestry. Historically, those Americans have been consistently racialized as "non-white" and most often as "negro," "black," or "colored." In order to make sense of this dynamic, it is necessary to understand the origins of "whiteness" and "blackness" in an historical context.

The first Africans to arrive in North America did not arrive as slaves and almost certainly did not conceive of themselves as "negros." The word, appropriated from the Latin word for "black" was a descriptive device divorced from any cultural or historical context for these people. Over time, that descriptive device would become a social designation constructed in opposition to and structurally inferior to "whiteness." The first Africans to arrive in Virginia may not have arrived as slaves, but legislation would ensure that black freedom would exist only as a misshapen simulacrum of white freedom. Where whiteness signified privilege, blackness had to signify subordination, a dynamic which was eventually codified in racial slavery. For those without claim to "whiteness," there was no recourse to white domination and so within this racialized caste system, "half-blackness" or "half-whiteness" were as problematic concepts as "partial-oppression" or "half-supremacy."

In an early example of racial legislation born out of white anxieties concerning mixed race people, a Legislative Act passed in Virginia in 1662 stipulated additional penalties for fornicators who sinned across color lines (Hening, 2010). Prior to this legislation, interracial fornication was not legally distinguished from intraracial fornication (Morgan, 1975, pp. 155–6). This public disapproval of sexual congress between Europeans and Africans speaks not only to a concern for public morality, but also articulates a clarification of the relative position of the negro caste as those who are forbidden from engaging with white people intimately, or as equals.

George M. Fredrickson, in his book *White Supremacy: A Comparative Study in American and South African History*, examines the origins of White-Anglo anxieties with regards to the sexuality of African people. He points to Shakespeare's characterization of Othello as a "lascivious Moor" as indicative of the Elizabethan characterization of uninhibited African sexuality. Indeed, promiscuous sexuality became identified with a concept of essential blackness (Fredrickson, 1981, pp. 99–100). Compared to Europeans, African sexuality was thought to be more primal, unrestrained and animalistic. Fredrickson examines the anti-miscegenation laws of Virginia, Maryland, and the Chesapeake Bay region in the 1600s and 1700s. According to Fredrickson, the majority of these laws seemed to fixate on the problem of white women and black men marrying, or perhaps more to the point, producing children of mixed heritage. Though such laws also included prohibitions on sexual relations between white men and black (or Indian) women, Fredrickson points out that "its stated purpose was to prevent 'that abominable mixture and spurious issue, which hereafter may increase in this dominion, as well by negroes, mulattoes and Indians intermarrying with English or other white *women* (italicized by author), as by their unlawful accompanying with one another'" (Fowler, 1963, quoted in Fredrickson, 1981, pp. 101–2, 307).

In one sense, the very existence of mixed race people, "that abominable mixture and spurious issue," represented a threat to a social order predicated on a binary caste division empowered by the mythology of race. This threat was articulated in essentialist terms, when some argued that the dilution of the mythical African libido with European blood was seen to be the cause of perversion and predisposition to a sordid sexuality, and as such, to be avoided in the interests of a rightly-ordered society. The unarticulated threat, of course, was the function that mixed race people played as "bridges" between the races, connecting white and non-white people through familial bonds. These connections, unchecked and un-moderated, were a threat to racial cohesion and thus undermined the racial logic of emerging American caste structures.

A little over a century after Virginians decided to discriminate against interracial fornicators, the political status of people with any traceable African ancestry would be articulated as being 3/5ths that of all other persons, for purpose of representation in the Congress of the United States of America, although this should not be misconstrued as evidence of democratic, political participation: these people would have no political voice at all, whether free or enslaved. The framers of the Constitution saw African slavery as a problematic issue in a nation founded, ostensibly, on the ideals of freedom and liberty, but agreed that the resolution to this problem would be a product of ongoing dialogue.

According to Fredrickson, by the 1820s, pervasive prejudices in the United States "taking the form of an implicit understanding that full citizenship was a white prerogative" would deny free African Americans rights that were enjoyed by European immigrants to the United States, even in the case of African Americans who had been free for generations (Fredrickson, 1981, p. 149). Yet, worse was still to come in one of the lowest points in America's ongoing dialogue on race.

One of the factors that directly contributed to the American Civil War would come in the majority Supreme Court decision in the case of *Dred Scott vs. Sanford* (1857). The inferior status of people of African ancestry, slave or otherwise, was clarified by the highest court in the land as "universally recognized as the natural position and real status of the negro" and that "no legal decision can be found in all America based on any other assumption" (Van Evrie, 2010).

Chief Justice Roger B. Taney, in giving the majority opinion was clear: "A free negro of the African race, whose ancestors were brought to this country and sold as slaves, is not a 'citizen' within the meaning of the Constitution of the United States," and furthermore, that

> The words "people of the United States" and "citizens" are synonymous terms, and mean the same thing. The question before us is, whether the class of persons described in the plea in abatement compose a portion of this people, and are constituent members of this sovereignty? We think they are not, and that they are not included, and were not intended to be included, under the word "citizens" in the Constitution, and can therefore claim none of the rights and privileges which that instrument provides for and secures to citizens of the United States. On the contrary, they were at that time considered as a subordinate and inferior class of beings, who had been subjugated by the dominant race, and, whether emancipated or not, yet remained subject to their authority, and had no rights or privileges but such as those who held the power and the government might choose to grant them. (Taney, 2010)

The Supreme Court of the United States had decided that no person of African ancestry had any claim to citizenship in the United States, nor any claim to any right or privilege of citizenship, at least in a U.S. Court. This is, perhaps, the definitive legal articulation of the aforementioned dynamic of white privilege/black subordination and the clearest definition of the limitations of the negro caste, prior to the Civil War. To be identified with the white caste was to be possessed of a validated political will and to enjoy the protection of the law, to be identified with the negro caste was to be bereft of any rights save those which were granted at the pleasure and convenience of the dominant white caste.

The American Civil War and the following period of Reconstruction was a chaotic period of great social change. The Emancipation Proclamation freed all enslaved people in the Southern States which chose to secede from the union, which did not include Kentucky, Missouri, Maryland, or Delaware. It was not until December of 1865, and the adoption of the thirteenth Amendment to the Constitution that slavery and involuntary servitude in the United States was abolished "except as a punishment for crime whereof the party shall have been duly convicted." Southern states would exploit that one exception to the prohibition against involuntary servitude to form chain gangs of imprisoned laborers who could be "rented" from the state by private business interests through convict lease arrangements.

The Thirteenth, Fourteenth and Fifteenth Amendments to the Constitution are known collectively as "The Reconstruction Amendments." The Fourteenth Amendment to the Constitution was adopted in 1868, effectively overruling the Dred Scott decision. It established that all persons born in the United States (including non-white people) would be considered citizens. The Fifteenth Amendment forbade the denial of a citizen's right to vote based on the citizen's "race, color, or previous condition of servitude." However, there remained a tragically substantial gap between the letter (and spirit) of the law and social practice, especially in the "Redeemed" South. African Americans nurtured aspirations of equality and opportunity after emancipation. Those aspirations were infused with momentum when their citizenship was recognized. Less than 30 years after the passing of the Fourteenth Amendment, the Supreme Court would dash those aspirations against the rocks of Jim Crow in the case of *Plessy vs. Ferguson* (1896).

In a dissenting opinion against establishing the legal principle of "separate but equal," Justice John Marshall Harlan suggested that "in the eye of the law, there is in this country no superior, dominant, ruling class of citizens. There is no caste here." Harlan's opinion was in the minority by a 7 to 1 margin. The Supreme Court had spoken: slavery or no slavery, there would be caste in the United States (Harlan, 2009).

The case of *Plessy vs. Ferguson* is taught in the United States, typically, as the test case which allowed racial segregation to fester and grow. Legally, "separate but equal" would be the foundation for all subsequent Jim Crow laws enacted in the United States until the case of *Brown vs. Board of Education of Topeka, Kansas* (1954) would provide the legal basis for the dismantling of legal segregation. However, what is often omitted from the standard narrative is that Homer Plessy was a mixed race Louisiana Creole from New Orleans and phenotypically "white."

In the words of Supreme Court Justice Henry Billings Brown, Homer Plessy "was a citizen of the United States and a resident of the state of Louisiana, of mixed descent, in the proportion of seven-eighths Caucasian and one-eighth African blood; that the mixture of colored blood was not discernible in him." However discernible or not, "blood quantum" laws and a tradition of determining the caste of mixed race people through hypodescent, expressed colloquially as the "one-drop rule," made Plessy "colored," and thus subject to the social conventions reserved for the negro caste in the United States (Brown, 2009).

Mary Niall Mitchell begins and ends her work, *Raising Freedom's Child: Black Children and Visions of the Future After Slavery,* with an analysis of a photograph of two recently emancipated slave children from New Orleans named Isaac and Rosa. Isaac is a very dark-skinned child with distinctly African features. Rosa is a fair-skinned child with distinctly European features. Mitchell raises a number of provocative questions in her analysis of this picture. "Light-skinned girls like Rosa...seemed to foreshadow the blurring of racial categories (such that 'white' people might be enslaved if slavery continued) and the difficulty of classification once 'white'-looking slaves became free" (Mitchell, 2008, p. 7). This blurring of racial categories made the world of the "one-drop rule" a confidence game at best and, at worst, it exposed the arbitrary nature of racial designation in the U.S. for what it was.

It was precisely for this reason that Plessy was chosen to challenge the law which demanded that white and black people be separated in railway cars in the first place. Plessy was *passé blanc,* or in English, able "to pass for white." The humiliation of being ejected from the train, argued Plessy's attorneys, had deprived Plessy of the property of his reputation as a white man. However, the Supreme Court had rejected his right to a reputation as a white man, *despite his appearance* based on his acknowledgement of his African ancestry, regardless of how remote it may have been (Lofgren, 1987, pp. 47–56).

In the end, Plessy did not prevail. Though perhaps it was the absurdity of the circumstances which led Justice Brown to offer Homer Plessy the advice to challenge his "blackness" under the law in Louisiana (Brown, 2009). As historians David Brown and Clive Webb have observed, although passing for white may have "improved the status of individual African Americans, it represented a tacit acceptance on their part of the southern caste system" (Brown and Webb, 2007, p. 224). Plessy did not bother to challenge his "blackness" in court. For Homer Plessy, "blackness" was not the issue.

As historian David Roediger points out, American racist ideological gymnastics would, at various times, designate the Irish and the Italians as 'non-white' or at least as "'situationally white,' 'not quite white,' 'off-white,' 'semiracialized,'(or only) 'conditionally white.'" American racial categories meant very little outside of a context in which the discrepancy "between the rights of people of color and of Europeans were at issue" (Roediger, 2005, pp. 12–13). If even the Irish and Italians were only conditionally and situationally allowed claims to the privilege of the "white caste," what was there to be gained in arguing over the "Africanness" of Homer Plessy?

Even in communities which had no history of segregation, laws which called for "separate but equal" facilities for "whites" and "coloreds" were passed with the hope that they might bring order to a society which struggled to redefine social norms in the wake of the upheaval of Emancipation, Reconstruction, industrialization, and urbanization. This new social order was defined by a new articulation of the negro caste with the same old characteristics of subordination, inferiority and subjugation as articulated by Chief Justice Roger Taney in the Dred Scott decision only 39 years prior, with one, crucial exception: the acknowledgement of citizenship and legal equality. The highest court in the land had approved the creation of two Americas within the United States, but because the law recognized, at least nominally, the inherent equality before the law of all citizens this "imposition of racial segregation...had the unintended effect of creating a greater sense of strength and cohesion within the black community" as "African Americans established informal and formal support networks" and community institutions, according to Brown and Webb (2007, p. 225). However, the legal realities of racial equality in the United States did not address the social realities of residual bigotry, left over from the previous 300 years of legislated racism. Still, autonomous (or at least semi-autonomous) black institutions, especially educational institutions, would allow African Americans to define themselves outside of the bounds of the arbitrary ascription historically reserved as the privilege of white dominators.

As time has passed, the nomenclature by which the negro caste is identified has changed over time. Or rather, it is changing. Over the course of the last hundred years, the negro has morphed into the "colored" which then morphed into the "Afro-American," which proceeded to morph into the American "black" before (arguably) settling on the contemporary "African American." Many of these changes have occurred only in the last 40 years as African Americans have struggled to define themselves in a social context in which the era of American white supremacy is, at least legally, over.

Barack Hussein Obama was born in Honolulu, Hawaii on August 4 1961 at 7:24 in the evening (Henig and Miller, 2010; for the image of the birth certificate itself, see Fact Check (2011), LA Times (2011), or White House (2011)). Three years after he was born, the Civil Rights Act of 1964 would become law, bringing Jim Crow to an end. Thus, it is safe to say that Barack Obama was born into a nation that did not fully acknowledge his political equality (not to mention social equality) with his own mother, or maternal grandparents, because of the color of his skin, the texture of his hair and the shape of his lips, and nose, not to mention the fact of his Kenyan father.

It is the history of a binary, racialized caste division that separated people into one of two caste positions, that makes Obama "black" or African American, as he identifies himself. The terms "multiracial" and "biracial" often may carry personal significance for those who identify themselves as such, indeed, it could be argued that there is an inherent protest against arbitrary racialization in such self-identification as well, but Barack Obama, at a glance, is not perceived to be the son of a Kenyan father and an Anglo American mother so much as he is perceived as a "black" man. In his own words, "I identify as African American—that's how I'm treated and that's how I'm viewed" (Associated Press, 2008). If there was any doubt to Obama's claim, a CBS news article published in November of 2007 followed up Obama's statement of self-identification with commentary from one nameless, white, South Carolina voter who said "I don't want to sound prejudiced or anything, but for one, I am not going to vote for a colored man to be our President" (CBS, 2007). It seems that even if some Americans may not want to *appear* prejudiced or bigoted, the fact remains that some Americans are very much prejudiced and bigoted and the fact of Obama's white mother does not immunize him from it.

The U.S. census of 2000 presented the first opportunity for Americans of multi-racial heritage to choose more than one racial category on the census. In times past, Americans of mixed ancestry (often regardless of proportion) were identified as "mulatto," an archaic term derived from the Spanish "mulo" or mule (i.e. the result of the union of a horse and a donkey). The offensive connotations of "mulatto" necessitated new nomenclature however, so new terms were evoked: biracial, or multiracial, for example. As a result of the revising of racial categorization, more than six million Americans identified themselves as multiracial (Carroll, 2008). Yet, in the months leading up to the presidential election of 2008, commentary on Obama's historic candidacy could hardly be described as post-racial.

Louis Chude-Sokei, in an opinion-editorial article for the *Los Angeles Times* in February of 2007, observes a very real distinction between immigrant Africans and African Americans. Chude-Sokei suggests that a "good proportion of [African or Afro-Caribbean] immigrants tend to be better educated than African Americans, don't have the 'chip' of racial resentment on their shoulder and exhibit the classic immigrant optimism about assimilation into the mainstream culture," in contrast to African Americans who are more "responsive to American racial traumas," and whose leaders "are unsure of Obama's loyalties to African American causes" (Chude-Sokei, 2007).

Leslie Fulbright, in an article in the *San Francisco Chronicle* in February of 2007, observed that many "insist he is not African American and is unsuited to be a black candidate, because he is not a direct descendant of slaves and hasn't had what they see as an authentic African American experience." The article goes on to frame the notion of an "authentic African American experience" as a personal connection to slavery and Jim Crow segregation, connections that Barack Obama's immigrant father lacked. Fulbright quotes the Reverend Al Sharpton to make the point: "Just because you are our color doesn't make you our kind" (Fulbright, 2007).

Lindsey Barrett articulated a similar argument in a January 2008 article for the Nigerian *Daily Sun*. Barrett observed that "strictly speaking Barack Obama is not an African-American—but an African who is American. He's not a descendant of the enslaved Africans who built America without reward or respect for their contributions. He is in fact a first generation American, while the real African-Americans are people whose lineage can be traced back fifteen generations and more." Barrett's identification of Obama as an "African who is American," like Chude-Sokei, conveniently ignores the reality of his maternal ancestry (which, extends to the mid-1600s in North America (Wade, 2007)), and although Barrett acknowledges that "because of the inherited racist perception in America that considers even a single drop of African blood as being the dominant factor in establishing one's ethnic identity, Barack, whose mother was a White lady, is seen as an African-American or 'Black' person," that insight apparently does not stop him from declaring Obama "African" despite the fact that Obama was born in Hawaii (Barrett, 2008).

In March 2008, in an opinion-editorial article for the *Los Angeles Times*, David Ehrenstein summoned the image of the "Magic Negro" in cinema to explain Obama's appeal. Ehrenstein draws a connection between Barack Obama and Sidney Poitier, Morgan Freeman and Will Smith. "He's there to assuage white 'guilt' (i.e., the minimal discomfort they feel) over the role of slavery and racial segregation in American history, while replacing stereotypes of a dangerous, highly sexualized black man with a benign figure for whom interracial sexual congress holds no interest" (Ehrenstein, 2007).

This insight would be seized upon by Rush Limbaugh and turned into a musical parody based on the children's song, "Puff the Magic Dragon." Assisted by an Al Sharpton impressionist, Paul Shanklin, Limbaugh would play "Barack the Magic Negro" periodically throughout the election season of 2008. The lyrics to the song referenced Ehrenstein's article directly:

> Barack the Magic Negro lives in DC
> The LA Times, they called him that
> Cause he's not authentic like me
> Yeah the guy from the LA paper
> Said he makes guilty whites feel good
> They'll vote for him, and not for me
> [...]
> (Rush Limbaugh Show, 2007)

The last verse of the song references comments made by Joe Biden on the campaign trail, who described Obama as "the first mainstream African American who is articulate and bright and clean and a nice-looking guy." After being criticized for his comments, Biden attempted to explain himself and even placed a call to Obama to apologize. Obama downplayed Biden's comments although he did challenge the historical accuracy of them (Thai and Barrett, 2007). This same graciousness would be on full display in January 2010 when Obama would deflect criticism from Democratic Senator Harry Reid after Reid was excoriated by both Democrats and Republicans alike for remarks made privately during the presidential campaign of 2008 that

Obama's success could be, at least partly, attributed to his relatively light skin and to his absence of a "negro dialect" (Preston, 2010).

Reid's comments were almost certainly absent of malice, but are telling in another way. Race, although sometimes articulated as a function of "blood" (genetics), is also understood as a cultural identification. Perhaps it is better understood this way: race as a social construct. Clearly, the attachment of cultural identifiers with race would suggest that as culture changes and evolves, so too would concepts of race within that culture. Certainly, Reid's comments would not have raised an eyebrow only 50 years ago, yet in 2008 to refer to an African American as a negro necessitated a public apology if Reid were to distance himself from the specter of racism which was responsible, culturally, for the creation of the negro caste to begin with.

Although Reverend Al Sharpton may muse on whether or not Obama is of "his kind" (i.e. African American), one thing is certain and that is that he is most definitely not white. The social reality of the historical binary division of race in America and the lingering traces of caste consciousness do not allow Obama a claim to the "property" of whiteness. Multiraciality and biraciality do not exist in the historical paradigm of American race and caste thus Obama's "blackness" is an "institutional fact," if not a "brute fact" (Searle, 1995). Nowhere is this more apparent than in the rhetoric of the far-right wing of the Republican Party.

The "Tea Party" is a particularly vitriolic sect of the Republican Party organized with funding from David H. Koch and Charles G. Koch, the sons of Fred Koch, a founding member of the far-right wing John Birch Society (*Arkansas Times*, 2009). Central to the Tea Party's political narrative is that Obama is, somehow, "un-American." Never mind the deeply totalitarian political sensibility entailed in labeling one ideological position or another as "American" or "un-American," the racist subtext of this criticism cannot be discounted. The most extreme examples of this sensibility can be found in the "Birther Movement" (whose members are derisively referred to as "Birthers") which maintains that Barack Obama's birth certificate is somehow inauthentic and that he perpetrated fraud to capture the White House (*Independent*, 2010). This "movement" operates, apparently, without any acknowledgement or respect for the historical struggle in which people of African descent have engaged in order to be considered citizens of the United States.

When confronted by the NAACP over the racism and bigotry expressed by Tea Party protestors, Tea Partiers responded by suggesting that their movement was "colorblind." Yet, according to researchers at the Kellogg School of Management at Northwestern University, a "colorblind" ideology does not promote tolerance or equality so much as it can serve to "lead people to turn a blind eye to even overt examples of racial discrimination and hamper the prospect for intervention" and furthermore, that it "can actually reduce individuals' sensitivity to meaningful racial differences. And as a result, when discrimination does occur, individuals with a colorblind mindset often fail to see it as such" (PR Newswire United Business Media, 2010). Is it possible that "colorblind" Tea Partiers have been rendered unable to perceive the racism within their own rhetoric?

For the Tea Party, and the Birthers, the election of the first black President was not seen as a sign of progress, much less the emergence of a "post-racial" America. For many in the Tea Party, Obama's election to the presidency represented something else, something terrifying. Latching on to comments uttered by a sobbing woman at a town hall meeting in Arkansas on August 5 2010, Tea Partiers in subsequent rallies producing signs proclaiming "I want my America back." Of course, this all raises the question: what "America" are they yearning for? Robert J. Elisberg, a comedy writer and blogger for the online journal *The Huffington Post* offered an interpretation:

> They want to go back to an earlier time, a friendlier time, a better time in America of our youth, a time when everything was taken care of for us by our parents, and the time of our grandparents. A time of that mythical Shining City on the Hill. A warmer time that we see in old movies. A happier time. "I want my country back," they say. Back. To that good, gracious wonderful time in America back where there were... No blacks in the White House. (Elisberg, 2010)

Far from ushering in a new "post-racial" America, Barack Obama has become one of the most racially polarizing figures in American politics. The fact of his biracial ancestry has not had a significant impact on the perception of Obama as a "black" man by his allies or his enemies. The hostility Obama has met from the American far right has been posed as a reaction against Obama's policies, which have been characterized as "socialism" despite the fact that Obama has consistently embraced political positions that no mainstream right-wing politician in the rest of the developed world would dare embrace for fear of being labeled a right-wing radical. Indeed, from domestic issues of taxation to the "War on Terror," Obama has embraced policies originally promoted by the Bush administration, so it is hard to take "colorblind" Tea Party critiques at face value, accentuated as they are with signs depicting Obama mugging Uncle Sam with a knife to his throat or Obama dressed as a witch doctor with a bone through his nose or describing his agenda as "White Slavery" (see Huffington Post, 2009; Think Progress, 2009; or CNN, 2009). Certainly, there are those who might desperately wish for a new, "post-racial" America but wishing it so does not make it so and Barack Obama, whether identified as biracial, multiracial, black or African American, has certainly not presided over a nation where race and, more to the point, racism, are things of the past.

Still, the reality of a non-white President in 2008 would have been unimaginable in 1908 and structurally impossible in 1808. The fact that President Obama identifies himself as African American is significant and, in itself, represents a challenge to racial preconceptions. Given the circumstances of his parents, he is undoubtedly "African" and "American" but what is a "black" man in the United States without the historical scars of slavery and Jim Crow? What is a "black" man without caste? The looming specter of "mixed race hegemony," to borrow Jolivette's interpretive device, only promises to further complicate such questions.

References

Arkansas Times. (2009) 'Weep No More, My Lady,' editorial published online, 27 August (www.arktimes.com/arkansas/weep-no-more-my-lady/Content?oid=948877).

Associated Press (2008) 'Obama's True Colors: Black, white...or neither?,' 14 December, MSNBC.com, sec. U.S. News/Race and Ethnicity (www.msnbc.msn.com/id/28216005/).

Barrett, L. (2008) *Obama May Win But He's No African-American, The Daily Sun, Nigeria* (http://worldmeets.us/dailysunna000003.shtml)

Brown, J. 2009, 'Brown, J., Opinion Of The Court, Supreme Court Of The United States, 163 U.S. 537, *Plessy Vs. Ferguson,*' Cornell University Law School, 1 February (www.law.cornell.edu/supct/html/historics/USSC_CR_0163_0537_ZO.html).

Brown, D and Webb, C. (2007) *Race in The American South From Slavery to Civil Rights,* Edinburgh: Edinburgh University Press Ltd.

Carroll, J. (2008) *Behind the Scenes: Is Barack Obama black or biracial?* CNN, *American Morning* (http://articles.cnn.com/2008-06-09/politics/btsc.obama.race_1_black-candidate-black-father-barack-obama?_s=PM:POLITICS).

CBS (2007) *CBS Evening News,* 'Obama's Racial Identity Still an Issue,' 27 November, News.com (www.cbsnews.com/stories/2007/11/27/eveningnews/main3546210.shtml)

Chude-Sokei, L. (2007) *Redefining 'black'* (Los Angeles Times Opinion, Viewed 15 March (www.latimes.com/news/opinion/la-op-chude-sokei18feb18,0,7298828.story?coll=la-opinion-center).

CNN (2009) (http://articles.cnn.com/2009-09-17/politics/obama. witchdoctor.teaparty_1_witch-doctor-tea-party-express-politics-and-african-american-studies?_s=PM:POLITICS).

Ehrenstein, D. (2007) *Obama the 'Magic Negro'*, *Los Angeles Times Opinion* (www.latimes.com/news/opinion/commentary/la-oe-ehrenstein19mar19,0,3391015.story).

Elisberg, R.J. (2010) 'The Nobel 'I Want My Country Back' Thing', *The Huffington Post*, published online on September 28, 2010, Viewed 22 June 2011 (www.huffingtonpost.com/robert-j-elisberg/the-noble-i-want-my-count_b_741606.html).

Fact Check (2011) 31 March (www.factcheck.org/UploadedFiles/birth_certificate_3.jpg).

Fowler, D. (1963) *Northern Attitudes Towards Interracial Marriage: A Study of Legislation and Public Opinion in the Middle Atlantic States and States of the Old Northwest*, Ph.D. diss., Yale University, 37–39; quoted in G.M. Fredrickson, 1981, *White Supremacy: A Comparative Study in American and South African History*, New York: Oxford University Press, pp. 101–2, 307.

Fredrickson, G.M. (1981) *White Supremacy: A Comparative Study in American and South African History*, New York: Oxford University Press, pp. 99–100.

Fulbright, L. (2007) *Obama's Candidacy Sparks Debates on Race: Is He African American if His Roots Don't Include Slavery?* San Francisco Chronicle Online (www.sfgate.com/cgi-bin/article.cgi?f=/c/a/2007/02/19/OBAMA.TMP).

Harlan, J (2009) 'Harlan, J., Dissenting Opinion, Supreme Court of the United States 163 US 537, *Plessy Vs. Ferguson*,' Cornell University Law School, 1 February (www.law.cornell.edu/supct/html/historics/USSC_CR_0163_0537_ZD.html).

Harnden, T 2008, *Racial Incidents Sour Barack Obama's Victory* 15 June, 2011, *The Telegraph* (www.telegraph.co.uk/news/worldnews/barackobama/3474135/Racial-incidents-sour-Barack-Obamas-victory.html).

Henig, J and Miller, J. (2010) *Born in the USA: The Truth About Obama's Birth Certificate* (http://factcheck.org/2008/08/born-in-the-usa/).

Hening, WW (ed). (2010) *The Statutes at Large: Being a Collection of All the Laws of Virginia, from the First Session of the Legislature, in the Year 161* [1809–23], 2: 170 (www.lva.virginia.gov/public/guides/rn17_tithables.htm).

Huffington Post. (2009) (www.huffingtonpost.com/2009/04/16/10-most-offensive-tea-par_n_187554.html).

Independent (2010) 'Born in the USA? Someone doesn't think so', *The Independent Online,* 31 March (www.independent.co.uk/news/world/americas/born-in-the-usa-someone-doesnt-think-so-1930680.html).

LA Times. (2011) 31 March (http://articles.latimes.com/2011/apr/27/nation/la-na-obama-birth-certificate-20110428) or 17 June, White House (www.whitehouse.gov/blog/2011/04/27/president-obamas-long-form-birth-certificate).

Lofgren, CA. (1987) *The Plessy Case: A Legal-Historical Interpretation,* New York: Oxford University Press, pp. 47–56.

Mitchell, MN. (2008) *Raising Freedom's Child: Black Children and Visions of the Future After Slavery,* New York: New York University, p. 7.

Morgan, ES. (1975) *American Slavery, American Freedom: The Ordeal of Colonial Virginia,* New York: W.W. Norton & Co.

PR Newswire United Business Media. (2010) 'In Blind Pursuit of Racial Equality,' published online on 22 September (www.prnewswire.com/news-releases/in-blind-pursuit-of-racial-equality-103516464.html).

Preston, M. (2010) *Reid Apologizes for 'Negro Dialect' Comment,* CNN Politics, Viewed 15 March (http://politicalticker.blogs.cnn.com/2010/01/09/reid-apology-for-negro-dialect-comment/?fbid=13cu_ApGngy).

Roediger, D. (2005) *Working Toward Whiteness: How America's Immigrants Became White; The Strange Journey from Ellis Island to the* Suburbs, New York: Basic Books, pp 12–13.

Rush Limbaugh Show (2007) Transcript, 26 April, *Drive-by Media Misreporting of 'Barack the Magic Negro' Song* (www.rushlimbaugh.com/home/estack_12_13_06/BarackSection/Drive-By_Media_Misreporting_of__Barack_the_Magic_Negro__Song.guest.html).

Searle, JR. (1995) *The Construction of Social Reality,* New York: Simon and Schuster, p 2.

Taney, RB. (2010) 'The Dred Scott decision: Opinion of Chief Justice Taney' with introduction by Dr. J. H. Van Evrie' *American Memory: Slaves and the Courts, 1740-1860,* 28 March, Library of Congress (www.archive.org/stream/dredscottdecisio00unit/dredscottdecisio00unit_djvu.txt)

Thai, X and Barrett, T. (2007) *Biden's Description of Obama Draws Scrutiny,* CNN Politics (www.cnn.com/2007/POLITICS/01/31/biden.obama/).

Think Progress. (2009) (http://thinkprogress.org/politics/2009/09/12/60525/912-signs/).

Van Evrie, JH. (2010) 'The Dred Scott decision: Opinion of Chief Justice Taney with introduction by Dr. J. H. Van Evrie' in *American Memory: Slaves and the Courts, 1740-1860* (Library of Congress Online), 28 March, Library of Congress (www.archive.org/stream/dredscottdecisio00unit/dredscottdecisio00unit_djvu.txt)

Wade, N. (2007) *Cheney and Obama: It's Not Genetic, New York Times* (www.nytimes.com/2007/10/21/weekinreview/21basic.html?_r=2&oref=slogin).

White House, 2011, 17 June (www.whitehouse.gov/blog/2011/04/27/president-obamas-long-form-birth-certificate).

Part II

Beyond black and white identity politics

CHAPTER FIVE

Obama Mamas and mixed race: hoping for "a more perfect union"

Wei Ming Dariotis and Grace J. Yoo

Introduction

In reviewing data from a national study, conducted in May 2009, of mothers and their feelings about the candidacy of Barack Obama for President, we saw a narrative emerge about his identity as a mixed race African American. Some of the mothers who responded themselves identify as mixed race, others identify as the mothers of mixed race children, and still others see Obama's mixed race identity as a metaphor for healing the racialized fissures in U.S. political and social culture and for mending the relationship of the United States with the international community. Mothers surveyed identified with Obama personally—especially if they were also mixed race—but they also identified with him as a member of a family. Thus, as one white 55-year-old with three grown children from Pennsylvania wrote so eloquently, they embraced the idea that Obama's daughters, "those two little girls running around on the White House lawn[,] will change the soul and heart of America." It is this hope that shines through the comments made by these Obama Mamas.

The original aims of this national study included a) examining reasons why mothers became supporters of Barack Obama, b) identifying how mothers involved themselves in the Obama campaign, c) understanding how mothers engaged others, including their children, in their support of Obama, and d) understanding their concerns for their children and the hopes they placed in the Obama presidency. What this self-selected group of women expressed were their concerns about race and race relations, and the persistence of racial inequality in the United States. For many mothers, Obama's candidacy represented a hope of healing the racial, economic, and political divisions within the U.S., and also between the U.S. and other nations.

Methodology

Data collection commenced during Mother's Day weekend, and continued from May 9 to 31 2008. Prospective participants were emailed a letter inviting them to take part in surveys. Identified as a Barack Obama supporter, the co-investigator, Grace J. Yoo, registered with the Barack Obama website and then, through the website, sent an invitation to several email networks including 34 networks focused on Obama Mama networks, seven Women for Obama networks, two Parents for Obama networks, and four more general and ethnic specific networks. Three-hundred and fifty-six women responded to the survey over a four-week period. Those who were interested in participating clicked on a designated link to the surveymonkey.com survey. From the outset of the survey, the voluntary nature of the study was stressed and participants were told they had the right to refuse to participate in the study. The survey, taking about ten minutes to complete, consists of questions about participants' demographic background, reasons why participants supported Obama for President, their involvement in the campaign, their top three concerns as mothers, their thoughts about the impact of a possible President Obama on their children's futures, and the possible significance of Obama as President for the nation.

In all, 356 women responded, between the ages of 22 to 75 with the mean age of 42 years of age (see Table 5.1). Survey respondents included mothers from all 50 states, but the top ten states where responding mothers resided were first California, followed by Pennsylvania, Illinois, North Carolina, Florida, New York, Texas, Minnesota, Oregon, and Maryland, in that order. The sample also consisted of women with 1 to 12 children with a mean of two children. Women had children of various ages, with 40 percent under the age of 4, 36 percent between the ages of 5 to 11, and 29 percent between the ages of 12 to17. Thirty-three percent had children over the age of 18. In terms of party affiliation, 86 percent were registered as Democrat, 10 percent Independent, and 4 percent as Republican—though some mentioned having switched from Republican to Democrat in order to be able to vote for Obama in their state's primary. The majority of the women (75 percent) were married, followed by 15 percent divorced, 8 percent single and 2 percent widowed. In addition, the majority of respondents reported a high level of education, including a majority with post-graduate education (43 percent), followed by college graduates (28 percent), those with some college education (26 percent) and those with a high school education (4 percent).

In terms of race, the majority of respondents identified as white (63.5 percent), followed by African American (22.5 percent), mixed race (7.3 percent), Latina (4.2 percent) and Asian American (2.2 percent), while no respondents identified as primarily Native American. In particular, the rate of response for African Americans and for mixed race people is significantly higher than the proportion of these groups in the general population (12 percent African American and 2.0 percent mixed race). This might indicate a higher level of identification with Obama as a mixed race African American, or a higher desire to speak to the issues because of their own identities.

Findings

There were several key themes that emerged from the surveys, including concerns about the status of African Americans, people of color, and people of mixed race; the relationships between racialized groups; and the persistence of racial inequality in the United States. Economic and political divisions within the U.S. and international political tensions were also problems an Obama presidency was seen as having the potential to solve.

Obama as a visible representation of African Americans, people of color, and people of mixed race

For women of color, Obama's race and ethnicity carries momentous historic import for their perception of more promising futures for their children. The election of Obama represents the possibility that anyone's child could become President because the election of someone who is African American and white would mean anyone could have the opportunity to attain political power. It means that the hopes for power and representation by people of various racial and ethnic backgrounds are possible in this lifetime.

For example, a divorced 39-year-old Latina woman with two children from Massachusetts wrote:

'I want America to be true to its word. Justice and equality for all its citizens. Electing the first black president in the U.S. would mean that a lifetime milestone has been accomplished for every citizen. That he has transcended race at least to become the President of the U.S.A. This will help empower others to keep reaching for your goals and dreams despite your background.'

Specific groups such as African American mothers, white mothers of mixed race children, and mixed race mothers each had particular perspectives on how Obama's racial identity might affect the status of African Americans, people of mixed race, and people of color generally.

Table 5.1: Background of Obama Mama survey participants

Background of Obama Mama survey participants N=356		
What are the ages of your children? Please check all that apply		
	Response Frequency	Response Count
0–4 years old	39.8%	140
5–11 years old	35.8%	126
12–18 years old	28.7%	101
Over 18 years of age	33.0%	116
What political party do you identify with?		
Democrat	85.9%	298
Republican	4.0%	14
Independent	9.5%	33
Decline to State	0.6%	2
Other (please specify)		13
What is your martial status?		
Single	8.0%	28
Married/Partnered	74.6%	261
Divorced/Separated	15.1%	53
Widowed	2.3%	8
How do you self-identify racially and ethnically?		
White	63.5%	226
African American	22.5%	80
Latina	4.2%	15
Asian American	2.2%	8
Mixed Race	7.3%	26
What is your highest level of education?		
High school graduate	3.7%	13
Some college	25.6%	90
College graduate	27.9%	98
Post graduate education	42.7%	150

African American mothers

Many African American mothers discussed how the election of an African American male would have an impact on how their children would and could see themselves. This election to the highest political office —the U.S. presidency—represents access to the most inaccessible reaches of U.S. society.

This view is expressed by a 39-year-old single mother, an African American with two children from New Jersey, who wrote: "If Senator Obama becomes President of the United States of America just having the job and seeing that America has elected an African American man to the presidency will impact my children's lives."

A 33-year-old African American single mother with one child from Washington DC argued that, "My son will be able to look to the White House and see someone who looks like him and his family. I think that will have a huge impact on how he views himself and his race."

A 39-year-old African American single mother with three children from New Jersey envisioned:

> 'changes in American similar to Dr. King's dream, where everyone is treated equally and color is not a factor. I envision peace and an America that considers itself equal to other countries not better than other countries. I envision an America where my daughters will have the same access and opportunity as our White sisters and brothers.'

An African American woman with three children from Pennsylvania stated emphatically:

> 'NO matter what, this election has already MADE HISTORY! IT is the first election that we have had a woman or an African American run for office... what's MORE IMPORTANT—he's a man of multi-ethnicity!!! Even 30 years ago NO one could have imagined that! SO really that IS HISTORY MAKING! I'm VERY encouraged to talk to my son about this and ALL the misconceptions about each of the candidates...and HOW important it is to KNOW the FACTS...FOR TRUTH is in the FACTS. SO it has a HUGE impact for U.S....it is in itself a learning thing!'

European American mothers

White mothers of mixed race children are particularly interested in how Obama's mixed race identity might affect their children's identity development. White mothers of mixed race children experienced a positive investment in seeing change work for their families. Many expressed the feeling that the election of Barack Obama would validate their own children's experiences growing up in a mixed race family, because his success indicates that mixed race people and interracial families are functional, in contrast to the stereotypes that pathologize them.

A 41-year-old white mother with three kids from California pointed out:

> 'My children are mixed race and for them to see a president who looks like them, to me, would be outstanding. My husband and I already tell them they can do whatever they put their minds to, but how extraordinary to see a man who's actually done that become president.'

A white 22-year-old mother with three children from Montana declared "I love that he cares so much about our youth. As a mother of three children I want them to grow up in country that cares about their people, no matter their age, race, gender, or finances."

A white 52-year-old woman with one daughter from Michigan wrote "Our daughter is mixed race and is so excited to see an African American person run for President. We talk in simple ways about different kinds of politics and how Obama exemplifies our values. She has requested and received Obama buttons and wears them proudly."

A white 49-year-old with two children from California affirmed: "My children are mixed race and for them to see a President who looks like them, to me, would be outstanding."

A white 63-year-old with 12 children from Georgia familiarized Obama by using his personal name and her son's in a way that connected the two: "My own son is mixed race like Barack. I tell Kevin that he is a child of tomorrow. When Barack is elected, tomorrow will have come : -)"

Several mothers who identified themselves as white and their children as being of another race, rather than being mixed race, may have been indicating that their children are transracially adopted. Their concerns are similar to those of the white mothers of mixed race children. They also realized the importance of visible representation and a powerful role model for the self-esteem of their children.

A white 55-year-old woman with one child from Vermont shared:

> 'Our daughter, who is Asian, watched the primary debate in New Hampshire and first saw the white Republican men debate, and then saw the diverse Democratic candidates. She listened to Obama's speech on race. She is part of dinner table conversation and often watches the news with us, she will march with the Obama contingent at the Fourth of July parade.'

A 32-year-old white woman with three young children from Illinois stated that:

> 'My children are all African American. I think it will make a huge difference to have a president who looks like them. My oldest daughter is already very excited that Barack Obama is 'brown' like her. Sen. Obama believes in equality for children in all the areas of concern that I have. I believe that he can bring the country together and improve education, health care, and race relations.'

Mixed race mothers

The mixed race mothers who responded tended to focus on their own identification with Obama as a mixed race person, rather than focusing as much as the African American and white mothers did on their children's future as represented by Obama. Based on their own experiences as mixed race people, mixed race mothers could see how Obama might serve as a bridge to U.S. and international racial and geo-political harmony.

A 33-year-old mixed race mother with two children from Ohio stated that: "As a biracial individual in America, I highly identify with his personal experience and agree with an overwhelming majority of his policies."

A 50-year-old mixed race mother with two children from New Jersey declared: "He is what I see when I look at America all blended together. He is for a fresh new change that I have never seen, a new approach!!!! He has worked in the communities (which is not just talk). He seems approachable and real. A change is gonna come!!"

Mending social, political, religious, and economic divisions in the U.S.

Many mothers feel that the election of Obama as President would represent a way to bring the country together—Obama's mixed race background is seen as not only healing racism in the U.S., but also to healing other social divisions threatening to tear apart the fabric of the country. According to many of these mothers, these divisions are not solely about race, but the other divisions in the U.S. regarding economic inequality and the differing viewpoints to solving many of the nation's crisis. For many of these mothers, Obama embodies change that could mend many of the fractures and fissues in U.S. politics and policy-making.

A 43-year-old African American woman with one child from North Carolina identified with Obama, stating "Barack Obama is from my generation with a multicultural view of the world politics."

A white 43-year-old mother with two children from Rhode Island considered the special significance of Obama's experiences of living in a Muslim country:

> 'I've lived in Muslim countries, even while I'm Christian, so I know how they're thinking about issues...electing a President that has lived in a Muslim country could not be a more effective message that we are breaking from Bush and Cheney policies. And it will make us more safe. It will give me more credibility on the world stage than any other candidate that is running.'

A white 41-year-old mother with four children from Pennsylvania wrote:

> 'I want to see all people come together, no matter what race, religion, gender, or political party, to save our country which in my opinion needs saving really bad. I want to see change in Washington, and I want people to look past color or gender and see the real people.'

A white 38-year-old mother with two children from North Carolina wrote:

'Bringing people together to work towards goals that benefit the greater population. Accepting differing points of views on topics/issues and continuing to work together to make this country better for all of us. Not leaving our neighbors out because they don't see things the way we do, finding common interests and motivators to keep everyone engaged and not feeling disenfranchised. Learning how to disagree with out being disagreable.'

A divorced African American 43-year-old mother with one child from North Carolina said:

'I think Washington has put forth a spirit of corruption and relationshp bias that has cost lives of Americans i.e.... Hurricane Katrina and the Iraq war. The working poor have become stressed and there is no end in sight if we continue the pace. I would like to be able to send my girl to college, pay for a wedding and to see her have success in a world that is fair and balanced. I would like grow old with a pension plan. I would like to see the U.S. get beyond the racial divide and show the world that we believe in the Constitution of the U.S. that all men are created equal and, yes, a man of color and modest means can become the President of the U.S.'

Easing international political tensions

Partially because of his political perspectives, but significantly also because of his mixed race and African American identities, Obama is seen as both having the potential to relieve international tensions—particularly in terms of the war in Iraq—and to elevate the moral status of the U.S. in the global community. Obama's mixed race and African heritage shows the world that the U.S. is open to relations with all countries. Obama's mixed race background shows the world that the U.S. was not threatened by diversity, but rather embraces it; we are open to working with diverse perspectives, backgrounds, world views, religions, nations, ethnic groups, and races.

A 37-year-old African American woman with one child from Ohio argued:

Also just the fact that our POTUS [President of the United States] will have diverse geneological background will help the children growing up in my children's generation to stop looking at skin color as an indicator of what kind of person someone is. It will normalize the diverse population that is america instead of seeing "mixed race" people as unusual or unique but the new norm. I never had any clue how truely segregated our country still is until I moved to NC in my 30s. Race relations feel very different here than they do back home on the west coast and southwest and while those areas are certainly not without their racial ills, there is a distinctly edgier tone to relations here. I think Obama will help smooth our transition to a nation that pays less mind to the color of skin and more to the quality of actions and words. This will go far in altering our approach to global relations.

A white 41-year-old mother with four children from Pennsylvania wrote: "We need the change; other countries aren't looking at us with respect any more, and if we don't change that soon I'm really worried about the future for my kids and grandchild."

A white 63-year-old woman with 12 children from Georgia suggested that: "Undoubtedly, many other nations will take note that a person of mixed racial groups has been elected in the United States."

Mixed race as a metaphor for healing

Given the struggles of the twenty-first century, the voices of mothers across the U.S. is a yearning not for the Great White Hope, but instead for the Great Mixed Race Hope. For many mothers, Obama's presidency is expected to heal race relations; divisions of political parties, socioeconomic class, gender, and religion; as well as to symbolize to the international community the triumph of the Great American Experiment of racial equality. All of these hopes are hung upon Obama specifically because he is *both* mixed race and African American. Mothers of various perspectives and races have a hope that electing a black president would be healing for a nation so riddled with a painful racist past.

Commenting on the historical significance of Obama's presidency, a 43-year-old African American mother of two children from North Carolina said "It will show our children that the U.S. is ready to turn a page in its history and move to a more Perfect Union."

A 31-year-old mixed race mother with two children from Nevada stated: "When I saw him on Oprah the first time, I was sold! Us mixed folks have a way of understanding both sides and that's what I noticed first! His ability to talk to both sides and still stay neutral."

A 52-year-old African American mother with two children from from New York said that: "I became a supporter of Obama as a result of his values, his ability to see and fully understand the world through others' eyes (because of his culture) and most importantly for my two daughters who deserve an opportunity in life and will only be possible through CHANGE."

A white 42-year-old Republican woman from Minnesota with two teenaged children said: "I support Barack Obama because of the way that he brings people together across all lines; race, gender, party, and economic. He can help heal our country's divisive wounds."

Conclusions

This survey of mothers who supported Obama, also known as Obama Mamas, reveals how Obama is seen by mothers of various racialized groups as a symbol of hope for a future healed of the myriad divisions between people. That hope is expressed through the discursive construction of Obama as a mixed race bridge between racialized groups, as a symbol of the end of racism, and as a sign of the ability of the United States to respect people of all races and religions internationally. The discourse around which this hope is built re-inscribes images of the mixed race person as bridge builder, and raises questions about the continued lived reality of racism. It is important to understand that these images and this language are not neutral—they are part of a larger discourse of race and mixed race in which mixed race people are figured not only as bridge builders and indeed as our saviors from racism, but also as race-traitors and signs of the dissolution of ethnic and racial communities. These negative associations are often just on the other side of the positive images.

The image of the mixed race bridge builder is a common trope for mixed race people. Whether with conscious or unconscious intent, many of these mothers reinscribed this view of mixed race people through their expressions of hope that Obama could bridge the wide chasms affecting our country, mainly in terms of the racial divide, but also including economic, social, and political divisions. Moreover, as we continually wage a war in Iraq and hope for peace, the image of Obama as a bridge builder becomes significant on an international scale as well. As they became invested in his candidacy, some did so with the hope that the election of a non-white, mixed race President could turn around the international tide of hate against Americans. Obama, to many of these mothers, represents a bridge to racial reconciliation, healing, and hope for a better future for their children in terms of improved race relations in the U.S. and peace in the world.

Unlike any other U.S. presidential election, the images of race projected during the campaign emphasized bridge building through the continual media coverage and images of his white grandmother, his white mother in Hawaii, and his white relatives in Kansas; his father's Kenyan roots; and his stepfather's Indonesian roots. Though some of these images were promulgated by opponents and detractors, for many mothers across the U.S., the images of a potential President with diverse roots proved to be something hopeful and beneficial for their children's future. People have been speculating and even declaring that the election of Barack Obama in November 2009 demonstrates that the U.S. is in a post-racial era, and that thus we no longer need to consider race. His election has been used as a justification for ending affirmative action programs upon the argument that if a black man can be elected President, "race" must no longer be a problem. However, there is a difference between being post-race and being post-racism. What the voices of mothers throughout the U.S. reveals is that there is a desire to be post-racism, which is not same as the desire to be color-blind, which the term "post-race" implies. Of the hundreds of mothers who responded to this survey, only one chose to declare her race as "human," while all of the others chose a racial category. Many of the mothers commented on how their children of color, especially their mixed race and or African American children, would see themselves and be viewed by others as having more potential because someone who looked like them, or who was identified similarly to them, had achieved this world-recognized position. This focus on the similarity between Obama and their children suggests that race does still matter.

The voices of mothers express concerns that mothers have for the next generation, and hopes that past racist pains can be transformed through the election of Obama. Respect and appreciation of differences and a movement toward the promise of racial unification, in other words, a "perfect union," are priorities for mothers. Moreover, mothers are concerned with how their children are perceived in the world, and how their children will be affected by larger social issues such as race and other factors that determine status for the majority of the U.S. population. Related to this concern, they are interested in how people in positions of power might serve as role models for their children; thus Barack Obama as President symbolizes the potential for every child of color—but especially for African American and mixed race children—to fulfill their potential; they, too, can grow up to be President of the United States.

Acknowledgements

The authors would like to thank the participants of this survey who were so willing and generous in sharing their thoughts and hopes of the Obama presidential campaign.

CHAPTER SIX

Is "no one as Irish as Barack O'Bama?"

Rebecca Chiyoko King-O'Riain

You don't believe me, I hear you say
But Barack's as Irish, as was JFK
His granddaddy's daddy came from Moneygall
A small Irish village, well known to you all
Toor a loo, toor a loo, toor a loo, toor a lama
There's no one as Irish as Barack O'Bama

(The Corrigan Brothers (with Shay Black))[1]

On May 23 2011 Barack Obama visited Ireland for the first time and, amidst an enthusiastic crowd of 50,000 people gathered in College Green, Dublin, began his speech thus: "My name is Barack Obama of the Moneygall Obamas. I've come home to find the apostrophe we lost somewhere along the way" (RTE, 2011). The crowd went wild despite the rain and high winds of the classic Irish summer. Obama's trip to Ireland, his warm embrace by the Irish nation as a "true son of Ireland" (Lord, 2011), and his own recognition of the trip to Ireland as a trip home, all served to underscore Obama's roots and his newfound Irishness. Why does being Irish matter for Barack Obama? What do people in Ireland see when they look at him? Is his biraciality a factor?

Debates about what Barack Obama actually is racially tell us more about the state of racial thinking in the U.S. and Ireland than they do about any racial reality that Obama represents as a multiracial man of both Kenyan and Irish ancestry. I argue that while some see Obama as the first black President of the U.S. and therefore a symbolic watershed in U.S. race relations, it might be more realistic to recognize that Obama has been unique in his ability to use flexible racialization to make claims to blackness, whiteness, "cosmopolitan-ness", and Irishness simultaneously. But what are the conditions and strategies that make this work?

This chapter focuses not on Obama's racial blackness or mixedness but instead his whiteness and specifically his Irishness through a content analysis, of print, television and popular cultural sources, from 2008–11, of the discovery of his Irish ancestry and his recent visit to Ireland.[2]

It analyzes: 1) what commentators say about Obama's racial and ethnic identity, 2) Obama's own racial and ethnic claims and those made upon him, 3) his reception in the U.S. in racial and ethnic terms focusing on when and where he is allowed to combine these various claims and why people allow him flexible racialization, and 4) his recent visit to the Republic of Ireland to understand why Irish people are now willing to accept a black person as authentically Irish thus allowing Obama to combine his black race with Irish ethnicity.

Commentary on Obama's racial and ethnic identity

When Barack Obama was elected the 44th President of the United States, he was most often touted as the first black President and a symbol of a post-racial America, inspiring new debates about the future of American race relations. Liberals and conservatives alike painted Obama as a collective symbol of the resolution of American race relations, and for many this claim hinged on his black background and his ability to point to having a black father from Kenya. Ward Connerly, a black conservative from California, famous for his attempts to overturn affirmative action, said "[T]he Presidential candidacy of Sen. Barack Obama is testimony that America is about ready to end the consideration of race in American life. In effect, he is the symbol of the American people 'overcoming' race" (Belton, 2008).

While Obama continues to identify himself as black and has not officially identified himself as mixed race personally, politically or publicly, he continues to invoke *both* whiteness and blackness and the connections and experiences that come with them in his speeches, his public comments, and books (see Ponder, Chapter Three).

Is Obama black...enough?

Some African American political pundits have argued that Obama is not really black due to historical experience, blood ancestry, political loyalties, or social position. Debra Dickerson, a well-known African American writer, claimed that Obama was not black on the grounds that he was not descended from slaves and did not represent the African American experience. Kimberly McClain DaCosta responded,

> The bulk of people protesting against references to Obama
> as a black man, however, grant that he is "part" black (by

way of his father), but assert that because he also has a white mother it is not "accurate" to call him black. He is in fact, "mixed," they say….what I find most interesting about the question of what racial label to assign Obama, is that we are asking the question at all. (DaCosta, 2008, p. 1)

Sociologists, who are at pains to point out that race is a socially-constructed concept and not real, also weighed in. Eduardo Bonilla-Silva in a discussion about the social significance of Barack Obama in August of 2008 described him as "black elite not because he is half-white, but because he has taken an almost raceless political stand and persona. This said, the legitimacy of Obama's blackness should be judged by his politics and, in my view, his are 'neo-mulatto' politics" (Bonilla-Silva, 2008).

Others, including white political figures like former Governor of Illinois, Rod Blagojevich, were quoted as saying, "I'm blacker than Barack Obama. I shined shoes. I grew up in a five-room apartment. My father had a little Laundromat in a black community not far from where we lived" (Rabb, 2010). Blackness, for Blagojevich, much like for Dickerson and Bonilla-Silva, was linked to social class, in particular poverty and economic struggle, and not skin color (for more discussion of class and Obama, see Chapter Nine). With the exception of DaCosta, all of these arguments essentialized race and linked blackness to race/blood, specific political stances, and class/economic conditions or experiences.

Senator Harry Reid of Nevada, the majority leader, stated that he believed Barack Obama could become the country's first black President because he was light-skinned and had the advantage of "carrying no Negro dialect, unless he wanted to have one" (Zeleny, 2010). Others agreed that Obama opened up the definition of blackness and expanded it to represent a much broader and more diverse community that could be considered essentially black. Enid Logan wrote,

> As for the issue of racial identity, I believe that what Obama is doing is opening up the space for new, expanded notions of blackness. The more time he spends in the national spotlight, the choices will hopefully, no longer only be to be seen as either a) "authentically black," i.e. in all ways identified with "the hood," poor blacks, and the "urban experience," or as b) "not really black," "honorary white," "black lite" (to use Eduardo's phrase), or "not black enough"…Barack Obama is not simply a "whitewashed" black man. He is, rather, someone who represents the

increasing diversity of the black community. Not all of us are from the hood. Some of us are biracial. Increasing numbers have parents from the Caribbean or from Africa. Obama seems to represent a blackness that is cosmopolitan, global, progressive, multifaceted, and forward-looking (rather than primarily referencing slavery, the Civil Rights Movement, and our glorious past as Kings and Queens in Africa). (Logan, 2008)

While for some this was liberating, to open up blackness as an internally extremely diverse category, for others it threatened the core of African American political solidarity allowing some African Americans, many of whom are of mixed descent, to distance themselves from the 'in the hood' stereotypes of blackness.

As DaCosta noted, some felt that Obama is in fact racially mixed. His mixed race status allows him to serve as a bridge between groups and throughout his campaign to supersede race and racial issues. But Michelle Elam writes, "Obama may often invoke and exploit the appeal of American exceptionalism and the melting pot mythology, but so far he has not used his mixed race status to herald any kind of post-race salvation" (Elam, 2011). Obama has been black, not black enough, white, not white enough and mixed. Eduardo Bonilla-Silva argues that this is because Obama is different things to different people.

White Obama supporters like him because he is the first "black" leader [with whom] they feel comfortable; because he does not talk about racism; because he tells them every time he can he is half-white (and it helps his father is from Kenya rather than from the South side of Chicago); because he is so "articulate" or, in Senator Biden's words, echoed later by Karl Rove, Obama is "the first mainstream African American who is articulate and bright and clean and a nice-looking guy"...for blacks, Obama is a symbol of their possibilities. He is, as Obama has said of himself, their Joshua—the leader they hope will take them to the promised land of milk and honey. They read in between the lines (probably more than is there) and think he has a strong stance on race matters. ...Poor blacks believe Obama will bring economic and social change to them—higher wages, health care, etc., and, for elite blacks, Obama is a symbol and a confirmation of their own standing, politics, and even behavior and manners—the genteel, aristocratic character of the black elite. (Bonilla-Silva, 2008)

Therefore, white people see a mixed race man raised by a white mother and white grandparents from Kansas—suitable Middle America. Asian Pacific Islanders from Hawai'i see a local guy who grew up on Oahu attending a predominantly API and Native Hawaiian school—Punaho. African Americans perhaps can relate to someone who has also undoubtedly experienced racism due to his physical appearance and who elects to identify with the black community. But what of his whiteness? His whiteness and the case of his newfound Irishness allows us perhaps to see the global, and, I would argue, more cosmopolitan, appeal of Barack Obama which is perhaps due not to his skin color, but down to his experience of being racially mixed—and to what George Kich calls, his "cognitive flexibility" (Kich, 1996, p. 275).

Unpacking Obama's whiteness is informed by the discussion of his blackness above because as always, race is hierarchical and relational at all times. His whiteness (and Irishness) is unique and interesting because he is predominantly seen as black.

Obama's own racial and ethnic claims

It is clear from the above that Obama, for many, does not measure up to their definitions of racial identity; this despite the fact that Barack Obama has clearly and consistently identified himself racially as a black man. He married a black woman, fathered black children, belongs to a traditionally black church, worked and lived on the south side of Chicago in a traditionally black neighborhood, and recalls experiences of racism as a black man. And yet, he is still not black enough, mixed enough, or post-racial enough to suit many.

Barack Obama proudly writes about his mixed race ancestry and clearly identifies that he has a father from Kenya (read black) and a white mother from Kansas and, yet, he does not identify racially as mixed race. His multiplicity is often also linked to his class background, which allows him to make non-racial and non-ethnic claims to being a cosmopolitan citizen of the world.

Barack Obama's flexible racial and ethnic portrayal is often one he draws on himself and he does this to connect to different types of people. He is the first black President for many African Americans; he is a local in Hawai'i and understands many of the Asian Pacific Islander cultural traits of the Islands; he is mixed race commenting that "I've got pieces of everybody in me" (Jordan, 2007, p. 2), and now he is ethnically Irish too.

What is fascinating about this is that Obama is involved in making multiple claims and many groups of people allow him to do so. Collective identities in the past have demanded of others that they choose identities to to be loyal to. In principle, many people have multiple and flexible identities but in practice they are not allowed by others to claim them. Obama manages to do this easily and that is why it is important to examine how audiences receive Obama's racial and ethnic claims and how they authenticate or reject them.

Irish America and the importance of O'Bama

It wasn't until 2007, during the lead-up to his presidential campaign that Barack Obama discovered that he was of Irish descent. Stephen Neill, a local Anglican rector in Moneygall, County Offaly, Ireland "found that Obama's great-great grandfather, Falmouth Kearney, was reared in Moneygall and left for America in 1850, when he was 19" (Jordan, 2007, p. 1). Descended from a relatively well off (Kearney was a shoe maker) Protestant family in Offaly, Obama seemed to relish the fact that he was Irish, commenting on St. Patrick's Day in 2009 to the Irish Taoiseach (prime minister) that, "when I was a relatively unknown candidate for office, I didn't know about this part of my heritage, which would have been very helpful in Chicago. So I thought I was bluffing when I put the apostrophe after the O" (Rooney, 2009).

Obama isn't kidding. When he invokes Irishness it gets votes and allows Irish Americans to connect with him in an ethnic way that they couldn't before. Maureen Dowd posited in the *New York Times*,

> Funnily enough, Obama had to take a foreign trip (*to Ireland*) to seem less foreign to Americans. Even though he did a best-selling memoir about his roots, he has had a persistent and puzzling problem coming across as rooted. A surprising number of Americans still find the President exotic and existentially detached, falsely believing he's either a Muslim or foreign born. (Dowd, 2011)

The visit to Ireland and claim to Irishness allowed Obama to present himself as an ordinary guy, like other white Irish ethnics in the U.S., who often had heretofore seen him as elitist—a class-based rather than a racial judgment. It also gave him documentable ethnic and ancestral roots to Ireland. Irish Americans embraced the discovery of Obama's Irishness. After the discovery that Obama had Irish heritage, it didn't take long for bumper stickers and t-shirts to appear with an Irish flavor to them (see Figure 6.1).

Figure 6.1: Irish themed logo

The accomplishment of whiteness in the U.S. (Ignatiev, 1996) allows Irish Americans to perhaps move beyond race and claim Barack Obama as Irish. The move to recognize and claim Irish heritage by Obama is important because it moved him out of generic whiteness or just being one of many African Americans who have white mothers, and gave him a country, a people and a place to point to and say "I am from and of Ireland." His resulting visit to Ireland and the acceptance of Obama as truly Irish, serves to underscore not just his own racial malleability but, in fact, the importance of his identity and presidency in racial terms—he is a black man who is also ethnically Irish. In effect he is making an ethnic claim without making a racial claim.[3] His flexibility is rooted in the power of black racial identity and the persistence of the cultural one-drop rule. Because he has chosen black as his racial identity, this perhaps gives him flexibility in U.S. politics to take on Irishness as a lesser symbolic ethnic claim to identity. Obama does not say that he is white and he is Irish. He does not relinquish his blackness. Instead he sidesteps a racial dilemma by claiming ethnic Irish identity but not a racial (white) one.

Obama's reception in Ireland

Ireland is a country that, until recently, saw itself as relatively homogenous and decidedly white. It is now changing rapidly in terms of race/ethnicity, primarily through increased migration, and is struggling to understand how Irish people should deal with increasing racial/ethnic diversity in schools, public policy, government, and politics. The presence, particularly of people of color, has challenged long-held notions of Irishness being an accomplished sense of whiteness and early indications are that there is an acceptance in Ireland that Irishness may be de-coupled, not from ancestry, as we see with Obama, but from skin color. For people in Ireland, it is Obama's cosmopolitan connections, of which being black is a large part, as well as his Irish ancestry, that matter. This means that Obama can claim both Irishness and blackness unproblematically.

Obama clearly stated that Ireland is unique in that it "punches above its weight" on the global stage. The visibility of its cultural contributions and its connections with not just Obama, but many past U.S. Presidents who continue to visit and feel connected to Ireland has paid off for Ireland in both financial and cultural ways (Wolf, 2011). The symbolic connection of Ireland to Obama and Obama's connection to Irishness more generally, pays off for both, however. For Obama, his visit and his now concrete ancestral connections to Ireland depend upon carefully managed and successfully translated notions of transnational Irishness that must be recognized and authenticated by Irish Americans in the U.S. People in Ireland are the key to that process and when they warmly welcomed and accepted Obama as a "true son of Ireland." In turn, Irish people get to claim the most politically powerful person in the world as one of their own thus making Irishness more cosmopolitan and multicultural. In addition, Ireland remains in the public eye, not only for its economic crisis, but also for its 'hard work ethic' identified by Obama in his speeches here and for access to political and economic power in the U.S. Obama gets from Irishness, through Irish ancestral connections, legitimate roots and perhaps success with the Irish American electorate.

In stereotypical Irish form, the discovery of Obama's Irish heritage in 2007 was solidified in cultural expression through a traditional Irish song. The Corrigan Brothers (with their band, Hardy Drew and the Nancy Boys), with later verses added by Shay Black, wrote a song in 2008 called "There's No One as Irish as Barack O'Bama" which became an overnight YouTube sensation with more than 1,000,000 hits. Unlike claims to Obama's blackness the song focuses primarily on his hitherto unknown Irishness. The claim that "no one is as Irish as Barack Obama" is a part of the broader phenomena of Obama's flexible racialization. It is also an example of how racial ideas can travel and transnationally get translated in different cultural and national contexts.

Does Obama's Irishness mean the same thing in the U.S. as in Ireland, however? It was much easier for Obama to be Irish in Ireland than perhaps it would be for him to claim such Irishness at home in the U.S. due to Ireland's identification with a post-colonial history and the identification of Irish people with oppression and solidarity with African Americans. It might also be because class differences and racism are more of an issue for him in Ireland than they are for Irish Americans. Ideas about race and interpretations of mixed race in the case of Obama and Irishness show how notions of whiteness are transnational in construction and can be translated back to the U.S. into political and ethnic capital.

When Obama finally landed in Ireland in 2011 on his first official state visit, it was overwhelmingly clear that Irish people were proud to welcome Obama as an Irish person. Ironically, it is the "Irish who became white" (Ignatiev, 1996) who openly recognized Obama, who publicly identifies as not white, but black, as being both black and now Irish. In doing so, Irish people in Ireland accepted and welcomed Barack Obama as Irish because he could prove his Irish ancestry by tracing a bloodline back to Ireland through his great, great grandfather. It is the importance of verifiable blood ties that mattered and allowed him to claim Irishness.

Others who are also black, who are born in Ireland, have lived their whole lives in Ireland, and often speak Irish (Gaelic)[4] cannot claim to be Irish. The difference between the two is of course, that Obama can trace his bloodline/race and ancestry to Ireland through whiteness and is in a position of power to assert his Irishness, and black Nigerian children born in Ireland are not entitled, under new citizenship requirements (changed in 2004), to claim Irishness or Irish citizenship and are powerless become so. Obama's move to claim symbolic Irishness, and the corresponding acceptance of Barack Obama by the Irish populace as authentically Irish, prioritizes ancestry/bloodlines as the only means by which to be Irish. It reinforces the increasing two-tiered hierarchy of Irishness with "certificates of Irishness" for those with Irish ancestry no matter how small, and nothing for those who are not. In effect, it also airbrushes out Irishness and Irish history linked with Irish anti-abolitionists and slaveholders. Ironically, Michelle Obama also has Irish ancestry, which was carefully not mentioned during President Obama's visit to Ireland, because her Irish ancestor was a slave owner who had possibly illicit sexual relations with a black enslaved woman (Geary, 2011). Obama then accomplishes having Irishness through racially mixed ancestry while still maintaining black identity. The importance of bloodline increases and the importance of whiteness seems to decrease. This is a fascinating case where it appears that two key elements of phenotypical race are going in opposite directions. Blood and ancestry are becoming more important and skin colour is becoming less so.

When Obama traveled to Moneygall, County Offaly on 23 May 2011, he spent an inordinate amount of time shaking hands, handling crowd-surfing babies, and hugging and kissing the 300 or so residents of this small Irish village where his great, great grandfather, Falmouth Kearney, had lived. He was greeted by Henry Healey, his cousin eight times removed, and other distant relatives and sipped a pint of Guinness in Ollie Hayes' pub, commenting that now he knows that they keep all of the "good stuff" in Ireland. During the trip to Ireland news reporters continually commented that he was relaxed in a way not seen during his campaign. The impact of the visit, however, was not solely or even primarily concerned with the Irish audience. Instead, the world press was focused on a black Irish man come home realizing that it was a public relations bonanza. *The Times* (2011) described it thus:

> There are no American votes in Moneygall, but for Mr. Obama yesterday there was electoral gold to impress the most jaded campaign manager. There was riotous confirmation of his role as a product of the melting pot, and for a man that never really knew his father, there were roots.

Even Stephen Neill who discovered Obama's Irish heritage commented that he doesn't look Irish: "It's not the first thing you think is it, when you see him, and that's another thing that's taken people aback, makes you realize how related we all are" (Lagorio, 2007). In the end, the popular notion that Barack Obama is not just the first African American President of the U.S., but *also* Irish, is gaining steam. His individual identification as Irish as well as black and his interactions with people as such, we hope may trickle up into Irish state meanings of race, but for now Irish people for the most part seem happy to call him one of their own.

Conclusions

Obama can be black and Irish to Irish people and Irish Americans precisely because he means different things to different people in racial terms. He embodies the racial expectations and understandings of heretofore different and separate racial groups. He can change his emphasis from black President to local Irish guy sipping a pint as it suits him and as the situation will allow. Some people would say that this is inauthentic or that Obama is using his situational ethnicity (Okamura, 1981) in order to gain strategic ethnic advantage. The argument that he is accurately black and is passing as white or that he isn't black enough (Dickerson, 2007) or that he is accurately mixed race (DaCosta, 2008) or even that there is "no one as Irish as Barack Obama" belie this understanding. He is accurately and *real*-ly all of these things at once. He is also culturally Hawai'ian and ultimately cosmopolitan (as a Harvard educated elite) (Sugrue, 2010). He is all of these and yet this does not make him dishonest in his representation of his racial self. He is like millions of other mixed race or multiracial people. He can have multiple identities and he can be strategically ethnic to further his political goals (as he joked that he could have done, in being Irish as a senator from Chicago).

Obama has "cognitive flexibility" which is, "the ability to tolerate and to manage increased levels of complexity and differentiation … the flexibility of constructs, relational competence and adaptability are potentially the skills of living with difference and in the margins" (Kich, 1996, p. 275). This doesn't make Barack Obama a racial imposter, devious or inauthentic, but comfortable in multiple settings, with ambiguity and with people of all kinds, because he has fallen between social categories and developed the skill to dwell in hybrid spaces. In turn, he projects this onto others and they feel comfortable with him because he represents different things to them.

This is both Obama's strength and perhaps a potential weakness as a harbinger of a change in the meaning of race in the U.S. When Obama became President, people thought that racial change was complete and that we had moved into a post-racial society. This has allowed people to turn away from the differential effects of the recession on racial/ethnic groups in the U.S. and hides much of the evidence to the contrary that race, and particularly class, still strongly divide the U.S. nation. Second, many thought that the symbolic election of Obama could bring hope and social change because he was a racial bridge (being *both* black and white) to heal racial tensions in the U.S., and yet, many also distrust him as not really black or white and feel that he has betrayed one or both of his backgrounds in his political achievement. It is precisely because people can't pin down his true racial identity, that they feel he is not to be trusted. Finally, by arguing endlessly over whether Barack Obama is black, but acceptable because he is well spoken and good looking, or whether he is black enough, we miss the underlying ability of Obama to connect with people, even though he is highly educated in elite institutions (Punaho and Harvard) through his connection to Irish people, his local village (and pub!) and the people of Moneygall.

Barack Obama's trip to Ireland and his move to accept and be accepted as Irish provided three important opportunities: access to 44 million Irish Americans who will be an important voting block in the upcoming 2012 election, a real and concrete ancestral connection to a culturally authentic white background (with an Irish language which Obama used in his speech—translating his campaign logo "Yes, we can!" into "Is Feidir Linn!"), and a chance to be seen as a man of the people, relaxed, chatting, and being embraced as a common working man of a small village in rural Ireland. Ultimately, though, Obama also provides an example of how race is changing in a global world where a black man can make claims to Irishness through ancestry without relinquishing black identity, hence possibly taking two aspects of race (ancestry and skin colour) and de-coupling them in ways not seen before.

Notes

[1] The author wishes to thank Ger Corrigan for his kind permission to reproduce the lyrics of "There's No One as Irish as Barack O'Bama" in this chapter.

[2] Media and journalistic sources are analysed as data better to understand how collective social actors understand and come to identify themselves through discourse, particularly in relation to race. Race, as we know, is socially constructed and any understanding of race, or by extension mixed race, must by definition be analyzed within specific social and cultural contexts as this chapter does. The research operates with an understanding that all social reality is mediated, including, and especially, ideas about race, which is considered not to be an empirical reality that can be measured by us out there. For more on this see Hesmondhalgh and Toynbee (2008), or for a discussion specifically about race see Lentin and Titley (2011, Chapter 2).

[3] Thanks to Sean O'Riain for this valuable insight.

[4] The Irish language is not referred to as Gaelic in Ireland but the "Irish language," or, in Irish, *Gaeilge*.

References

Belton, D. (2008) 1 April 2008 (http://blacksnob.blogspot. com/2008/04/ward-connerly-likes-obama-but-would.html).

Bonilla-Silva, E. (2008) "What is the Social Significance of Barack Obama?" (http://contexts.org/obama/#comments-list).

DaCosta, K. (2008) "Viewpoint: Is Barack Obama black?" 18 November, BBC News (http://news.bbc.co.uk/2/hi/americas/ us_elections_2008/7735503.stm).

Dickerson, D. (2007) "Colorblind". 22 January 2009 (www.salon.com/ opinion/feature/2007/01/22/obama/).

Dowd, M. (2011) "Don't Be a Stranger" *New York Times.* 24 May 2011 (www.nytimes.com/2011/05/25/opinion/25dowd. html?ref=maureendowd).

Elam, M. (2007) "Obama's Mixed Race Politics", from "ObamaRama" in *Mixtries: Mixed Race in the New Millennium.* Palo Alto, CA: Stanford University Press.

Geary, Daniel. (2011) 'Michelle Obama: The Irish Connection' *Irish Times,* 26 May.

Hesmondhalgh, D and Toynbee, J. (2008) *The Media and Social Theory,* London: Routledge.

Ignatiev, N. (1996) *How the Irish Became white,* New York: Routledge.

Jordan, M. (2007) 'Tiny Irish village is latest place to claim Obama as its own' *Washington Post,* 13 May.

Kich, GK. (1996). 'In the Margins of Sex and Race: Difference, Marginality, and Flexibility' in Root, Maria PP *The Multiracial Experience: Racial Border as the New Frontier,* Newbury Park, CA: Sage Publications.

Lagorio, C. (2007) 'O'Bama's Irish Roots?' CBS News. May 16, 2007. (www.cbsnews.com/stories/2007/05/16/eveningnews/main2819352. shtml).

Lentin, A and Titley, G. (2011) *The Crisis of Multiculturalism: Racism in a Neoliberal Age,* London: Zed books.

Logan, E. (2008) 'The Social Significance of Barack Obama' August 2008.

(http://contexts.org/obama/#comments-list).

Lord, M. (2011) 'The Day O'Bama Stormed Moneygall' *Irish Times.* 24 May.

Marlowe, L. (2011) '"Ireland Carries a Blood Link With U.S." says Obama', *Irish Times.* 24 May.

Okamura, JY. (1981) *Situational Ethnicity,* London: Routledge and Kegan Paul.

Raab, S. (2010) "The Notorious Blago" *Esquire Magazine*. 11 January (www.esquire.com/features/people-who-matter-2010/rod-blagojevich-interview-0210).

Radio Telefis Eireann (RTE) 2011 (www.rte.ie/news/av/2011/0523/6news.html).

Rooney, K. (2009) "Raining on the St. Patrick's Parade" *Time Magazine*. 17 March 2009 (www.time.com/time/specials/packages/article/0,28804,1889908_1893754_1893876,00.html #ixzz1Q0Mg4U2S) [site no longer active].

Sugrue, T. (2010) *Not Even Past: Barack Obama and the Burden of Race*, Princeton, NJ: Princeton University Press.

The Times, 2011, 24 May (www.thetimes.co.uk). Article by Giles Whittnell 24 May 2011. "Pub forgot Obama's change but hands him pure electoral gold" (www.theaustralian.com.au/news/world/pint-of-guinness-gives-barack-obama-a-taste-of-electoral-gold/story-e6frg6so-1226061813943).

Wolf, R. (2011) 'Obama: Ireland Punches Above Its Weight' *USA Today*. 23 May 2011. (http://content.usatoday.com/communities/theoval/post/2011/05/obama-ireland-punches-above-its-weight/1).

Zeleny, J. (2010) "Reid Apologizes for Racial Remarks About Obama". *New York Times*, January 9, 2010. (http://thecaucus.blogs.nytimes.com/2010/01/09/reid-apologizes-for-racial-remarks-about-obama/).

Appendix: Lyrics to 'There's No One as Irish as Barack O'Bama' by The Corrigan Brothers (with Shay Black)

There's no one as Irish as Barack O'Bama
O'Leary, O'Reilly, O'Hare and O'Hara
There's no one as Irish as Barack O'Bama
You don't believe me, I hear you say
But Barack's as Irish, as was JFK
His granddaddy's daddy came from Moneygall
A small Irish village, well known to you all
Toor a loo, toor a loo, toor a loo, toor a lama
There's no one as Irish as Barack O'Bama

He's as Irish as bacon and cabbage and stew
He's Hawaiian, he's Kenyan, American too
He's in the White House, he took his chance
Now let's see Barack do Riverdance
Toor a loo, toor a loo, toor a loo, toor a lama

There's no one as Irish as Barack O'Bama
From Kerry and Cork to old Donegal
Let's hear it for Barack from old Moneygall
From the lakes of Killarney to old Connemara
There's no one as Irish as Barack O'Bama
O'Leary, O'Reilly, O'Hare and O'Hara
There's no one as Irish as Barack O'Bama
From the Old Blarney Stone to the great hill of Tara
There's no one as Irish as Barack O'Bama

2008 the White House is green,
They're cheering in Mayo and in Skibereen.
The Irish in Kenya, and in Yokahama,
Are cheering for President Barack O'Bama
O'Leary, O'Reilly, O'Hare and O'Hara
There's no one as Irish as Barack O'Bama
The Hockey Moms gone, and so is McCain
They are cheering in Texas and in Borrisokane,
In Moneygall town, the greatest of drama,
For our famous President Barack O'Bama
Toor a loo, toor a loo, toor a loo, toor a lama
There's no one as Irish As Barack O'Bama

The great Stephen Neill, a great man of God,
He proved that Barack was from the Auld Sod
They came by bus and they came by car,
To celebrate Barack in Ollie Hayes's Bar
O'Leary, O'Reilly, O'Hare and O'Hara
There's no one as Irish as Barack O'Bama.

CHAPTER SEVEN

Mixed race kin-aesthetics in the age of Obama

Wei Ming Dariotis

Many years ago I was not referred to as anything [racial or ethnic], and now I always am. Now that Obama is President—because he is biracial, I would hope that it would have an impact. But I don't think we are "post-racial" at all.

(Li-lan)

Barack Obama's decision to mark "Black/African American" on the 2010 census would seem to affirm mixed race Asian American artist Li-lan's feeling that we are indeed not in a "post-racial" time at all. And what would such a label mean? How would we measure the start of a post-racial era? Would President Obama, born in 1961, or Li-lan, a Chinese and European American artist born a generation earlier, be part of the post-racial era? How so, given that both have lived through significant watersheds in U.S. racism? Their identities are shaped just as much by racism as by being Americans. Can we mark a moment and say that from this moment on, all children born will be part of the post-racist era? What happens to post-racialism when racism keeps on happening? This essay examines notions of self within the context of lived experience, cultural politics, and moves conversations beyond mixed race as a black–white phenomenon. More specifically, I trace the experiences of President Obama and mixed race artist Li-lan within a U.S. and a global context to suggest that racism is real even though "race" is a social construct, and that mixed "race" plays a slippery role when it comes to the negotiation of one's public self-representation. How do Li-lan and President Obama present themselves publically in their professional lives and how does this presentation in the arts and in politics—disparate, though some might say related, fields—allow each to bring together people from various backgrounds, building a new American majority that is ethnically, economically, and politically diverse, but certainly not post-racial?

Both Obama and Li-lan have been shaped by being Americans, but Americans of a particularly "cosmopolitan" stripe. Obama's experience of having lived in Hawai'i and Indonesia, and having family members who are white, black, and Asian, and Li-lan's experiences of growing up with a Chinese modernist painter father and European American mother in New York City, then having been married to a Japanese man and lived in Japan, have shaped their cosmopolitanism in particular ways. Cosmopolitanism is a peculiar club; and though Li-lan and Obama have not yet met within its walls, Li-lan's friendship with another "cosmopolitan" American—the modernist sculptor Isamu Noguchi—sparked this essay. In the work of both Li-lan and Noguchi we can read an aesthetic impulse towards cosmopolitanism, while in their friendship we might read a certain kind of tribalism. Neither of these things is positive or negative. Both, however, lie squarely outside the bounds of any imagining of a post-racial era, even in the era of Obama's presidency.

After meeting her at an event for the "Experiences in Passage" exhibit at the de Young Museum in San Francisco, in April 2009 I interviewed, by telephone, mixed Chinese and German American artist Li-lan about her life, her art, and her friendship with Isamu Noguchi. During our discussion about mixed race identity, the subject of Barack Obama as a symbol for the end of racism was raised. Li-lan's work has focused a great deal on representations of the self and her take on Obama as a "post-racial" figure sheds light on the continuing significance of race and particularly on nuanced, and specifically Eurasian, contexts of mixed heritage identity.

Before Obama's election, I received a phone call from a journalist seeking a quote about Obama. The journalist, who identified himself as a "Hapa" (a Native Hawaiian-rooted word, which has been taken by some to mean an Asian American of mixed heritage, and by others to mean a person of Native Hawaiian mixed heritage, and by others to mean anyone of mixed heritage with a connection to Hawai'i) from Hawai'i, asked me if I thought Obama was "Hapa." Clearly, the reporter was familiar with some of my work on mixed heritage Asian American identity and community, but not with my recent repudiation of the use of the term "Hapa" by non-native Hawaiians (Dariotis, 2009). We talked for an hour, but ultimately I would not give him the quote he wanted—I would not declare that Obama was "Hapa." He did not quote me in the article. I could not give this reporter what he wanted for two reasons: 1) because I no longer think that "Hapa" should be used outside of the Hawaiian context nor should it be used to describe people who are not part Native Hawaiian, and 2) because when I did use the word, as a member of Hapa Issues Forum, we fought to maintain the integrity of the word as relating specifically to Asian and Pacific Islander Americans of mixed heritage, rather than being a general mixed heritage term. In the 1990s and early 2000s, I used the word because it provided an alternative space for identifying and representing a public self as an Asian American. I stopped using the word "Hapa" to refer to myself and to other mixed Asians because of the power and colonial history attached to it. Some want to claim Obama not only as a post-racial figure, but as a mixed race person who can thus "be all things to all people"; he can be Irish (see Chapter Six), he can be black, and in Hawai'i some feel he can be claimed as "Hapa" and therefore as a kind of "native son." The problem with this is that Obama, while he is a mixed race public figure that has personal connections with people from practically every racialized group, is still not a Native Hawaiian, just as mixed heritage Asian Americans as a group are not Native Hawaiians (although some are through virtue of their mixed ancestry) thus using "Hapa" to describe President Obama or other non-Native Hawaiians can reinscribe the colonial traumas still being experienced by the Native peoples of the Hawaiian Islands. I wrote about this choice in a 2007 edition of *Hyphen Magazine*:

> The controversy has not gone away, it has only grown stronger, and it is time for me—and other mixed heritage Asian Americans—to recognize that when we use the word "Hapa" it causes some people pain. What is so troubling about this is that the word "Hapa" was chosen because it was the only word we could find that did not really cause us pain. It is not any of the Asian words for mixed Asian people that contain negative connotations either literally (e.g. "children of the dust," "mixed animal") or by association (e.g. Eurasian). It avoids the confused identity and the Black–White dichotomy implied by English phrases (e.g. mixed blood, biracial). It was adopted to enhance an Asian-focus to our mixed identity, thereby allowing us to use the word to participate more fully in our Asian American communities—rather than being separated into the larger mixed race community (and perhaps being subsumed under the Black–White dichotomy). (Dariotis, 2009)

Developing a kin-aesthetic

A kin-aesthetic is a kind of mixed aesthetics that appeals to multiple people, views, ideas, and attitudes all at the same time, as though we are all part of one extended and rambling mixed heritage nation/family. More than this, it is the way we recognize each other as mixed race "kin" or create community through friendships and cultural signs. Artists like Li-lan do this through the creative work and politicians like President Obama achieve this through rhetoric, speeches, and sometimes through policy. President Obama and Li-lan have been deeply influenced by the work of others who might be seen as "authentic ethnic community brokers." Here I explore the influence of Isamu Noguchi (an artist of mixed heritage from a generation earlier) on the work and self-representation of Li-lan along with impact of the Rev. Jeremiah Wright on the public and racialized representation of Barack Obama.

Li-lan, born in New York City in 1943, and mixed Japanese and Irish American artist, Isamu Noguchi, born in Los Angeles in 1904, are both recognized, though to different degrees, for their contributions to American modern art. Reflecting an earlier interracial relationship pattern during a time of relatively fewer Asian female immigrants, both had Asian fathers and European-American mothers. Noguchi and Li-lan met in 1962, when Li-lan, then the young daughter of expatriate Chinese painter, Yun Gee (1906–63), was 19 years old, and they maintained a friendship until Noguchi's death at age 84 in 1988. An enduring aspect of their friendship was the bond they shared as mixed race Asian Americans, which was a frequent topic of discussion between the two friends. They recognized each other as mixed heritage Asian Americans and artists; through this connection they saw and sought a kind of *kinship* of mixed race identities, which is expressed in varying degrees through their art.

Laura Kina, in her article, "The Arts and Mixed Heritage Experience," argues: "many [mixed heritage] artists share an interest in negotiating, exploring, celebrating and/or complicating intersections of identity. Artists play a crucial role in envisioning, forming and reflecting (and disrupting) our communities. The mixed heritage community," she asserts, "will be no exception." Both Li-lan and Noguchi certainly "share an interest in negotiating, exploring, celebrating and/or complicating intersections of identity" (Kina, 2010).

Reviewing these two mixed Asian artists' and their work through the lens of critical mixed race studies, in the context of Obama's election, helps us negotiate, explore, and complicate our understandings of the intersections that contribute to mixed Asian–American identities in the twenty-first century. If President Obama was a post-racial figure, like the art created by both Li-lan and Noguchi, he could be something other than what he appears to be on the surface. He could be culturally Hawaiian or culturally part Asian, but we as a nation are still fixated on color, on phenotype, and on the performance of racial identity. Recall the media reactions to the Obamas' famous fist-bump, or the references to Obama's ability to dance, or play basketball. These signs of his "blackness" reflect a society more deeply affected by racial stereotypes and ethnic performance than anyone realizes. These public symbols and gestures are not innate, however: they are learned. These public enactments of identity are critiqued and negotiated by mixed race artists like Noguchi and Li-lan.

Noguchi, the better known of the two, was born in 1904 as the illegitimate son of Yone Noguchi, a Japanese poet who had gained great acclaim in the United States, and Irish American Leonie Gilmour. Raised in both the United States and Japan, during Noguchi's years as a young man in Indiana, he was known as Sam Gilmour, and he identified as a "Hoosier" (Anonymous, 2011). "Sam" was a truncated version of Isamu, and Gilmour was his mother's name. Later, he adopted his father's name and then nothing in his name signified his European American heritage. Li-lan uses just her first name. Like Noguchi, she had a famous artistic father; unlike Noguchi, she chose not to identify herself by her father's Chinese surname. This may be seen by some as a rejection of her Chinese heritage, though it is just as likely to be a rejection of her father's fame, or more specifically the burden of his reputation on her as an artist. But perhaps these are not so easily separable, as part of Yun Gee's fame was his Chinese heritage. How can Li-lan's identity, or that of any mixed Asian person, be separated into different sides, as though any aspect did not already reflect on every other aspect? According to Li-lan's interviewer, Joyce Brodsky,

> In her early years in school, Li-lan desired to be Caucasian [sic], like her friends and classmates; she rejected all things Chinese and was particularly upset when her mother dressed her in Chinese costumes [sic].… She suffered enough because she looked different from other young girls, with her "Oriental"-shaped eyes. (Brodsky, 2008 p. 102)

In the quote above I have objected to a number of terms used by Brodsky to interpret Li-Lan, particularly the terms "Caucasian," "Chinese costume" and of course the term "Oriental," which Brodsky herself sets apart in quotation marks. Brodksy presents a paraphrased version of her conversation with the artist, rather than direct quotes from Li-lan, so it is impossible to know to what extent these symbols and racial markers are based on Brodsky's own views. And yet every interview is structured by the interviewer—it is a conversation in which what one hears and what one wants to hear or expects to hear rather than allowing interviewees to speak for themselves. We are always doing the work of interpreting individuals and communities. For people of color, and especially for people of mixed descent, interpretation can lead to mis-categorization, oversimplification, and stereotypes.

Lisa Lowe begins her essay, "Heterogeneity, Hybridity, Multiplicity: Marking Asian American Differences," with a discussion of mixed Asian author Diana Chang's story, "The Oriental Contingent," in which Lisa, a Chinese transracial adoptee, and Connie, of mixed Chinese heritage, obsess over which one of them is more Chinese. Lowe emphasizes the "horizontal" relationship between the two women, as opposed to a more hierarchical familial one as a way to move away from the "homogenizing of Asian Americans as exclusively hierarchal and familial" (Lowe, 2004, p. 256). Noguchi and Li-lan, like Lisa and Connie and other mixed race people cannot rely on their parents for a hierarchical transmission of identity, however, "in one another they are able to find a common frame of reference" (Lowe, 2004, p. 256). But what are they, or we, to call this frame? What are the names that allow these artists, or any Asian Americans of mixed heritage, to be grouped within a community? A similar struggle was faced by Obama, who was taught by his former pastor, Jeremiah Wright, to negotiate "blackness" in the public sphere. Like Obama, who was questioned as to whether he was "black enough" or "too white," Li-lan and other mixed heritage Asian Americans are still seeking ways to name themselves without the use of symbolic markers to gain community credibility; they are seeking a mixed kin-aesthetic—a connection with others who share similar lived experiences.

If I were still using the word "Hapa" to describe Asian Americans of mixed heritage (Dariotis, 2009), I would be tempted to a-historically reclaim Li-lan and Noguchi under the term, in the way that writers or artists or political leaders who practiced or expressed something that might be today recognized as a Queer sexuality are reclaimed under that identity label as part of a project of building a lineage, or depth of community identity. But I no longer use the word "Hapa" to describe Asian Americans of mixed heritage, so I struggle with what to call Li-lan and Noguchi. The terms by which they have been labeled and by which they have called themselves—cosmopolitan, biracial, etc.—all are problematic for various reasons. These terms like those applied to President Obama are often either race-neutral, post-racial, or steeped in symbolism. Biracial, a term Li-lan uses to describe herself is more often used to refer to people of mixned African American and European American heritage, because of the extreme black–white binary oppositional structure of the American racial hierarchy. The term Eurasian, which might be functionally accurate, also carries a layer of meaning associated with the buffer or "middleman" identities deliberately constructed by British, Dutch, and other colonial masters in India and Indonesia. Li-lan, in response to my question, "How do you feel about being labeled a 'mixed race' artist or a 'cosmopolitan' artist?" said, "I guess in a way I like 'cosmopolitan' because it is the broadest—I am all of those things and none of those things. It is awkward if people say, 'Oh, you're Chinese or Chinese American' because I'm not totally" (phone interview, April 17 2009).

"Cosmopolitan" is a word with which both Li-lan and Noguchi have been associated, because of the idea of them as transnational, and also at least partially because of their strong associations with New York City and Tokyo. But "cosmopolitan" invokes a post-race type of future where hybrid or blended identities and experiences are often equated with sophistication and chauvinism.

In *Nation and Narration*, Homi Bhabha says the following about the concept cosmopolitan: "Why does this label, 'cosmopolitan' trouble me so? Partially it is the elitism implied by a supposedly jet-setting/metropolitan lifestyle, it is the implication that such a person lives without borders, always ungrounded" (Bhabha, 1990 p. 60).

Rather than use the word "cosmopolitan" for either Li-lan, Noguchi or for President Obama I would offer that "kin-aesthetic" implies dynamic and sensitive movement through space as it connotes visual culture and the recognition of the other as kin. Thus, the connections made through words, imagery, and shared meanings can be much more revealing than simply saying someone is cosmopolitan. For President Obama this kin-aesthetic connection was often made at rallies with crowds in the hundreds of thousands and at other times with much smaller audience. In each venue people were able to connect and relate to some aspect of his story as an "American" story. Despite possibly being very different there was a kinship formed between Mr. Obama and his supporters. Not unlike Obama, Li-lan sees her art as connecting the lives, experiences, and stories of different people to find common ground.

In my interview with Li-lan, she spoke for some time about her series of paintings featuring various eyes. She wanted to be very clear that they were not portraits of her eyes literally, but figuratively, in the collective, they represent her eyes or her identity as a mixed Asian person. She said,

Sometimes a few people wrote that they were all my eyes—
but I was able to correct them before publication. Some were
Korean—one is from a German postcard ... I did those eyes
mostly in the 1990s, one was from a self-portrait exhibition,
and I did the other painting of the German eyes—I thought
if you put the two together it would be my eyes: the German
eyes and the Chinese eyes. (phone interview, April 17 2009)

In paintings such as "Two Views, Bridged" (2000), "Fly By" (2000),
and "Bird of Passage" (2001), pairs of women's eyes, framed as though
images on a stamp, or a graphic part of a post card, hover near the top
and center of the flat field. In "Look Out" (2004), the eyes are off-center,
and are not individually boxed, as are the others, but rather are part of
a whole center-strip of an Asian woman's face, with her hair puffing
slightly out and framing this much smaller scale feature.

Li-lan's 1971 painting, "Evening Profile of a Lady, 2," features a
honey-colored woman in profile—a red ribbon wrapped around her
high hair-bun and a red apple in her hand. Her skin tone, hair, and
eyes are various shades of honey. The view, framed by a painted picture
frame, is of her shoulder and up; the apple is held up at shoulder-level.
In front of this figure is its own shadow, flipped so that it faces right,
the opposite direction of the left-facing figure, and also situated as to
partially obscure the figure behind it. The shadow is in the place in
front of the painted frame of the painting, so that it is closest to the
viewer, reversing the typical spatial relationship of object and shadow.
The shadow is also graduated, where the lightest color, a medium
periwinkle blue, is at the front of the face, and the back of the bun and
the neck and shoulders are almost black. This painting reminds me of
the poem, "Ideal," in which mixed Chinese American poet Mei-mei
Berssenbrugge writes about the spaces between people that are also
the spaces within people:

> Here is the body of the person, his torso facing you, head
> and feet in profile.
>
> There is a twist of space between the front arm and the
> back arm. Time goes there.
>
> The arm that turns toward you is personal, the arm that
> turns away is the impersonal.
>
> (Berssenbrugge, 2006 p. 67)

Following this observation, I connected Li-lan's images of frogs in her painting, "Lottery" (2003), to the idea of "amphiberasians" from *My Own Private Sukiprata*, a play written by Michael Chi-ming Hornbuckle and the Asian-American skit-comedy troupe, the 18 Mighty Mountain Warriors. She described that she had included the image of frogs in recognition of her godson, who like her, is mixed heritage, and thus lives between identities. Li-lan was very isolated, in her childhood, from other people of color generally, from other Asian Americans, and from other mixed race people. My conversation with her and this essay are both ways for me to bring her into dialogue with a larger portion of the mixed Asian American community. The friendship between Li-lan and Noguchi, the way she described to me their almost instant recognition of one another as being the same kind of different, struck me in a personal way; mixed race people often don't look like members of their own family—they don't look like their usually mono-racial parents. I am the only person in my family who looks like me, so I have sometimes found myself developing a strong feeling of kinship with other mixed people who look like me despite not sharing any ethnic heritage. Li-lan described to me a similar feeling, saying: "I look very Asian, I would have a different kind of life if I didn't look so Asian. I talked with [mixed Asian author] Lisa See about this. I think you grow up with a different attitude about the world" (phone interview, April 17 2009).

When Li-lan described the way Noguchi immediately said to her, "You are mixed, like me," I could hear the echo of relief in her voice, even now, almost 50 years later. She was 19, and he was her father's age—neither of them had known others like themselves—mixed white–Asian artists. Neither had known very many other Asian Americans, period. "With my double nationality and double upbringing," Noguchi wrote in his 1968 memoir, *A Sculptor's World*, "where was my home, where was my identity? Japan or America—both?" (Noguchi, reprinted 2009). For people of mixed descent finding these connections to others is often difficult. It produces conflict within a person about loyalty and legitimacy, and yet in choosing to identify as mixed these individuals are going against the status quo. They—contrary to some arguments out there—do not seek a post-racial existence, instead by engaging a complex blended identity, they are keeping their ethnic identities intact. President Obama, perhaps due in part to the influence of Rev. Wright chooses a different public self. He identified himself as being monoracial black on the census. It is a choice that is at the same time political as it is self-preserving. It is easier to choose one monoracialized identity to quell questions about one's allegiance to one group over the other. People of mixed descent are clearly developing their own unique kin-aesthetic for making connections like the one between Li-lan and Noguchi. And yet despite identifying as monoracial on the census, in his daily life and even in how he is represented, Barack Obama continues to be seen as multiracial. In his autobiography (see Ponder, Chapter Three) Obama writes about his ability to learn over time to connect with different people because he grew up in Hawai'i; he had to "learn how to be Black," and he had to learn to connect with people who are different from him phenotypically, but similar in experience. Thus, while Li-lan and Noguchi's sense of mixed kin-aesthetics is based upon being mixed heritage Asian American artists, for Obama his mixed kin-aesthetic is that his story resonates with the stories of so many people in the United States and globally.

On Li-lan's website, in the section labeled "About," there is only a single black-and-white photograph of Li-lan and the following description of her written by Noguchi for a 1980 solo exhibition of her work:

> Li-lan belongs in the same way as I do to that increasing number of the not exactly belonging people. I understood her sense of isolation and escape to Europe soon after I met her in early 1960.

> Since then it has always been a pleasure to see her in Tokyo or New York where she traces the steps I know so well. How fortunate are those of us who have gained the constancy of art to guide and welcome us. Li-lan has found that blank page of our school notebook, which we may all claim as our own. Upon it we can write our thoughts freely, beyond race and without prejudice. (Noguchi, 1980)

Noguchi, Li-lan, and Barack Obama are like the millions of mixed race people living across the world seeking connections, seeking kinship; they found theirs through the arts and through politics respectively. Through their work they share both public and private identities that, while hybrid, cannot lead to a post-racial era because in many ways their success is—at least in part—based on race, even while racialization also has limited them. Ultimately their success is rooted in the connections they make with others through recognitions of kinship. Noguchi, Li-lan and President Obama have created networks of support, socio-cultural stories of convergence, and ultimately a mixed race kin-aesthetic.

References

Anonymous (2011) "A Hoosier Story: Sam Gilmour Becomes Isamu Noguchi", 3 January (http://homepage.mac.com/gralston/oneNoguchi_000.htm).

Berssenbrugge M (2006) *I love artists: new and selected poems. New California poetry* University of California Press.

Bhabha H. (1990) *Nation and Narration*. Psychology Press

Brodsky J. (2008) *Experiences of Passage: The Paintings of Yung Gee and Li-lan,*. University of Washington Press.

Dariotis, WM. (2002) 'Developing a Kin-Aesthetic: Multiraciality and Kinship in Asian and Native North American Literature', In *Mixed Race Literature*, edited by Jonathan Brennan, Palo Alto, CA: Stanford University Press.

Dariotis, WM. (2009) 'To Be "Hapa" or Not to Be "Hapa": What to Name Mixed Asian Americans?' *At 40: Asian American Studies at San Francisco State*, San Francisco, CA: Asian American Studies, San Francisco State University.

Kina, L. (2010) "The Arts and Mixed Heritage Experience" from Mixed Heritage Center e-articles. Accessed 3 January 2011 (www.mixedheritagecenter.org/index.php?option=com_content&task=view&id=880).

Lowe, L. (2004) "Heterogeneity, Hybridity, Multiplicity: Marking Asian American Differences" in *A Companion to Asian American Studies* ed. Kent Ono, Wiley-Blackwell.

Noguchi, I and Bonnie Rychlak, B. (2009) *A Sculptor's World*. Isamu Noguchi Foundation; Steidl,

Noguchi I and Shuichi Kato and Li-lan (1980) *Li-Lan, Solo Exhibition.* Nanteshi Gallery, Tokyo.

CHAPTER EIGHT

Mutt like me: Barack Obama and the mixed race experience in historical perspective

Zebulon Vance Miletsky

In an attempt at humor, in his first press conference as President-elect, Barack Obama made an awkward joke in regard to choosing a puppy for his daughters. As many will recall, there had been much talk about adopting a dog during the campaign after Obama had promised his daughters that they could have one if he won the election. It became the kind of fun political issue that media pundits began reporting on as a light alternative to the heavy issues of the long and drawn-out, and often negative campaign. "We have two criteria that have to be reconciled. One is that Malia is allergic, so it has to be hypoallergenic. There are a number of breeds that are hypoallergenic," Obama said. "On the other hand, our preference would be to get a shelter dog, but, obviously, a lot of shelter dogs are mutts like me" (Fram, 2008).

A few nervous chuckles could be heard from the reporters covering the event. During the campaign, Obama had celebrated his biracial background as the son of a white mother from Kansas and an African father from Kenya—and many biracial Americans celebrated with him—including this author. But what was one to make of this new comment, one of the first uttered publicly as President-elect? During the campaign, Obama had become known for his self-deprecating style. Most people considered this an amiable expression of humility and audiences seemed to appreciate it. It did not hurt that it had the added bonus of softening his reputation as an elitist. However, the first African American President in history describing himself as a mutt? This simply would not do. Not only was it demeaning to African Americans, but to all Americans who come from a mixed race background. To that group in particular, it is considered perhaps the worst insult one could utter and a slur that carries with it a very specific history of hatred and fear of race mixing. From a purely political perspective, it made the President-elect appear weak and sounded like racial pandering at a time when Obama's reputation and anticipation about his presidency and what it would portend for America was at its absolute highest. After such a momentous victory, was this an ominous sign of things to come? Would Obama need so desperately to be accepted by white Americans, even after the election, that he would make comments at the expense of his own background? Would it affect his governing style? Was there lurking underneath the surface of this seemingly proud African American a self-loathing, desperate need to please white people?

Mutt, mongrel, mulatto: the significance of race and etymology

Although the United States may have been ready for its first African American President, it apparently was not ready for its first self-identified biracial President. It bears repeating the somewhat obvious truth that Obama is not only the first African American President, but also the first biracial President in American history (as far as we know). Despite this fact, because of some very real and long-standing historical imperatives, which dictate an acceptable identity for a person of mixed black–white ancestry, Obama has largely constructed an African American identity for himself. This essay attempts to provide some historical perspective and context for what has shaped the contours and parameters of that identity.

Obama is in many ways a simple manifestation of these imperatives for an acceptable public identity for a biracial individual. Drawing from Obama's experience and rise to power, it seems clear that one must embrace the one-drop rule in order to have any viability as a candidate in need of the African American vote. One must consider whom one marries, where one lives, how they express themselves, in order to be "black enough." At the same time, however, Obama utilized his mixed race heritage in order to reach out to white voters and mainstream sensibilities. I argue that this is a manufactured public identity, not to be confused with Obama's private identity as a biracial person. The question that this essay poses then is a simple one—do we have a full and complete picture of our President? My argument is that a new lens is needed to understand more fully President Obama's multiraciality because it is part of his core being. In addition, there are multiple examples of the ways in which, although the man himself may not publicly identify as mixed race except at times when it's politically expedient for him to do so, his experience with mixed race offers evidence of a more complex identity and therefore calls into question the notion that Obama is "black only."

Indeed, had Obama run as a self-identified biracial candidate, he most certainly would not have received the outpouring of eventual support from African Americans, and therefore might not have been elected to the nation's highest political office. Before the African American community rallied around Obama's candidacy, he also had to pass the, "Is he black enough?" test. Had he not campaigned as a strongly identified African American, he may have jeopardized his candidacy. Thus, his comment about "mutts like me" was really his first public (and direct) utterance and more importantly, public recognition of his multiraciality. This was well documented in his autobiography and other interviews, mostly before the presidential campaign. Yet Obama's self-description in his first press conference was much more personal. It went beyond his more typical and comparatively more oblique projection of his multiraciality by simply mentioning his white mother from Kansas and African father from Kenya. Certain questions still linger about that first public coming out. Was he setting a dangerous precedent by labeling himself as such? Was it now acceptable for others to begin using the term?

For some mixed race people, the term hits with the sharpness of a dagger the way that the N-word may feel for African Americans or other pejorative ethnic slurs may sound to other groups. For others, it is an endearing way of poking fun at the fact that we are all really just mutts anyway, mixed-up and cross-bred over many generations, aren't we? It is something one occasionally hears mixed race people say about themselves in jest. Certainly, many people of a mixed race background will recognize this as a typical feature of the mixed race experience. Often the argument is made that people are "reclaiming" the term—by applying the ultimate insult to themselves, thus, taking away its power to hurt—as other oppressed groups have reclaimed hateful terms.

One wonders, however, whether the public at large is aware of the term's association with "mongrelization" (another term applied to dogs), which was used to refer to the mixing of the races in the late nineteenth and early twentieth centuries. During that period, interracial marriage brought on the worst fears of many white Americans and foretold a terrifying future in which one could not determine the race to which an individual belonged. Perhaps people are unfamiliar with the history of the use of terms that apply to the breeding and domestication of animals to describe mixed race people. Indeed, in popular thought, the term "mulatto" is said to derive from the Portuguese word for mule (*mulo*). Supposedly, it was an epithet referring to the fact that the latter was the sterile offspring of a donkey and a horse, and that the mulatto, as the offspring of a black and a white person, was degenerate and low in fertility, if not actually sterile. That said, there have been alternative etymological explanations. Linguistic evidence suggests that as a legacy of the Islamic occupation of Iberia, the Arabic word used to refer to individuals of blended African–Arab descent—*muwallad*—may have actually evolved into the Portuguese word *mulato* to refer to individuals of blended African European descent (Buscaglia-Salgado, 2003; Daniel, 2006; Forbes, 1988).

Whatever the etymological origin of the term, by the twentieth century, certain specific and negative stereotypes about the mulatto could be found throughout scientific literature and in popular imagination. Because of the extensive legacy of race mixing in the African American population (which is more than 85 percent mixed), this notion was eventually extended to all African Americans. An example of this is Frederick Hoffman's extinction thesis, which predicted that African Americans as a race were destined to die out, and therefore could not receive life-insurance because the financial risk was too high. It is the main reason that the "M" for mulatto, used in the census between the years 1850 to 1920, was employed, not to count mulattoes or legitimize identities, but to measure this slow decline to eventual African American extinction. Yet even in the face of this history many people still feel very comfortable using terms like "mutt," "half-breed," or "mongrel" to describe human beings. These terms are all problematic in that they reify a biological view of race that most anthropologists, biologists, and social scientists now reject. Furthermore, terms like this reintroduce a taxonomy of human beings that is mostly associated with nineteenth-century pseudoscientific efforts to prove the superiority of the white race—a categorization that is aligned with efforts to categorize human beings into races—which simply *does not* work.

Black and mixed race: Obama's public and private identities

In light of this historical perspective, what is needed is a re-consideration of the identity of President Barack Obama. I offer this essay as a scholarly thought piece to invite and encourage further research on this newly emerging topic. Although there are no hard-and-fast conclusions, I am suggesting that although Obama may have won the election by identifying as an African American candidate, there is at the core of his identity an important biracial dimension. This exhibits many of the features of what I would call a mixed race experience, one rooted very strongly in blackness.

What is more important, though, is the racial sleight-of-hand at work here. Obama and his handlers went to great lengths to convince the electorate that Obama was on the one hand, black enough, tied to an authentic African American experience. On the other hand, he was projected as someone who could draw from his biracial heritage to bring people together. One could argue that Obama may have moments, particularly private ones, when he resonates with a multiracial identity, or at least with the mixed race experience, notwithstanding choosing to identify publically as black. However, one is not yet simply black by choice (McClain, 2004). Despite the increasing availability of a multiracial identity, one is still largely black by popular demand. This is attributable to the continuing external imposition or ascription of the one-drop rule in U.S. racial commonsense, however attenuated, as compared to previously (McClain, 2004, p. 114).

It is important here to underscore the fact that the "black enough" argument is not a biological argument, but one that is tied to an important commitment to African American issues, cultural experiences and historical travails or even traumas. More difficult than Obama's problems with being "black enough," however, is his questionable commitment to important African American policy issues, and the fact that he has demonstrated time and again a retreat and mishandling of issues of race. Indeed, one could make the argument that his misreading of issues of race, for example, the Gates arrest, or the firing of Shirley Sherrod, suggests a sense of privilege that may stem from Obama's biracial identity which caused him to perhaps think that he was somehow an exception to this rule.

Although Obama realized, wisely, that in order to win the highest office in the land, he would have to run as an African American, using his mixed race background to highlight his ability to work with many different groups, he has made mistakes that simultaneously demonstrate a *naïveté* about race. One could argue that there was a glide of opportunism in this strategy, but it has also been a double-edged sword. Cultural theorists have referred to this phenomenon as "strategic essentialism" or more precisely, in the case of Obama, as "strategic blackness" (Landry and MacClean, 1996).

In some ways, Obama's strategic blackness is thus similar to Spivak's concept of strategic essentialism. This concept refers to a tactic that nationalities, racial/ethnic or "minority" groups can use to present themselves to achieve certain goals. Significant differences may exist between members of these groups. Yet it can be advantageous for them to project their group identity in a reductionist manner that focuses on one axis of experience, identity, and ultimately, oppression.

Although mainly applicable to groups, one could argue that Obama in a similar fashion has "simplified" his racial identity by focusing on one component of his background as a strategy for affirming his connection with the struggles of African Americans as well as for garnering their critical support (and social approval) in his bid for the presidency (Daniel, 2002).

Indeed, it was a lesson Obama learned very bitterly after having lost the 2000 Illinois Congressional race against Bobby Rush in which Jesse Jackson and Bill Clinton, who both supported Rush, said Obama was "not black enough" (Remnick, 2008). Apparently, the electorate agreed and Obama lost that campaign badly to Rush. By the Senate. race in 2004, Obama's campaign style had changed and he clearly shifted toward an identity and a campaign style that was more African American in orientation (so much so that he joined a church with very strong roots in the African American community led by a Pastor, Jeremiah Wright. Although it should be said that he had already been a member of the Church. His history with Wright extended over at least a decade).

Certainly this was a long way from young Barry Obama of Hawai'i, or even the compromiser who was able to become the first African American editor of the *Harvard Law Review*. Also, the extent to which Michelle Obama played a role in helping Obama reshape his identity and re-connect him through her own family's roots to an authentic African American experience cannot be overstated. It is important to emphasize that this was more of a political concern than a biological one. That is to say, there is more complexity to this issue than the rather simplistic picture that is often presented by the media. It is not simply a matter of being "black enough" but of having a commitment to black issues. It is Obama's support for "post-racial" policies like supporting the education "reforms" of Arne Duncan and his backtracking on the Gates arrest, the firing of Shirley Sherrod, and his systematic funneling of resources to corporate interests that raise these concerns even now. Is there any connection with the ways in which Obama sees himself and these missteps with regard to race in his presidency? Does his divided racial allegiance make it more difficult for him to govern in these areas of racial sensitivity?

That being said, even with Obama's strong identification with blackness, many of the facets of his experience are consistent with the typical mixed race experience in the United States. I believe it is this commonality of experience that ultimately binds the disparate elements of today's mixed race community in America. Accordingly, what is needed is a different lens through which to view Obama—his candidacy and his presidency. That is to say, Obama's triumph as the first African American President and the celebration of this historical fact has somewhat distorted our perception of the more encompassing "true" nature of the individual and who he is at his core. We should not confuse the fact that although it was necessary to run as an African American to become elected by the American public, this is not entirely who Obama is. Even the comment about "mutts like me" belies a certain insecurity, a lack of ease with his identity, which suggests that he is not always the confident African American many of us have come to recognize.

Some in the mixed race community may have seen this comment as unfortunate; still others privately rejoiced over this statement as Obama's "coming-out" moment, stated clearly, albeit humorously in his first press conference. Yet with the campaign safely behind him, perhaps Obama was finally able to reclaim part of his true identity. However one interprets this moment, for important historical reasons, it clearly resonates with the experience of multiracial Americans. These individuals at one time or another may have felt the same way or made the same kind of comment about themselves, either as a bold act of reclamation or as a way to explain mixed race identity in a popular context. For historians and social scientists who have studied multiracial identity, it is a very identifiable part of the contemporary and historical mixed race experience; I will discuss in detail the patterns, facets, and archetypes that make up that experience.

Until a clearer picture emerges of Obama, his actions, policies, governing style, personal decisions, and the very way in which he is perceived by the public, will indeed remain distorted or at least incomplete. Glenn Beck, formerly of Fox News, has stated that Obama has "over and over again [exposed himself as] a guy who has a deep-seated hatred for white people or the white culture" (Bauder, 2009). This argument is myopic at best and egregiously distorted and inaccurate at worst, one that forgets the fact that Obama was raised by his white grandmother. Have we forgotten the lessons that Obama so thoughtfully wrote about in his autobiography? A new picture is needed, one that is not only informed by the current euphoria of those who believe Obama embodies a post-racial present, but also tied to the very real racial past, which culminated in the system of legalized American apartheid. I will attempt to rethink President Obama in that past by recasting him in terms of his relationship to the historical mulatto and his identity in the context of the American mixed race experience.

Obama may have won the election by identifying as an African American candidate. Yet he utilized his racial "hybridity" or multiraciality as a strategy to project himself as a person who could or at least sought to bridge the racial divide, this was not purely strategic or spontaneous (Daniel, 2009). Yet Obama's construction of an African American identity began much earlier as documented in his autobiography and was reinforced by several incidents that shaped his "political identity." This is something very different and apart from his personal racial identity and the potential costs of not appearing "black enough." Beyond all the speculation about whether Obama was "black enough" leading up to the presidential election, race is clearly a demon with which he had wrestled for many years, indeed all his life. His first memoir, *Dreams from My Father*, published in 1995, was so raw, so honest and unvarnished that it almost became a political liability when Obama ran for President in 2008. He is eloquent in many parts of the autobiography about his thoughtfulness about issues of race at a very young age. It clearly became part of his overall strategy for political success and in this way, as many autobiographies do, serves as a map that leads the reader through the geography of the mixed race experience if not of mixed race identity.

Mixed race *identity* and the mixed race *experience*

Obama is representative of the angst, challenges, and archetypal experiences, of what it means to biracial in America. It is this multiracial identity which, I argue, is held together by common experience. Sociologist G. Reginald Daniel has written extensively on this question.

> Resistance to the binary racial project, which originates in identification with more than one racial group, is what binds multiracial-identified individuals together most powerfully. This racial liminality, or sense of being "betwixt and between," becomes a fundamental part of the self-conception of multiracial individuals and a defining component of the multiracial experience. (Daniel, 2002)

Accordingly, readers of *Dreams from My Father* react when they read that white people challenged Obama for denying his white heritage, as white people are often wont to do. Or, then there is the inevitable "What are you?" question, which becomes so common that it has attained the status almost of some kind of rite of passage for people of mixed race. The inexorable questions of whom to marry, of how to think, even as a very young person, about perhaps ending a relationship, because of worry over what race the offspring of such as relationship will be. Then there is the concern about becoming lost in a white world, and loss of one's own identity because of the ability to move back and forth between the two worlds, or in the case of some biracial people, and even monoracially-identified African Americans, who are light enough to pass for white. Many of these individuals experience unintentional passing and involuntary beneficiaries of white privilege. Although not so applicable to Obama, this latter slice in the spectrum of the African American experience is one that poses many specific problems in the multiracial experiential paradigm.

Another aspect of the multiracial experience that has only recently become further explored is that of passing for other racial groups—for Latina/o, Native American, some even going so far, as many black–white biracial people do, especially in parts of the northeast, of learning Spanish, becoming culturally Hispanic and, in effect, disappearing into this already multiracial, mixed race group. This makes sense when we consider that many Latin American nationalities have a very different formulation of race in their home countries than we do in the United States, and therefore offer a ready-made community in which many biracial people find an identity.

James Weldon Johnson ventured into this territory famously in his *Autobiography of an Ex-Colored Man* (1927). In this sense, the autobiography becomes a tradition in which certain archetypes, certain tropes emerge. In much the same way that the *Autobiography of Malcolm X* became a sort of representative text, an archetypal map of the various obstacles that confronted young black men in urban areas, so does Obama's own autobiography become an interesting testimonial to the racial landscape of the various obstacles that confront young mixed race people today in this country. However, Malcolm's red hair, gray eyes, and light skin posed some questions about his authenticity as a black man when he was growing up—when some of the local black children of Lansing teased him about his "high yellow" appearance, called him "Eskimo" and "milky" and "snowflake." Consequently, his experience would also resonate with some of the issues of the mixed race experience (Perry, 1985).

In many ways, Obama's story provides a possible model for black-descended multiracial people in that racial acceptance and success depends on an identity that is closely tied to blackness. In the larger sense, Obama reconciles the tensions between what G. Reginald Daniel has called "multigenerational multiracials," that is to say, the category that most African Americans fall into as a racially mixed people, and "first-generation" multiracial people who have one parent that identifies as monoracially white and another that identifies as monoracially black. The question is: does this require an African American identification or can it simply be a multiracial identity that affirms one's connection to the African Diaspora and the black experience? Had Obama identified more with the white side of his parental lineage, or even more strongly as a mixed race person, many Americans might not today know the name Barack Obama. The important point to take away from this memoir is that in the end, the protagonist, the hero, does not choose a mixed race identity but, rather, an African American one. To do otherwise would surely have antagonized and alienated African American support and acceptance. Anything less than full and absolute acceptance of an African American identity would have cost Obama severely.

That said, Obama's embrace of a black identity notwithstanding, Daniel points out that African American educator, activist, political commentator, and Democratic Party affiliate, Donna Brazile, emphasized Obama's "affirmative connection to whiteness" in courting European Americans who might not vote for Obama simply because he is an African American rather than because they disagreed with his political platform (Daniel, 2009). He writes, "Brazile strategically emphasized that the Harvard-educated Obama is 'biracial'" and "spent nine months in the womb of a white woman. He was raised for the first eighteen to twenty-one years by his white grandparents" (Daniel, 2009). For a people who have for so long been the targets of this most specific kind of racial rejection, the slightest hint of preference for whiteness raises eyebrows.

So then, this, in many ways, constructed African American identity is based not only on the preference of Obama himself, but also the unique set of rules, strictures, and etiquette that has arisen alongside the unique history of race in this country, much of which comes out of the experience of slavery. The important ways in which the "one-drop rule" functions and dictates this set of values and expectations about the ways in which one must identify, further complicates the picture. It is only through the very precise and careful adherence to this seemingly strange set of rules and values that Obama's meteoric rise to the top of the world of politics, his success and acceptance in the most competitive, elite quarters of academic distinction and achievement in the world are even possible.

One may speculate about the way the world could, and perhaps should be; but Obama has had to live, and indeed thrive, in that world. Yet even this does not give us a complete picture of who Obama is.

To truly understand that, we must understand Obama at two different levels: his "public" racial identity, that is to say, the identity Obama constructed for himself to navigate society, to grow more powerful, and eventually to become elected; and the other, perhaps more important, and more accurate personal, that is to say, "private" identity of Obama. We also need to understand the nexus at which the two levels meet. His personal (or "private") identity is that of a biracial man in America, trying to find an identity, sometimes being ingratiating to white people, self-deprecating in his discussion about his mixed race background, which could result in comments such as the "mutts like me" statement.

He writes in *Dreams from My Father*,

> I learned to slip back and forth between my black and white worlds ...One of those tricks I had learned: People were satisfied so long as you were courteous and smiled and made no sudden moves. They were more than satisfied; they were relieved—such a pleasant surprise to find a well-mannered young black man who didn't seem angry all the time. (Obama, 2007)

Obama began to observe that when people discovered his mixed race heritage, they made assumptions about who he was. Once again, in this "archetypal" mixed race experimental testimony, Obama writes, "I ceased to advertise my mother's race at the age of 12 or 13, when I began to suspect that by doing so I was ingratiating myself to whites" (Obama, 2007).

His musings on biracial identity and the mixed race experience do not dominate the story; this is after all a mostly African American autobiographical account. Yet Obama does discuss recognizable archetypes that exist in American myth and have perhaps been most expressed in literature, observing that when people discover Obama's mixed race heritage, they make assumptions about

> the mixed blood, the divided soul, the ghostly image of the tragic mulatto trapped between two worlds.... the constant, crippling fear that I didn't belong somehow, that unless I dodged and hid and pretended to be something I wasn't, I would forever remain an outsider, with the rest of the world, black and white, always standing in judgment. (Obama, 2007)

The contemporary mulatto: multiraciality and the multiracial movement

Since the 1967 landmark Supreme Court decision of *Loving vs. Virginia*, in which a Virginia state law banning interracial marriage was overturned and declared unconstitutional by the United States Supreme Court, America has witnessed a major demographic shift, and more importantly, a sea-change in accepted racial identification. Debates over the race and identity of people—particularly those who consider themselves to be of mixed race—have increasingly come to dominate contemporary dialogues about racial identity and multiculturalism. Scholars such as Kathleen Korgen have written about a bi- and multiracial "baby boom" which has occurred since the 1967 *Loving vs. Virginia* case, which made laws barring interracial marriage illegal in the United States (Korgen, 1998). However, as Spencer asserts in *Challenging Multiracial Identity*, since 1967, the "bi- and multiracial baby boom" is actually due, not only to black and white marriages after the *Loving vs. Virginia* case, but also to the relaxed immigration statutes of the 1965 Immigration Act (Spencer, 2008). Similarly, Spencer points out that even earlier statute changes such as the War Brides Act of 1945 had the effect of bringing larger numbers of Asian war brides who married and had children with American white people (Spencer, 2006). That said, since the late 1960s, growing numbers of individuals have challenged the rule of hypodescent by asserting identities that reflect their various backgrounds.

Consequently, a multiracial identity is more common among the offspring of contemporary interracial marriages, including black–white individuals, born in the post-civil rights era. Many individuals display more traditional single-racial identities. Indeed, the extant data indicate that black/white offspring of racial intermarriages have a strong connection to blackness, but many also retain a black identity even with the more recent availability of a multiracial identity. That is to say that, for black-descended multiracial people, identity is problematized in ways that it is not for other multiracial people due to the one-drop rule. Like Obama, many younger multiracial people who now have multiple identities available to them still choose a black identity for important historical and sociological reasons.

Taking a multidimensional approach to identity and drawing on reflected appraisals (how they think others see them), in her article "'If You're Half Black, You're Just Black': Reflected Appraisals and the Persistence of the One-Drop Rule," Nikki Khanna examines racial identity among black–white adults in the South and the lingering influence of the one-drop rule. Most respondents internally identify as black and when asked to explain these black identities, they describe how both black and white people see them as black. While quantitative studies suggest that the one-drop rule still has an impact on identity in the South, little qualitative work examines black–white identity within this context (Khanna, 2010). This data is also reinforced by others who have examined the identity preferences of children of black–white parentage.

According to Carol McClain,

> It was only after the advent of the civil rights and black power movements of the 1960s and 1970s that the children of black/white parentage began to consider themselves as other than or as more than black. Before these transforming events, mixed race children were typically raised in black families, having been uniformly rejected by white society, if not their white relatives, and grew up in black neighborhoods and communities. The white mothers of black children were also accepted, if not embraced, by the same communities, even when estranged or divorced from the black fathers of their children. Until the last 30 years, the combination of the one-drop rule, phenotypical variation in the black population, the willingness of black families and communities to accept as their own people with known mixed race parentage, and Jim Crow segregation—all interacted to assure that mixed race individuals were socially defined as black. That they identified themselves as black as well is hardly surprising. (McClain, 2004)

Yet beginning in the late 1970s, a multiracial consciousness was reflected in a movement that sought to change standards in official racial-data collection that have required individuals to identify with only one racial background. By the 2000 census, this movement succeeded in making it possible for individuals to express a multiracial identity by checking more than one box in the census race question.

Some scholars see the election of Obama as the logical extension of that movement, if not a completely related phenomenon, one that has had the consequence of reinvigorating debates around mixed race identity. Of course, the complexities of multiracial identity are not limited to the experiences of individuals of partial African descent, but encompass a wide variety of backgrounds. However, the movement has been disproportionately composed of black–white couples—particularly those involving European American women and African American men—and their offspring. This is particularly true of the support groups (I-Pride, Biracial Family Network, Multiracial Americans of California, Interracial Family Circle, etc.), which were primary vehicles of the movement in the 1990s. Though only a small percentage of the larger national population of interracial families, their overrepresentation is due to the unique legacy of attitudes and policies that have crystallized around blackness in race relations—and more specifically, racial jurisprudence—in the United States.

Still, much of the contemporary research continues to focus on the offspring of black–white unions since black and white people continue to be the two groups with the greatest social distance and therefore the strongest impediments against interracial marriage. Two of the leading intellectual voices in research on biracial identity are Kerry Ann Rockquemore and David L. Brunsma whose *Beyond Black: Biracial Identity in America*, offers some potential models in which to categorize biracial identity. Their research used survey data collected from biracial college students to help to give voice to the complexities of biracial identity, and how it can be influenced by physical appearance, surroundings, situation and other factors. Based on their surveys, Rockquemore and Brunsma describe four major variations on biracial identity: the "border" identity, which encompasses both socially accepted racial categorizations of black and white yet includes an additional element from its combination; the "protean," which involves multiple identities and personas that can be called up in appropriate contexts; a "singular" identity as either black or white, rather than biracial; finally, a "transcendent" identity, consciously denying having any racial identity at all. Using that lens to examine Obama, one would have to conclude that he would most likely fall into the "protean" identity, one in which a racial self-understanding is based on a fluidity of identity which allows one to move comfortably through the world.

About the protean identity, they write, "the biracial person possesses multiple racial identities and personas that may be called up in appropriate contexts. Instead of identifying as biracial, black, or white consistently, the individual will sometimes identify as black, at other times as white, and still other times as biracial" (Rockquemore and Brunsma, 2002). The common element that holds them together is the mixed race experience, a commonality, not so different from what W.E.B. Du Bois, in his classic *Souls of Black Folk,* called the "double-consciousness." "One ever feels his two-ness—an American, a Negro; two souls, two thoughts, two unreconciled strivings; two warring ideals in one dark body, whose dogged strength alone keeps it from being torn asunder" (Du Bois, 1903). Notwithstanding the fact that African Americans are multiracial in terms of ancestry, if not identity, Du Bois was positing a cultural rather than racial two-ness, yet this timeless quote should remind us that many African Americans also share an affinity with the mixed race experience, and therefore have a very nuanced understanding of it (Gaines, 2002).

Tim Wise writes in *Between Barack and a Hard Place,*

> In the case of Barack Obama, of course, as many have noted he is a man of biracial ancestry: the son of a white mother from Kansas and black father from Kenya. That said, it is valid and valuable to note Obama's biraciality—especially given the growing number of biracial persons in the United States whose racial identity is often ignored, or feel as though they are forced to "choose sides" in claiming an identity for themselves. Yet, it is also worth pointing out that throughout U.S. history and still today, to be black/white biracial hardly erases one salient fact: a person so designated will typically be seen as a member of the lowest in the racial hierarchy. So, to be black and white in terms of parentage is to be black. And so, while ancestrally biracial, in the social sense, as a resident of the United States, Barack Obama is incontestably black. (Wise, 2009)

Authenticity and identity: African America and the fact of blackness

One article appearing on CNN.com dated June 9 2008, looked at this issue at an early point in the campaign when "candidate Obama," a relatively newly-elected Senator from Illinois, was still largely unknown to most of America. The article states,

> Included in the multiracial category is the Democratic presumptive nominee, Sen. Barack Obama. With a white mother from Kansas and a black father from Kenya, Obama is the nation's first biracial candidate for President. The media, however, have continually called Obama the nation's first major party "black candidate," saying he could make history as the first "black President." But is that accurate? A columnist examining Obama's background summed up

his racial identity into one equation: white + black = black. (Carroll, 2008)

Interesting still is that Joe Biden who, before he was selected as Obama's running-mate, said of Obama, that he was the "first mainstream African American who is articulate and bright and clean and a nice-looking guy" (Balz, 2007). It was thought by many at the time that perhaps the two would not be able to work together after such a comment was made. In an article entitled "Is Obama Black Enough?" he writes,

> In calling Obama the "first mainstream African American who is articulate and bright and clean and a nice-looking guy," the implication was that the black people who are regularly seen by whites—or at least those who aspire to the highest office in the land—are none of these things. But give Biden credit—at least he acknowledged Obama's identity. (Coates, 2007)

The authenticity argument reared its ugly head again when the author made the argument that Obama may still have had to prove his race credentials in running for the highest office in the land. "As much as his biracial identity has helped Obama build a sizable following in middle America, it's also opened a gap for others to question his authenticity as a black man." (Coates, 2007). This issue alone perhaps caused the greatest hue-and-cry in the beginning of the election when elected officials and many of the African American spokespersons openly questioned Obama's blackness.

The same cannot be said for others. "Obama's mother is of white U.S. stock. His father is a black Kenyan," Stanley Crouch recently sniffed in a *New York Daily News* column entitled "What Obama isn't: Black Like Me." "Black, in our political and social vocabulary, means those descended from West African slaves," wrote Debra Dickerson on the liberal website Salon. Writers like *New Republic* columnist, Peter Beinart, have argued that Obama is seen as a "good black," and thus has less of a following among black people (Crouch, 2006).

He concludes,

> Back in the real world, Obama is married to a black woman. He goes to a black church. He's worked with poor people on the South Side of Chicago, and still lives there. That someone given the escape valve of biraciality would choose

to be black, would see some beauty in his darker self and still care more about health care and public education than reparations and Confederate flags is just too much for many small-minded racists, both black and white, to comprehend. Barack Obama's real problem isn't that he's too white—it's that he's too black. (Coates, 2007)

Much of Obama's overall appeal stems from his image as a post-racial politician. Not only does he have a mixed race background, but his rhetoric, most notably his 2004 Democratic National Convention speech, also emphasizes the importance of Americans moving beyond political, religious, and racial differences. He rarely makes explicit appeals based on his race the way Jackson did. "A lot of black people aren't ready to get beyond race, because race puts them in the situation they're in," said Ron Walters, a political scientist at the University of Maryland who worked on Jesse Jackson's presidential runs. "But many whites want to get beyond the past, they want to support a black person who doesn't raise the past and in fact gives them absolution from the past" (Bacon, 2007a).

The transcript for an NPR news broadcast, entitled "Why Obama Chooses 'Black' Over 'Biracial,'" broadcast on January 9 2008, read this way:

> Mr. Larry King (CNN): Can a black man be elected President of the United States?
>
> Mr. Alex Cohen (CNN's *Day To Day*): What you don't often hear is Barack Obama could be the first biracial President, nor do you hear the candidate refer to himself that way. And that's been a sore spot for many Americans who do identify as biracial.
>
> Ms. Joy Zarembka (author, "The Pigment of Your Imagination"): Friends of mine who are sort of part of the multicultural community very much feel like he should come out and be sort of a proud biracial American. (Chadwick, 2008)

Several prominent commentators were also interviewed for the radio broadcast and their opinions also mirrored that of the larger audience, which saw African American as the only politically viable choice for

Obama. G. Reginald Daniel was among those interviewed and stated the case plainly,

> Prof. Daniel: To say you're a biracial, a multiracial person, is really asking for trouble, because first of all, nobody's going to know what you're talking about.

> Mr. Alex Cohen: After all, biracial is a bit vague. It could refer to someone who's half Korean and half Jewish or half Iranian and half Puerto Rican.

Daniel goes on to say there's another much more perilous consequence Obama would face if he identifies as biracial.

> Prof. Daniel: African Americans are likely or possibly going to say, "Oh, you just don't want to be black."

> Mr. Alex Cohen: And that's not something a candidate wants voters saying in an election, says Fred Harris.

> Mr. Fredrick Harris (Center on African American Politics and Society): Should the candidate become invisible to its black roots. I think that would turn off a lot of voters. (Cohen, 2007)

In an article in which Stanley Crouch weighs into the debate, entitled, "What Obama Isn't: Black Like Me (Stanley Crouch Eats His Own)," He writes,

> Obama's mother is of white U.S. stock. His father is a black Kenyan. Other than color, Obama did not—does not—share a heritage with the majority of black Americans, who are descendants of plantation slaves....So when black Americans refer to Obama as "one of us," I do not know what they are talking about. In his new book, *The Audacity of Hope*, Obama makes it clear that, while he has experienced some light versions of typical racial stereotypes, he cannot claim those problems as his own—nor has he lived the life of a black American. (Crouch, 2006)

Although Crouch may have jumped the gun, making these comments as he did in 2006, well before Obama was even nominated, he may have been somewhat prophetic in his commentary. After only one year of having been in office, many members in the black leadership, especially the Congressional Black Caucus, have become critical of President Obama in ways that seek to distance and separate him from slave-descended African Americans.

Conclusion: Obama's multiraciality and hybrid blackness

In many ways the situation in which Obama finds himself in terms of racial identity is the same struggle with which many biracial Americans must contend. These memories provide important directives for Obama's identity, which is a profoundly biracial identity. His struggles and experience are profoundly biracial and his personal or internal identity may be biracial. At the same time, however, this is a profoundly African American experience as well, and Obama's public identity is African American but also what Daniel has characterized as profoundly "hybrid" (Daniel, 2002). Daniel writes,

> For all his hybridity, Obama's identity is situated in the black community and extends outward from that location. This differs from a multiracial identity, which manifests itself "betwixt and between" the boundaries of traditional U.S. racial groups. It extends outward from this liminal location depending upon individuals' orientation toward the groups that compose their background. (Daniel, 2002)

Once again, we can draw some conclusions from Obama's autobiography *Dreams from My Father*. He writes, "The year that my parents were married, miscegenation was still described a felony in over half the states in the union. In many parts of the South, my father could have been strung up from a tree for merely looking at my mother the wrong way" (Obama, 2007). In another important trope for the biracial experience is the contradiction of being raised as a person of color by a white mother. In reminiscing about how he was raised, Obama recollected.

> She came into my room at 4:00 in the morning, force-fed me breakfast and proceeded to teach me my English lessons for three hours before I left for school and she went to work. I offered stiff resistance to this regimen. She would patiently

repeat her most powerful defense, "This is no picnic for me either, buster." (Obama, 2007, p. 48)

David Mendell, author of *Obama: From Promise to Power*, has commented in a *Frontline* documentary on Obama,

> I think she felt like, here's this African American child whose father has left him. He may suffer from some self-esteem issues. So she built his character up from the very beginning. She told him he was from almost a superior race of people, that he was a special person to the point that he seems to still believe that today. (Kirk, 2009)

Obama clearly wrestled with that identity, but in the final analysis he did what many biracial people have done, which is to cling to an African American identity. As a public person Obama was perhaps pushed in that direction. He had to construct a black identity by teaching himself to be a black man in America. This was something he could not learn from his white family. This is only possible because although African Americans do not identify as multiracial, they are "multigenerational multiracial" in terms of ancestry. In other words, they are monoracial in identity and multiracial in background. Obama has stated, "I am rooted in the African American community. But I'm not defined by it. I am comfortable in my racial identity. But that's not all I am" (Daniel, 2009).

Perhaps there is no way of knowing with any certainty how Obama self-identifies. All we have are our clues or hints that point to a particular identity informed by experience. In order to gain some perspective on the way that Obama truly self-identifies, it becomes interesting to look at the way that he has handled some of the issues in which race weighs heavily which have confronted Obama's administration. During the summer of 2009, Harvard professor Henry Louis Gates Jr., one of the nation's pre-eminent African American scholars, was arrested at his home by Cambridge police investigating a possible break-in. The now infamous incident provoked Obama to step into the mess by remarking that the "Cambridge police acted stupidly," and eventually offered to invite both the arresting officer and Professor Gates for the now famous beer at the White House. There was President Obama, at the nexus of race and class, black and white trying to help find common ground on one of the most polarizing modern issues we face, racial profiling, serving as a bridge between the races. The incident was one in which Obama was strongly rebuked by his handlers for having made the comment at all and the incident is now remembered by most for having been a situation which was bungled. He was forced to make an apology to the Cambridge Police department and others for having made the remark. But what are we to make of this situation? What does it tell us about Obama's identity?

In hindsight, the incident stands out more than anything for being the first of several situations which demonstrated Obama's eagerness to please. Many people felt that he was trying to have it both ways, on the one hand standing firm as an African American leader and speaking out about an issue that affects many African Americans, particularly in urban areas, much as Henry Louis Gates himself was doing. At the same time, he did not want to alienate white Americans, or the law enforcement community and it was interpreted by some as having caved in too quickly.

For all its awkwardness, what emerged from all this was "a teachable moment" on race. As with Obama's comment about "mutts like me," these first few forays certainly demonstrated that this would be a new style of governing, especially with regard to issues of race. After all, this was in part what Obama ran on as a candidate. He utilized his mixed race background to present himself as a candidate who could help America heal its racial wounds. Daniel writes,

> Obama's skillful deployment of bargaining and conciliating is integrally connected to his experience as the son of a white mother from Kansas, in the heartland of the United States, and black father from Kenya, the African homeland of humanity. This has imbued his consciousness with a broader vision and wider ranging sympathies in forming an identity. (Daniel, 2009)

So perhaps it is safe to say that Obama, while he does not self-identify as multiracial, identifies with the mixed experience.

In what was perhaps the most telling moment, in April 2010, the *New York Times* reported that when asked to declare his race, Obama checked "Black."

> A White House spokesman confirmed that Mr. Obama, the son of a black father from Kenya and a white mother from Kansas, checked African American on the 2010 census questionnaire. The President, who was born in Hawai'i and raised there and in Indonesia, had more than a dozen options in responding to Question 9, about race. He chose

"Black, African Am., or Negro.'" Mr. Obama could have
checked white, checked both black and white, or checked
the last category on the form, "some other race," which he
would then have been asked to identify in writing. There is
no category specifically for mixed race or biracial. (Roberts
and Baker, 2010)

There was some reaction in the mixed race community, many
of whom expressed disappointment in the President's choice. *The
Washington Post* carried a story by Elizabeth Chang entitled, "Why
Obama Should Not Have Checked 'Black' on His Census Form." She
stated in that article,

I have always considered Barack Obama to be biracial, and
I had hoped that his election would help our country move
beyond the tired concept of race....The federal government,
finally heeding the desires of multiracial people to be able
to accurately define themselves, had changed the rules in
2000, so he could have also checked white. Or he could
have checked "some other race." Instead, Obama went with
black alone. (Chang, 2010)

In many ways, this was a view that was echoed throughout the mixed
race community and one finds this same sentiment reflected throughout
the blogosphere. Many mixed race identified individuals saw this as a
disappointment and felt very strongly about choosing more than one
race on the census and could not understand why Obama would not
as well. She continues,

The President's choice disappoints me, and it seems
somewhat disingenuous. Obama, who has also referred
to himself as a "mutt," made a big deal during the 2008
campaign of being able to relate to Hawaiians and
Midwesterners, Harvard grads and salespeople, blacks,
whites, Latinos, whatever—precisely because of his
"unconventional" background and multicultural exposure.
On the census, however, he has effectively said that when
it counts, he is black. (Chang, 2010)

In the final analysis, instead of strategically using blackness to get
elected, Obama may be an African American who strategically used
his mixed race background to present himself as the ideal candidate.

As Chang stated, when it counts, he's black. Yet the few times that Obama has spoken publicly about his identity have usually been in those contexts that called for the healing of race relations. Whether it was the speech given in the wake of the Reverend Jeremiah Wright scandal "A More Perfect Union" or Obama's famous keynote address at the 2004 Democratic National Convention in Boston, in which he stated that "There's not a black America and white America and Latino America and Asian America; there's the United States of America." Many African Americans bristled at the assertion that there was not a black America, but most were still very receptive to the speech because it was coming from someone who was perceived to be at the nexus of all these communities and somehow possessed a different perspective of the problem because of his mixed race background.

In perhaps a fitting bookend to the "mutt" comment, Obama appeared on the daytime talk show, *The View*, in August 2010, in which he classified African Americans as a "mongrel people." Needless to say there were some in the African American community who bristled at this statement. Then in the next sentence Obama suggested white Americans are also of a "mongrel" class. Here was another comment then about Obama's ethnicity that borrowed from the parlance of dog breeding in which to explain his identity. If there was any doubt that Obama's first use of the term was just a throwaway comment, here is yet another suggestion that perhaps Obama truly sees himself this way. Was this another biracial "coming out" moment or another flawed attempt at ingratiating himself with white people?

It is the experience of being mixed that ties the various elements of Obama's personal identity together and in the end, it is that experience that he hearkens back to again and again. In his most poignant and soul-searching moments, Obama pays tribute to the experience of having two families who self-identified differently as the thing that made him. It is the part of his identity that in his most honest moments, he always comes back to. And yet, Obama is a contradiction. He slips in and out of different identities and yet claims them all equally but never completely. Although Obama may not personally identify as multiracial, he most certainly identifies with the mixed race experience and variously draws from it as a source of strength, particularly in times of need. And in the final analysis, is that not the quintessential expression of the mixed race experience—racial fluidity, ease with differing identities, and strategic identification with one or more of them? Perhaps we must let Obama's own words speak for him from a stump speech he made in New Hampshire during the presidential campaign. He said,

I'm an African American, but I am somebody, like many African Americans, who has all kinds of stuff in him...You should have seen Thanksgiving, we were like the United Nations... But I self-identify as an African American. That's how I am treated and that's how I am viewed and I'm proud of it. (Bacon, 2007b)

Reference

Bacon, P. (2007a) 'Can Obama Count On the Black Vote?', *Time*, 23 January (www.time.com).

Bacon, P. (2007b) 'Rock Solid Support for Obama, but Will the Black Vote Follow?', *Washington Post,* 30 November 2007 (www.washingtonpost.com).

Balz, D. (2007) 'Biden Stumbles at the Starting Gate: Comments About Obama Overtake Bid for President,' *Washington Post*, 1 February, p. A06.

Bauder, D. (2009) 'Glenn Beck: Obama Is a Racist Fox News Commentator Says He Believes Obama Has "Deep-Seated Hatred" of White People.' *Associated Press,* 29 July.

Brunsma, D.L. (2005) *Mixed Messages: Multiracial Identities in the "Color-Blind" Era*, Boulder, CO: Lynne Rienner Publishers.

Buscaglia-Salgado, JF. (2003) *Undoing Empire: Race and Nation in the Mulatto Caribbean*, Minneapolis, MN: University of Minnesota Press.

Carroll, C. (1900) *The Negro a Beast*. St. Louis, MO: American Book and Bible House.

Carroll, J. (2008) 'CNN Behind the Scenes: Is Barack Obama black or biracial?' (http://articles.cnn.com).

Chang, E. (2010) 'Why Obama Should Not Have Checked "Black" on His Census Form', = *Washington Post,* 29 April (www.washingtonpost.com).

Coates, TP. (2007) 'Is Obama Black Enough?', *Time*, 1 February.

Cohen, A. (producer) (2008) 'Why Obama Chooses 'Black' Over "Biracial"', NPR (www.npr.org).

Crouch, S. (2006) 'What Obama Isn't: Black Like Me', *New York Daily News,* 2 November (http://articles.nydailynews.com)

DaCosta, KM. (2009) 'Interracial Intimacies, Barack Obama, and the Politics of Multiracialism', *The Black Scholar*, vol. 39, no. 3/4.

Dalmage, HM. (2004) *The Politics of Multiracialism: Challenging Racial Thinking,* Albany, NY: State University of New York Press.

Daniel, GR. (2002) *More Than Black? Multiracial Identity and the New Racial Order*, Philadelphia, PA: Temple University Press.

Daniel, GR. (2006) *Race and Multiraciality in Brazil and the United States: Converging Paths?*, University Park, PA: Penn State Press.

Daniel, GR. (2009) 'Race, Multiraciality, and Barack Obama: Toward a More Perfect Union?', *The Black Scholar*, vol. 39, No. 3/4.

Du Bois, WEB. (1903) *Souls of Black Folk*, New York: Penguin Classics.

Forbes, JD. (1988) *Black Africans and Native Americans: Color, Race and Caste in the Evolution of Red-Black Peoples*, Blackwell, London, pp. 131-50.

Fram, A. (2008) '"Mutts Like Me" Shows Obama's Racial Comfort', *Associated Press*, 8 November (www.msnbc.msn.com).

Gaines, Jr., SO. (2002) 'The "Two Souls" of Barack Obama', *The Western Journal of Black Studies,* vol. 34, no. 3.

Johnson, JW. (1927) *Autobiography of an Ex-Colored Man,* New York: A. A. Knopf.

Khanna, N. (2010) '"If You're Half Black You're Just Black": Reflected Appraisals and the Persistence of the One-Drop Rules', *The Sociological Quarterly,* no. 51, pp. 96–121.

Kirk, M (producer). (2009) Dreams of Obama (videorecording), *Frontline*. Boston: PBS.

Korgen, KO. (1998) *From Black to Biracial: Transforming Identity Among Americans,* Westport, NY: Praeger.

Landry, D. and MacClean, G. (eds) (1996) *The Spivak Reader: Selected Works of Gayatri Chakravorty Spivak*, New York: Routledge. pp. 7, 54–71, 159, 204, 295.

Leroy, J. (2005) 'Chasing Daybreak: A Film About Mixed Race in America', Seattle, WA: MAVIN Foundation.

McClain, CS. (2004) 'Black by Choice: Identity Preferences of Americans of Black/White Parentage', *The Black Scholar*, vol. 34, no. 2.

Obama, B. (2004) Transcript: Illinois Senate Candidate Barack Obama Keynote Address at the 2004 Democratic National Convention (www. washingtonpost.com).

Obama, B. (2008) *The Audacity of Hope: Thoughts on Reclaiming the American Dream,* New York: Vintage.

Obama, B. (2007) *Dreams from My Father: A Story of Race and Inheritance*, New York: Crown Publishing.

Perry, B. (1985) 'Neither White nor Black', *Ethnic Groups,* no. 6, pp. 293-304.

Remnick, D. (2008) 'Race and the Campaign of Barack Obama', *The New Yorker*, 17 November.

Reuter, E.B. (1918) *The Mulatto in the United States: Including a Study of the Role of Mixed-Blood Races Throughout the World*, Boston: Richard G. Badger.

Reuter, E.B. (1931a) 'The Hybrid as a Sociological Type' in *Race Mixture: Studies in Intermarriage and Miscegenation*, New York: McGraw Hill Education, pp. 183–185.

Reuter, EB. (1931b) *Race Mixture: Studies in Intermarriage and Miscegenation*, New York: McGraw Hill.

Roberts, S. and Baker, P. (2010) 'Asked to Declare His Race, Obama Checks "Black"', *New York Times*. 3 April 2010, p. A9.

Rockquemore, KA and Brunsma, DL. (2002) *Beyond Black: Biracial Identity in America*, Thousand Oaks, CA: Sage Publications.

Rockquemore, KA, Brunsma, DL and Delgado, DJ. (2009) 'Racing to Theory or Retheorizing Race? Understanding the Struggle to Build a Multiracial Identity Theory', *Journal of Social Issues*, 65, no. 1, pp. 13–34.

Sexton, J. (2008) *Amalgamation Schemes: Antiblackness and the Critique of Multiracialism*, Minneapolis, MN: University of Minnesota Press.

Spencer, JM. (1997) *The New Colored People: The Mixed-Race Movement in America*, New York: New York University Press.

Spencer, R. (1999) *Spurious Issues: Race and Multiracial Identity Politics in the United States*, Boulder, CO: Westview Press.

Spencer, R. (2006) *Challenging Multiracial Identity*, Boulder: CO: L. Rienner Publishers.

Spencer, R. (2008) 'New Age Multiraciality: Generation Mix and the Fascinating Phenomenon of non-Mulatto Mulattoes', Paper presented at the Conference on Race: Future of an Illusion, Future of the Past, Monmouth University, West Long Branch, NJ.

Spivak, G. (1988) 'Can the Subaltern Speak', in *Marxism and the Interpretation of Culture*, eds. C Nelson and L Grossberg, Champaign, IL: University of Illinois Press,.

Williamson, J. (1995) *New People: Miscegenation and Mulattoes in the United States*, Baton Rouge, LA: Louisiana State University Press.

Wise, TJ. (2009) *Between Barack and a Hard Place: Racism and White Denial in the Age of Obama*, San Francisco, City Lights Books.

Wu, FH. (2002) *Yellow: Race in America Beyond Black and White*, New York: Basic Books.

Part III

The battle for a New American majority

A different kind of blackness: the question of Obama's blackness and intraracial variation among African Americans

Robert Keith Collins

Introduction

Prior to that amazing day of January 20 2009, many African Americans talked about Senator Barack Obama as if he was not "black enough," would not understand "the black experience," and that most Americans— by the time they realized that he was not a "real black man"—they also believed that he would not be able to execute the office of President of the United States. This notion of what counts a "true blackness" is receiving much revitalized attention as a result of CNN's Solidad O'Brien's critical discussion series "Black in America": "the black experience" may be much more varied than the notion suggests. This chapter engages in the taboo discussion of intraracial variation among people recognized in the United States as African American.

Using a person-centered ethnographic[1] approach and drawing on the works of early African American anthropologists and psycho-cultural anthropological scholars of motivation, this chapter examines the lived realities behind the racial variation that exists among African Americans as described in ethnographic interviews and participant observation (Levy and Hollan, 1998; Crapanzano, 1977). The analysis presented here relates their racial variation to the animosity that many experience from other African Americans, the acceptance or rejection that results and the need for a renewed discussion of the variation of racial compositions that exist within those recognized as African American (Davis, 1999; Mintz and Price, 1976). Although American culture encourages us to think of African Americans as racially and culturally homogenous, the argument presented here asserts that African American people are racially and culturally varied and that an understanding of this diversity is imperative if Americans—especially African Americans—are to understand the heterogeneous nature of this population (Herskovits, 1928; Foster, 1935; Davis, 1999).

Intraracial variation among African Americans

The broader issue here is one that is perennial for American understandings of African Americans: can some African Americans be more than one race (Sampson and Milam, 1975; Smith and Moore, 2000)? This question is central because it lies at the intersections between the social construction of being African American or black in the United States to which some conform and the genealogical realties to which others belong. Anthropologist Melville Herskovits (1928) engaged the importance of this inconsistency in *The American Negro: A Study in Racial Crossing*:

> A maxim which is never challenged in fact—since the fact is self-evident—is that two human groups never meet but they mingle their blood. It is this fact that makes the position of the American Negro peculiarly valuable for biology. Because the Negroes were slaves, the law of the masters was paramount; and the masters, as in all slave lands, took the slave women for themselves. But the offspring of a slave was also a slave, and so the mixed-bloods were regarded as "Negroes," while the White stock remained largely free from the introduction of Negro blood. Furthermore, there were American Indian peoples throughout the Southeast in the early days, and with these the Negroes mingled to a degree that Whites usually fail to recognize, though to a Negro knowledge of Indian ancestry is a matter of pride. This mingling also took place in the West Indian Islands, whence came many of those who later formed part of the American Negro community. Thus to the Negro–White mixture a third element was added, so that in the American Negro of today we find represented the three principal racial stocks of the world: Negro Ancestry from Africa, Caucasian from northern and western Europe, and Mongoloid (American Indian) from southeastern North America and the Caribbean Islands. (Herskovits, 1928, pp. 3-4)

To relate this literature review and participant observations to the understandings of genealogical heritage that individuals possessed at Howard University, Harlem in New York City, and in rural West Virginia. Samples of his findings were as shown in Table 9.1 (Herskovits, 1928, p. 9).

Table 9.1. Samples of Herskovits' (1928) findings

Class	Number of individuals	% of total
Unmixed Negro	342	22%
Negro, mixed with Indian	97	6.3%
More Negro than White	384	24.8%
More Negro than White, with Indian	106	6.9%
About the same amount of Negro and White	260	16.7%
The same class, with Indian mixture	133	8.5%
More White than Negro	154	9.3%
More White than Negro, with Indian	75	5.5%
Total	1,551	100%

The pioneering research of Caroline Bond Day (1930), who by her own calculations was approximately 7/16 white, 1/16 Indian, and 8/16 Negro, illustrated how notions of race and class were intertwined. It was particularly this aggregation of race and class that brings about the divisions seen among individuals of African descent. The black middle class tended to include—although not exclusively—populations that frequently fit neither the black nor white racial categories. Populations which according to Day,

> lived in worlds of their own, tucked away here and there on some quiet street, or in little peaceful neighborhoods, frequently unknown and unobserved by those about them. The average tourist in the South never suspects their existence. If he is shown Negro life at all, he is usually conducted through a slum district, the squalor of which probably seems heightened to him by the fact of physical difference. If he were to see this group, in which physical differences are less striking, he would probably be impressed with similarities to any other middle class group of American people, rather than differences. (Day, 1930, p. 3)

Day's research illuminated great similarities between the black middle class and white middle class in the areas of family life, occupation, and

171

salaries. This work also revealed the inconsistencies between racist expectations of African Americans and the true lived realities of the people. It must be noted that Day—like Foster after her—was keen to talk about the race complex and not only how this group experienced prejudice from white people but also from other African Americans in tandem with the social and economic advantages the color, features, and wealth afforded them both within and outside their own community (Day 1930).

Later, Laurence Foster (1935) furthered the research made evident by Herskovits's and Day's findings in his dissertation on *Negro–Indian Relationships in the Southeast*. Foster's work revealed that the interactions African Americans had were as varied as the blood lines found among the people and what implications this mixture held for understanding the heritage of individuals of African American descent in the Americas. According to Foster,

> Physically, to some Indians it has almost meant absorption by Negroes; to others it has meant a large infusion of Negro blood; to still others, through admixture, it has meant the mixing of a small amount of white blood by way of a Negro–white hybrid progenitor. To the Negro, it has meant an infusion of Indian blood and occasionally an infusion of white blood through an Indian–white hybrid progenitor. In certain Latin American countries we have seen special classes of the population bearing names which are significant of mixture of whites, Indians, and Negroes. (Foster, 1935, p. 73)

For Foster, this variation has created the skin color differences found among individuals of African descent in the United States and the variations in cultural practices among those recognized as Negro and later as African American.

A scholar and writer frequently forgotten for her research in comparing black cultures in the United States and the Caribbean was Zora Neal Hurston. Influenced by Franz Boas and Ruth Benedict, Hurston used oral history and literary texts to examine cultural differences among black populations in the Americas before it became a common anthropological technique. It has been argued that it was even Hurston's technique—used in her research on voodoo in New Orleans and Haitian cultures—which influenced Boas' ultimate acceptance of the method (Mikell, 1998, p. 61).

Despite the empirically sound nature of the research supporting these arguments, there continues to be a serious lack of attention on the relationship between being African American and being of mixed race. In anthropology, this issue is usually isolated in discussions of mixed race, with African American identity being an identity which one is denied from claiming by other African Americans. To what extent does mixed race preclude one from being accepted as an African American? Is mixed race, defined as pertaining to individuals of more than one racial background as constructed in the United States, a state of being not found among African Americans? Or conversely, is being African American an identity so fixed that ambiguity in being and belonging is never subjective? How these questions have been answered academically has had an important impact on the ways in which mixed race is negated from discussions of African American race and culture (Mintz and Price, 1976; Root, 1997; Russell, 1913; Russell, et al. 1990; Stephenson, 1910; Zack, 1995).

Where being African American is assumed to have a relationship to mixed race, the analytical focus has been on the preferential treatment lighter-skinned individuals are assumed to receive from white Americans. On the other hand, where mixed race is assumed to have a relationship to being African American, the analytical focus has been on the battles between African Americans over light skin and dark skin or so-called "good" and "bad" hair textures (Davis, 1991; Russell, 1990; Root, 1997; Russell, et al. 1993; Woodson, 1918b). However, within these approaches social opinions and public policy are made central, which renders elusive the origins behind the incredibly beautiful variations in skin color, hair textures, and physical characteristics found among the people.

In the person-centered approach that guides this analysis, the relationship between being African American and of mixed race is formed from family-based understandings of self and negotiated in social interactions. In this context, the individual comes to internalize racial models, language, and symbols, as a means for asserting an understanding of self (Holland, 1992). According to Raymond D. Fogelson (1998), this process may cause an individual to cultivate contextually varied identities. For example, because individuals are at the same time both themselves and extensions of groups, one may

> comprise an ideal identity, an image of oneself that one wishes to realize; a feared identity, which one values negatively and wishes to avoid; a "real" identity, which an individual thinks closely approximates an accurate representation of the self

or reference group; and a claimed identity that is presented to others for confirmation, challenge, or negotiation in an effort to move the "real" identity closer to the ideal and further from the feared identity. (Fogelson, 1998)

Although Fogelson did not specifically use a person-centered ethnographic approach to his study of identity struggles, his work did illuminate the subjectivity in self-understanding that individuals evoke when dealing with identity struggles (Holland, 1992; Wallace and Fogelson, 1965). All of these selves add up to more than one person wants to meet in basic everyday interactions. However, to get at the root cause of the need for situational variations in self-understanding, an examination of the literature beyond that which deals solely with African Americans—particularly that which deals with motivations—is necessary (D'Andrade, 1992; Holland, 1992; Fogelson, 1998).

For most scholars of African American identity—within and outside of anthropology—the major problem encountered in assessing the relationship between being African American and of mixed race has been trying to understand what motivates an African American individual to claim a race other than black (Russell, et al 1993; Woodson, 1918ab). One could make the common social assumption that the individual is a "wannabe" and discuss the kinds of privileges that the individual maybe trying to get over other African Americans; however, illustrations of exactly when, where, and in which contexts these privileges are being sought would be absent. When a dark-skinned African American—who has a Choctaw father and an African American mother—asserts that he or she is Choctaw to other African Americans who wonder why his or her hair is "good," is it really that difficult to understand the motivation behind the person's claim of a Native American ancestry (Collins, 2006; Jolivette, 2006). In a similar vein, when a light-skinned African American says that he or she is not mixed, but that his or her African American heritage is Creole from New Orleans and his or her family has been light skinned for generations and fought in the Civil Rights Movement in Louisiana, is he or she attempting to be better than other African Americans? In 1995, as a lawyer in Chicago, Barack Obama wrote about the implications such questions hold in his own life:

As a result, some people have a hard time taking me at face value. When people who don't know me well, black or white, discover my background (and it is usually a discovery, for I ceased to advertise my mother's race at the age of twelve or thirteen, when I began to suspect that by doing so I was ingratiating myself to whites), I see the split-seconds adjustments they have to make, the searching of my eyes for some telltale sign. They no longer know who I am. Privately, they guess at my troubled heart, I suppose—the mixed blood, the divided soul, the ghostly image of the tragic mulatto trapped between two worlds. And if I were to explain that no, the tragedy is not mine, or at least not mine alone, it is yours, children of Africa, it is the tragedy of both my wife's six-year-old cousin and his white first grade classmates, so that you need not guess at what troubles me, it's on the nightly news for all to see, and that if we could acknowledge at least that much then the tragic cycle begins to break down…well, I suspect that I sound incurably naïve, wedded to lost hopes, like those Communists who peddle their newspapers on the fringes of various college towns. Or worse, I sound like I'm trying to hide from myself. I don't fault people their suspicions. (Obama, 1995, p. xv)

For many scholars of African American identity it is not obvious which field methods can be used to illustrate comprehensive questions to these answers; however, the words of Barack Obama offer great insight into the importance of focusing on lived realties rather than racial expectations derived from the illusion of uniformity in African American lived experiences (D'Andrade, 1992; Davis, 1991; Ross, Adams, and Williams, 1997; Jolivette, 2007; Mintz and Price, 1976).

Current anthropological studies of African American identity while informative about race formation, racism, urban culture, educational issues, and identity formation, have yet critically to engage mixed race as it related to the motivational forces behind African American identities (Mikell, 1997; Mintz and Price, 1976; Smedley, 1990; Sturm, 1994). This issue will not go away by merely criticizing discussions of mixed race as subversive attempts to create a new racial category— although given the hostile reception the discussion receives, I can't blame those who have attempted such efforts in the United States. Instead, it is therefore relevant to look to—if not back at—methods that offer insight into the realities of African American genealogy and family composition that have created the diversity represented by the term "African American" (Crapanzano, 1977; Levy and Hollan, 1998; Root, 1997; Woodson, 1918b).

The salience of racial variation in African American lives

To what extent can the salience of this discussion be seen in historical and contemporary lived realties of African Americans? The answer to this question is as follows: of the considerable amount of ethnographic work done on African Americans, a very small subset actually contains ethnographic documentation of experiences with racism in the lives of individuals. Consequently, the discussion presented here utilizes the "Works Progress Administration" (WPA) slave narratives, my own ethnographic fieldwork among individuals of blended African American and Choctaw heritage, and the narratives found in the detailed works of President Barack Obama (Collins, 2006; Obama, 1994).

My interest in the relationship between being African American and being of mixed race came from my own recent ethnographic research on the current Smithsonian exhibit "Indivisible: African–Native American Lives in the Americas" (Collins, 2009). Using a person centered approach, it was found that individuals of blended African and Choctaw, African and Creek, as well as Garifuna heritage possessed not only incredible variations in their understandings of self as indigenous Americans but the degree to which being African Americans was salient in their identities. In some cases respondents discussed being both African American and Native American. While in others, being African was part of being Native American or vice versa. These statements led me to consider this racial variation in other African American lives. The basic inspiration was that a person–centered approach might reveal even greater subjectivity in conceptualizations of being black among African Americans of blended racial ancestries (Collins, 2009; Davis, 1999).

The first examples of this variation in being African American can be seen in the narrative of ex-slave Ms. Julia Grimes Jones Ocklbary who offers an example of the challenges that being mixed African American and Choctaw could pose to other African Americans within one's own family. According to Ms. Ocklbary,

> Ma's name was Melissa Gimes. She was married twice, the second time to Ap Moore. I called my step-fathaw Pappy; but I called my own fathaw Pa, and his name was Arthur Grimes. Pappy Moore was good to me, though. He never hit me. One reason was dat de white folks made him treat me good. Pa was a full-blooded Choctaw Injun. Mistress Abbie's grandfathaw captured him f'om de Injun nation,

when he was jes' a little boy. He couldn't talk plain, and de white folks had to learn him how to talk dere way. Pa always knowed dat he was a Injun. Mawster Henry Grimes made him a overseer over de niggers on his large cotton plantation. Pa was de head boss, but he had a cabin among de niggers in dere quarters, near de Big House. De niggers treated him lak a boss, and dey loved him... Aw, I know dat I was a spoiled child. De white folks has spoiled me to dis day. I remembah dat de biggest cry dat I ever had was when Ma, who was mad at me 'cause I was so spoiled, told me dat I wasn't nuthin but a nigger child. Mistress Abigail would act lak she was goin' to tear her to death fo' sayin' dat. Den Ma would say to me, "Come here, nigger, and bring me dat chair." (Minges, 2004, p. 191)

What motivated Ms. Ocklbary's mother to make the statements that she did? And, what was she saying to her daughter? One could argue that Ms. Ocklbary, as a young girl, had forgotten her place or that she might think herself better than her mother. On the other hand, one might think that Ms. Ocklbary's mother was simply trying to save her daughter from the disappointment that came to slaves who thought that they were deserving of good treatment from white people; however, given that the words of Ms. Grimes provoked a quarrel with Mistress Abigail, it is possible that Ms. Grimes did not want her daughter—whose father was the overseer—believing that she was worth more attention than her own mother (D'Andrade, 1992).

Further research into African Americans of blended ancestries like Ms. Ocklbary's is very important because, subjectively, many talk about being "part Indian" as if it is a convenient explanation for the presence of "good hair' and "high cheek bones" and "keen features" within the population. While participating in such conversations, from southeastern Oklahoma to the San Francisco Bay Area, one often hears some African Americans talking more about their heritage in a culturally specific manner than the generic assertions of "Indian" heritage made by others. This Native American heritage may be part of an individual's commonsense understandings of family: a commonsense understanding that occasionally is met with the following statements:

"Just because you are Indian, you think that you are better than everybody."

"That hair Pocahantas, ain't going to make you white."

"What we are talking about is a Black thang. You ain't enough to understand."

"Why you always got to tell people you are Indian, I see it, it ain't like you Black anyway."

The previous statements point to the type of attitudes that a respondent from my own contemporary studies of African–Native American lives has dealt with for most of his life. Mr. Sun is a retired janitor in his sixties, who has lived in Foi Tamaha (fictitious name) all his life. Mr. Sun is the third eldest of nine siblings. While he was growing up, both English and Choctaw were spoken in the home, as Mr. Sun's mother was three-quarters Choctaw and a quarter African American and his father was one-half Choctaw and one-half African American. According to Mr. Sun, his parents often reinforced Choctaw culture and language at home more than African American cultural practices; however, he lived and attended church on the "colored side of town." Knowledge of family and relatives was very important to Mr. Sun's mother and father and he was encouraged from a young age not to, as he puts it, "pay too much attention to what people looked like." Growing up, he explained was easy because his family (that is, his brothers, sisters, and cousins (second, third, and fourth)) were always around and they stuck together and stuck up for one another. Outside of the family, however, he remembers people having a problem with him because he stood out, sometimes, as the Indian and that made his peers jealous.

Mr. Sun said:

> When I was younger, if I tell you this, forgive me if I get mad, but I use to have so much fun. Me and friends would go down the way here to the hall for the dances and would go all night long. If you was lucky, then you got to walk a foxy little thang home. We didn't do what ya'll do now: all that going all the way. No, I was happy if she kissed me. Boy, I'd smile from ear to ear….

> See, back then, this side of town was really nice. Everyone was so friendly. Everybody said good morning. Do ya'll do that where you from? I would put on my nice shirt and slacks and boots and walk proud down the street. Not a whole lot of riff-raff. Well, this one night, after my mom had made my favorite dinner. Oh, I can still taste it [laughing]! She made cobbler for dessert, corn bread, good ole greens, and chicken and dumplings. I was so happy and full that night. I was ready to dance. Well, I told her that I would be home early and my sister and my cousin were going

together, you know. This way we were responsible for one another. My mother would not have it any other way. Well, that night, I met this beautiful girl. Man, oh man. I had to fix my hair [laughing]. She had these big ole eyes and batted them like that. So I went to ask her to dance. That was a mistake. See she was looked at by everyone. And why the hell she said yes, I don't know, but she did. We danced, danced all night. I got her punch and we danced some more. Well, when we got ready to go, I ask her could I walk her home. My sister and cousin were already ready to leave. This ugly guy kept flirtin' with my sister and she was mad. My cousin has his girl with him. She said no. Her mom did not allow that. So I fixed my shirt and went outside. When I got there, I ran into this guy that was trying to cut in. He pushed me and said why don't you stick to own, Indian. I told him that I did not want no trouble. He say, just because you live on the colored side of town, don't mean that you can be colored. I told him that my grand daddy was colored and I am too. He is my grand daddy. He pushed me again and before I knew it, he sliced my stomach open from east to west. I heard him say, you ain't colored on the inside, you red. That was a bad night.

Such examples of policing blackness should raise serious concerns about the manner in which African American identities, which are conceptualized, policed, and understood socially, are not discussed academically. The implications of these explanatory gaps can be seen in the rationales created behind the question of Senator Obama's "blackness" before he became President of the United States. It must be noted, however, that this notion of questioning the authenticity of African Americans is not limited to the black community. On June 25 2008, James Joyner and others reported that Ralph Nader—a politician and activist whom I respected, had voted for in previous elections (when he was a Green Party Candidate), and was prepared to vote for again—suggested that,

There's only one thing different about Barack Obama when it comes to being a Democratic presidential candidate. He's half African American…Whether that will make any difference, I don't know. I haven't heard him have a strong crackdown on economic exploration in the ghettos. Payday loans, predatory lending, asbestos, lead. What's keeping him from doing that? Is it because he wants to talk white?

According to Joyner, when Nader was given the opportunity to clarify whether he thought Obama does try to "talk white," Nader said:

> Of course, I mean, first of all, the number one thing that a black American politician aspiring to the presidency should be [able to do] is to candidly describe the plight of the poor, especially in the inner cities and the rural areas, and have a very detailed platform about how the poor is going to be defended by the law, is going to be protected by the law, and is going to be liberated by the law…Haven't heard a thing. (Joyner, 2008)

Is there no irony—as Joyner questioned—in a white man telling a black man that he should talk black and how to talk black? More importantly, for the purpose of this analysis, is it not ironic that anyone would tell an African American how to talk black or that they should talk black when this individual has not lived the reality of the person to which the suggestion is directed? President Obama's recollections in *Dreams from My Father: A Story of Race and Inheritance* illuminated not only the problems of such misplaced assumptions about why some African Americans may not behave according to racial expectations:

> Look at yourself before you pass judgment. Don't make someone else clean up your mess. It's not about you. They were such simple points, homilies I had heard a thousand times before, in all their variation, from TV sitcoms and philosophy books, from my grandparents and my mother. I had stopped listening at a certain point, I now realized, so wrapped up had I been in my own perceived injuries, so eager was I to escape the imagined traps that white authority had set for me. To that white world, I had been willing to cede the values of my childhood, as if those values were somehow irreversibly soiled by the endless falsehoods that white spoke about black. Except now I was hearing the same thing from black people I respected, people with more excuses for bitterness than I might ever claim for myself. Who told you that being honest was a white thing? They asked me. Who sold you this bill of goods, that your situation exempted you from being thoughtful or diligent or kind,

or that morality had a color? You've lost your way, brother. Your ideas about yourself—about who you are and who you might become—have grown stunted and narrow and small…. My identity might begin with the fact of my race, but it didn't, couldn't, end there. (Obama, 1995, pp. 110–11)

Obama's words may have modern trappings; however, they are directly comparable to the sentiments and rationales found by early African American ethnographers among whom self determination—not racial determination—was central to their understanding of self as black or African American people.

Implications

What implications do these narratives hold for understanding intraracial variation among African Americans? Erik Erickson (1959), who introduced the term identity to the social sciences, reminds us that scholars of history often forget that people are born of mothers. The mothers teach their children how to be viable members of their families and communities regardless, which often includes strategies for navigating social rules and taboos that they might disagree with or see as detrimental to the wellbeing of their children (DeMallie, 1996; Erikson, 1959; Thornton and Nardi, 1975). A major implication of the analysis and narratives presented in this chapter is that the deconstruction and critical examination of the intraracial variation found among African Americans is vital to understanding the sentiments that made Senator—now President—Obama not "black enough" for some African Americans and their votes, but also how this practice of assessing the "blackness quantum" has created barriers to African Americans—and Americans in general—understanding the love- and policy-based partner choices which created the heterogeneous racial composition and cultural practices found in African American communities throughout the United States (Brodkin, 1999; Davis, 1999; Kawash, 1997; Minges, 2004).

The ethnographic methods and narrated lived realties described in the previous sections are engaged through a person-centered perspective. x Regardless of approach, however, most of the scholars discussed here—including Obama—articulate the importance and difficulties of illuminating the complexities of African American family composition and the varied meanings which blended ancestries hold in individual lives. Whether a person-centered, standard ethnographic, or political anthropological approach is taken, the racial diversity that exists and continues to grow within the African American population seems like a starting point conducive to teaching tolerance of difference in being African American and creating "brothers" and "sisters" who embrace the efforts and achievements of individuals like President Obama, rather than policing the extent of their racial loyalty through questions which challenge the legitimacy of their blackness.

More ethnographic studies of African American lives will encourage readers to ponder the inconsistencies between what African Americans represent to American society versus what they represent to themselves. In Ms. Ocklbary's narrative, one is offered a window into the motivational forces behind jealousies which her blended ancestry evoked for her own mother. Such jealousies we premised merely on the belief held by Ms. Ocklbary's mother that she was forgetting her "place" as a slave. In Mr. Sun's narrative, readers are offered a glimpse of the motivations behind the rejection of his efforts to socialize with people whom he was raised to see as his own and the directive forces behind the violent lengths to which individuals will go to police who can and who cannot call themselves African American and date African American women. President Obama's statements illustrate how many of the problems often projected onto African Americans of blended ancestries are not their own. Instead, they reveal the aspects of being African American upon which misplaced expectations of mixed race individuals are based. There should be renewed investigations into these phenomena and the race complex among African Americans that they evoke (Cialdini, 1984; Jolivette, 2006; Obama, 1994).

If unity is truly a goal that African Americans hold dear, then the narratives of President Obama and others mentioned in the previous sections should exemplify the importance of this type of reflexive investigation (Woodson, 1918b; Obama, 2005). They have the potential for revealing the truths and falsehoods behind the motives of mixed race African Americans and those that assume or know themselves to be purely of African descent. Expectations of evoking "light-skinned" economic and social privilege, light skinned not liking dark, dark-skinned contempt for the light skinned, etc., can all be grounded in the aspects of individuals' actions upon which they are assumed to be based, rather than—as President Obama experienced—the assumptions made by people who really did not know their "brother." Conditions which all the people mentioned in the narratives endured persistently over time.

Census 2000 reveals that the time for non-holistic examinations of African American populations is over. Data collected on African Americans reveals an ever-growing and changing population. For example, Table 9.2 is an excerpt on the most common blends of ancestries found among African Americans revealed by Census 2000.

Table 9.2 The most common blends of ancestries found among African Americans revealed by Census 2000

African American in combination	Population
Black or African American; White	784,764
Black or African American and Some other race	417,249
Black or African American; American Indian/Alaskan Native	182,494
Black or African American; White; Am. Indian/Alaskan Native	112,207
Black or African American; Asian	106,782
Black or African American; White; Some other race	43,172
Black or African American; Hispanic	710,353
All other combinations including Black or African American	114,576
Total	**2,471,597**

One use of these data and the ideas presented here is to begin building on the ethnographic frameworks established before the Civil Rights Movement, not just after, which are often neglected in African American ethnography. With greater ethnographic investigation it should be possible to revitalize an ethnography of mixed race identities within African American communities. This would be reflective of a vision not only held by African American pioneers in ethnography. In the words of the first African American President of the United States:

> I have witnessed a profound shift in race relations in my lifetime. I have felt it as surely as one feels a change in temperature. When I hear some in the black community deny those changes, I think it not only dishonors those who struggled on our behalf but also robs us of our agency to complete the work they began. But as much as I insist that things have gotten better, I am mindful of this truth as well: Better isn't good enough. (Obama, 2005, p. 233)

Conclusion

The central focus of this chapter is on the relationship between being African American, mixed race, and how this relationship manifests itself in the diversity of lives represented by the term "African American." It is the author's sincere hope that this discussion will illustrate the need for a critical discussion of intra-racial diversity among African Americans. Phenotypical advantage of light over dark has always been a concern and fear among African Americans. If it can be understood that skin color preference by white people—as well as other African Americans—is not always the motivational force behind why some African Americans take pride in asserting their multiracial heritage, then perhaps these fears and concerns can be alleviated and addressed and the color complex deconstructed (Meyers, 2005).

The "pro-person-centered" stance taken in this chapter raises a perennial objective for scholars of African American identity: the need for academic specification of when, where, and in which contexts intra-racial variation is related to African American understandings of self. If this chapter has any moral implications, then it is that it is no longer sufficient to assume that mixed race African Americans are "not black enough" or that they "wannabe" a race other than black without specific examples from their own lived experiences that support such accusations. Such assumptions are wrong on several levels. One, they lend the illusion of consistency between African American racial expectations of their black brothers and sisters and the lived realities behind the "blackness" of those individuals. Two, they ignore the reality that being African American and African ancestry is not uniform. To borrow from Roy D'Andrade (1992), much of being African American remains "at the cliché level" or the "ideal identity" discussed by Fogelson (1998) and does not encompass all aspects of African American answers to the following basic question: "Who am I?" Three, different African Americans hold different family members and heritages dear in different ways, so that the statement "not black enough" severely negates the degree of racial variation found among African Americans. For is it not wrong to expect unity from antagonism? And, if not, then who, other than those that fit the parameters upon which such antagonism is based, will want to belong? Perhaps being "not black enough" is merely a different kind of blackness. The election of President Obama has made this different kind of blackness a central question socially, culturally, and political in thinking about the changing demographics of the United States. Thus, as this article highlights, questioning the construction "not black enough" is not only a push toward accepting different forms of blackness, but is also moving us toward a new American majority where culture and not just race are at the center of our lived experiences.

Note
[1] Person-centered ethnography differs from other forms of ethnography in that it takes individuals as active agents in the creation and maintenance of culture and self understanding (see Levy and Hollan, 1998).

References
Appiah, A. (1996) *Color Conscious: The Political Morality of Race*, Princeton, NJ: Princeton University Press.
Banton, M. (1987) *Racial Theories*, Cambridge: Cambridge University Press.
Barth, F. (1969) *Ethnic Groups and Boundaries*, Boston: Little, Brown, and Company.
Berger, PL and Luckman, T. (1967) *The Social Construction of Reality*, New York: Doubleday.
Berry, B. (1969) *Almost White*. MacMillan Publishing Company.
Bhaba, H. (1983) 'Difference, Discrimination, and the Discourse of Colonilaism', *In The Politics of Theory, New Formations*, vol. 5, pp.194-211, edited by Francis Baker, Peter Hulme, Margaret Iversen and Diana Loxley, Colchester: University of Essex.
Blu, K. (1980) *The Lumbee Problem: The Making of an American Indian People*, Cambridge, NY: Cambridge University Press.
Boster, J. (1987) 'Intracultural Variation' in *American Behavioral Scientist*, vol. 31, no. 2, pp. 150–2.
Brodkin, K. (1999) *How Jews Became White Folk and What That Says About Race in America*, New Jersey: Rutgers University Press.
Burnett, SM. (1889) 'A Note on the Melungeons', *American Anthropologist*, vol. II.
Census. (2000) (www.census.gov/prod/2001pubs/c2kbr01-5.pdf).
Cialdini, R.B. (1984) *Influence: How and Why People Agree to Things*, New York: William Morrow.
Collins, RK. (2005) 'When Playing Indian is a Misplaced Assumption: Evidence From Black Choctaw Lived Experiences' in *Race, Roots, and Relations: Native and African Americans,* Terry Strauss, ed, New York: Albatross Press.
Collins, RK. (2006) 'Katimih-o Sa Chata Kiyou? (Why am I Not Choctaw?): Race in the Lived Experiences of Two Black Choctaw Mixed Bloods' in *Crossing Waters, Crossing Worlds: The African Diaspora in Indian Country*, Sharon P. Holland and Tiya Miles, eds, Durham: Duke University Press.

Collins, RK. (2009) 'What is a Black Indian? Racial Expectations and Lived Realities', in *Indivisible: African-Native American Lives in the Americas,* Smithsonian.

Crapanzano,V. (1977) The Life History in Anthropological Field Work. *Anthropology and Humanism Quarterly*, vol. 2, pp. 3-7.

D'Andrade, RG. (1992) 'Schemas and Motivation', in *Human Motives and Cultural Models*, Roy D'Andrade and Claudia Strauss, eds, Cambridge: Cambridge University Press.

Davis, JF. (1991) *Who is Black? One Nation's Definition*, University Park, PA: Pennsylvania State University Press.

Day, CB. (1930) 'Race Crossing in the United States', *Crisis*, vol. 37, no. (3, pp.): 81–82.

DeMallie, RJ. (1998) 'Kinship: The Foundation of Native American Society', in *Studying Native America: Problems and Prospects*, Russell Thornton, ed, Madison,WI: University of Wisconsin Press, pp. 306-56.

Erikson, EH. (1959) *Identity and the Life Cycle*, London:W&W Norton and Company, Inc.

Fisher, JB. (1872) 'Who Was Crispus Attucks?', *American Historical Record*, vol. I.

Flores,WV and Benmayor, R. (1996) *Constructing Cultural Citizenship: Claiming Identity, Space, and Rights*, Boston: Beacon Press.

Fogelson, RD. (1982) 'Self, Person, and identity: Some Anthropological Retrospects, Circumspect, and Prospect', in *Psychosocial Theories of the Self*. Benjamin Lee, ed, New York: Prenum Press, pp. 67–109..

Fogelson, RD. (1998) 'Perspectives on Native American Identity', in *Studying Native America*, Russell Thornton, ed, Madison,WI: University Wisconsin Press, pp. 40-59.

Foster, L. (1935) *Negro Indian Relations in the Southeast*, New York: AMS Press.

Gregg, GS. (1991) *Self-Representation: Life Narrative Studies in Identity and Ideology*, New York: Greenwood Press.

Hallowell,AI. (1955) *Culture and Experience*, Philadelphia, PA: University of Pennsylvania Press.

Herskovits, M. (1928) *The American Negro: A Study in Racial Crossing*, New York: Alfred A. Knoff.

Hollan, D and Wellenkamp, JC. (1994) 'Methodological Developments in Psychocultural Anthropology' in *Contentment and Suffering: Culture and Experience in Toraja*, New York: Columbia University Press, pp. 3-10..

Holland, D. (2001) *History in Person: Enduring Struggles, Contentious Practice, Intimate Identities*, Santa Fe, NM: School of Americans Research Press.

Holland, D. (1992) 'How cultural systems become desire: a case study of American Romance', in *Human motives and cultural models*, Roy D'Andrade and Claudia Strauss, eds, Cambridge: Cambridge University Press.

House of Representatives. (1997) *Federal Measures of Race and Ethnicity and the Implications for The 2000 Census. Subcommittee on Government Management, Information, and Technology of the Committee on Government Reform and Oversight.* One Hundred Fifth Congress, First Session.

Johnson, JH. (1929) 'Documentary Evidence of the Relations of Negroes and Indians' *Journal of Negro History*, vol XIV.

Jolivette, A. (2007) *Louisiana Creoles: Cultural Recovery and Mixed-Race Native American Identity*, Lanham, MD: Lexington Books.

Joyner, J. (2008) 'Ralph Nader: Obama Not Black Enough', *Outside the Beltway* (www.outsidethebeltway.com/archives/nader-obama-not-black-enough).

Katz, WL. (1984) *Black Indians: A Hidden Heritage.* New York: Atheneum.

Kawash, S. (1997) *Dislocating the Color Line: Identity, Hybridity and Singularity in African-American Narrative*, Stanford, CA: Stanford University Press.

Levy, R and Hollan, D. (1998) 'Person Centered Interviewing and Observation in Anthropology' in *Handbook of Research Methods in Anthropology*, Russell Bernard, ed, Walnut Creek, CA: Altamira Press.

McKinnon, J. (2001) 'The Black Population: 2000 Census Brief', U.S. Census Bureau (www.census.gov/prod/2001pubs/c2kbr01-5.pdf).

Martin, M. (2007) 'Sen. Barack Obama: Is He Black Enough?', NPR (www.npr.org/templates/story/story.php?storyId=11868091).

Meyers, M. (2005) *Thicker Than Water: The Origins of Blood As Ritual and Symbol*, Abingdon: Routledge.

Mikell, G. (1998) 'Feminism and Black Culture in the Ethnography of Zora Neale Hurston', in *African American Pioneers in Anthropology*, Ira E. Harrison and Faye V. Harrison eds), Chicago: University of Illinois Press.

Minerbrook, S. (1994) *Divided to the Vein: A Journey Into Race and Family*, New York: Harcourt Brace & Co.

Minges, P. (2004) *Black Indian Slave Narratives*, Winston-Salem, NC: John F. Blair Publishing.

Mintz, SW and Price, R. (1976) *The Birth of African American Culture: An Anthropological Perspective*, Boston: Beacon Press.

Mooney, J. (1907) 'The Powhatan Indians', *American Anthropology*, vol. 9.

Obama, B. (2006) *The Audacity of Hope: Thought on Reclaiming the American Dream*, New York: Crown Publishers.

Obama, B. (1995) *Dreams from My Father: A Story of Race and Inheritance*, New York: Three Rivers Press.

Obeyesekere, G. (1990) *The Work of Culture*, Chicago: University of Chicago Press.

Omi, M and Winant, H. (1994) *Racial Formation in the United States: From the 1960s to the 1990s*, New York: Routledge Press.

Parsons, EC. (1919) 'Folklore of the Cherokees of Robeson County, North Carolina', *Journal of American Folklore*, vol. 32.

Perdue, T. (2005) *Mixed Blood Indians: Racial Construction In the Early South*, Atlanta, GA: University of Georgia Press.

Prince, JD. (1907) 'Last Living Echoes of the Natick', *American Journal of Anthropology*, vol. IX.

Reuter, EB. (1918) *The Mulatto in the United States*, Boston: The Gorham Press.

Roosens, EE. (1983) 'Creating Ethnicity: The Process of Ethnogenesis' in *Frontier of Anthropology* 5, Newbury Park, NY: Sage Publications.

Root, MP. (2000), 'Rethinking Racial Identity Development', *in We Are a People: Narrative and Multiplicity in Constructing Ethnic Identity*, P. Spickard and J, Burroughs (eds),. Philadelphia: Temple University Press.

Ross, HB, Adams, AM and Williams, LM. (1997) 'Caroline Bond Day: Pioneer Black Physical Anthropologist', in *African American Pioneers in Anthropology*. Ira E. Harrison and Faye V. Harrison (eds), Chicago: University of Illinois Press.

Rotberg, RI. (1990) *The Mixing Peoples: Problems of Identity and Ethnicity*, Stamford: Greylock Publishers.

Russell, JH. (1913) *The Free Negro in Virginia. Studies in Historical and Political Science*, Baltimore, MD: Johns Hopkins University, series 31, no. 3.

Russell, K. et al. (1993) *Color Complex: The Politics of Skin Color Among African Americans*, New York: Harcourt Brace Jovanovich.

Sampson, WA and Milam, V. (1975) 'The Intraracial Attitudes of the Black Middle Class: Have They Changed?', *Social Problems*, vol. 23, no. 2, pp. 153-165.

Smedley, A. (1990) *Race in North America: Origin and Evolution of a Worldview*, Boulder, CO: Westview Press.

Smith, SS and Moore, MR. (2000) 'Intraracial Diversity and Relations among African-American: Closeness among Black Students', *The American Journal of Sociology*, vol. 106, no. 1, pp. 1-39.

Speck, FG. (1913) *Nanticoke Community of Delaware*, New York: The Museum of the American Indian.

Steinberg, S. (1980) *The Ethnic Myth: Race, Ethnicity, and Class in America*, Boston: Beacon Press.

Stephenson, GT. (1910) *Race Distinctions in American Law*, New York: Cornell University.

Sturm, C. (1994) 'Blood Politics, Racial Classification, and Cherokee National Identity: The Trials and Tribulations of the Cherokee Freedmen', *The American Indian Quarterly*, 22 (1&2).

Thornton, R and Nardi, PM. (1975) 'The Dynamics of Role Acquisition', *The American Journal of Sociology*, vol. 80, no. 4, pp. 870-85.

Valbrun, M. (2007) 'Black Like Me? Those Asking if Barack Obama is "Black Enough" Are Asking the Wrong Question', *Washington Post* (www.washingtonpost.com/wp-dyn/content /article/2007/02/15/).

Wallace, FC and Fogelson, Raymond, D. (1965) 'The Identity Struggle', in *Intensive Family Therapy: Theoretical and Practical Aspects*, Ivan Boszomenyi-Nagy and James L. Framo (eds), New York: Harper and Row, pp. 365-406..

Woodson, C. (1918a) 'The Relations of Negroes and Indians in Massachusetts", *Journal of Negro History*, vol. V.

Woodson, C. (1918b) 'The Beginning of Miscegenation', *Journal of Negro History*, vol. III.

Woodson, C. (1922) *The Negro in Our History*, Washington: Kessinger Publishing.

Zack, N. (1995) *American Mixed Race: The Culture of Microdiversity*, Landham, MD: Rowman & Littlefield Publishers.

CHAPTER TEN

Avoiding race or following the racial scripts? Obama and race in the recessionary period of the colorblind era

Kathleen Odell Korgen and David L. Brunsma

The United States is founded upon many stories and scripts. Individualism, property, ownership, rights, democracy, white supremacy, patriarchy, and empire are some of the stories that have been woven into the fabric of dominant U.S. institutions and interpersonal relationships. There are also embroidered patterns etched upon this fabric—us/them, individual/structure, black/white, men/women, etc. Such a fabric also structures the scripts from which individuals, like the President of the United States, can draw to resonate with the people, create laws and policies, and to *do* the job. Acknowledgement of this reality helps us to begin understanding that President Barack Obama cannot effectively address racial issues during his presidency.

In this chapter we look at how Obama, as a black/multiracial President, has operated within the racial scripts available to him during the recessionary period of the colorblind era. Recognizing the dominant lens through which Americans view the racial world—colorblindness—and its associated ideology is crucial to insights about the scripts from which it is possible to draw and which scripts will resonate with audiences in the twenty-first century. We look closely at a key speech of Obama's—"A More Perfect Union" or the "Race" speech—to analyze the scripts utilized in the speech and how the American public responded to them. We also describe the influence of the Great Recession on Obama's ability to address racial inequality in the United States.

Obama's racial identity

Barack Obama's racial identity, like so much else about President Obama, tends to be defined and interpreted in various ways by those who observe him. Though people hold a dizzying array of identities and statuses and exist in a matrix of identities (Brunsma and Delgado, 2008) and meanings—racial scripts in the United States have historically and contemporarily worked to limit that variation and to portray individuals' racial identities as monolithic. Many older Americans, raised when the "one-drop rule" was prevalent, are wary of what they see as Obama's "obvious" black racial background and fear that he may take a special interest in—and favor—racial minorities because of it. Many younger Americans are more likely to resonate with Obama's multiracial background and view him as someone who can transcend race, and not become bogged down in "old" issues like racial discrimination, racism, and racial inequality.

Obama's racial self-identification is clear. While he openly acknowledges his biracial heritage and multiracial family (and argues that this background is a positive symbol for America), he racially identifies as black (Cohen, 2008). This racial identity is common among those Americans with both a black and a white parent who, like Barack Obama, grew up during the Civil Rights Movement but before the influence of the multiracial movement (Korgen, 1998). Born in 1961, Obama's formative years were after the passage of civil rights legislation but before the multiracial movement in the 1980s and 1990s.[1]

The multiracial movement was led, in large part, by the middle-class offspring of the "biracial baby boom" after the Civil Rights Movement and the 1967 *Loving vs. Virginia* decision that outlawed anti-miscegenation legislation (DaCosta, 2007). This late twentieth-century multiracial movement led to a significant change in the 2000 U.S. Census, allowing people to choose more than one race. This change had an impact not only on the identity formation processes of many young multiracials, but also on how others see race in the United States. This movement helped drive home to young Americans that race is a social, rather than biological, construction. While most black people and multiracial people who grew up under the "one-drop rule" do not understand why there would be any debate about Obama's racial self-definition as black, many young multiracial Americans don't understand why Obama would check off *only* "black" on the census. Many other young Americans cannot fathom why Obama, or anyone else, has to racially define themselves at all in this "post-racial" era.

The colorblind ideology and the "post-racial" era

The colorblind era began in the late 1970s with conservative attacks against affirmative action programs as anti-white and "reverse-racism."

The notion that affirmative action programs are examples of reverse-racism gained traction after the *Regents of the University of California vs. Bakke* Supreme Court case in 1978 that struck down racial quotas and declared that the white applicant Allan Bakke had been discriminated against by the University of California medical school when he was denied admission in favor of a black applicant. In the 1980s and 1990s conservatives effectively disseminated the colorblind racial ideology as one based on the Civil Rights Movement notion that race should not be a factor in how people are treated (Thernstrom, 1987; Thernstrom and Thernstrom, 1997; Gingrich, 1997). Using Martin Luther King's phrase that people should be judged on "the content of their character rather than the color of their skin," colorblind advocates framed their movement as a fight against reverse-racism and for racial justice. Such claims focused on individual rather than structural understandings of racism. In spreading this individualistic perspective of racism they created a racial script to support the racial ideology of colorblindness.

Promoters of the colorblind ideology maintain that we should act as though we are "colorblind" when it comes to race (Bonilla-Silva, 2006; Brunsma, 2006; Carr, 1997). According to those who adhere to this ideology, we live in a post-racial society in which discrimination against racial minorities is no longer a serious issue and race, itself, is no longer important (see Chapter One). Drawing from the individualism-infused racial script, many go so far as to say that people who talk about and notice racial differences are actually causing racial friction that would otherwise not exist. Thus, taught to ignore racial differences, and to never question the structural and institutional basis of racial inequality, many young Americans were very comfortable with the multiracial Obama, who seemed to embody the notion that race no longer matters in the United States. Here was a person with both a black and a white parent, who was raised by white people but appears black, and who "appeared" to fit in among all races. Moreover, he was not campaigning on racial issues; he spoke of hope and uniting Americans for a better future.

Barack Obama was very aware of most of the electorate's desire to avoid discussing issues of race and/or fear of a potentially "racial" (i.e. not white) candidate (Kornblut, 2008). During the presidential campaign, Obama largely kept his distance from older black political figures like Jesse Jackson who highlighted racial justice issues. He focused on a positive message of "hope" and "change" that promised to bring together Americans of all backgrounds. Those who were most frustrated by the dearth of conversations about racial issues during the campaigns were those who did not adhere to the colorblind racial ideology: activist racists and anti-racists (as well as political operatives who wished to stir up opposition to Obama). The former were frustrated by the fact that Americans did not perceive the "nightmare" that they could be electing a black man as President. The latter were frustrated that Americans could feel comfortable electing a person of color but not acknowledge the racial inequality that still exists in the U.S.

Electing a black/multiracial President by (largely) ignoring racial inequality

Obama did confront racial issues head-on at any point during the 2008 Democratic presidential primary. Under tremendous pressure to refute the "racial perspective" of his former pastor, Reverend Jeremiah Wright (who was perceived to be "anti-white"), Obama gave a speech that focused on his view of race relations in the United States. In his March 2008 "A More Perfect Union" speech, Obama addressed and contextualized the race-based resentments of both black and white Americans clearly and eloquently, according to most commentators (Kornacki, 2008; Baker, 2008). In doing so, he acknowledged the perspectives of both racial groups, and argued that each must make efforts to overcome the racial divide.

According to Obama, the path toward "a more perfect union" requires black Americans to embrace

> the burdens of our past without becoming victims of our past. It means continuing to insist on a full measure of justice in every aspect of American life. But it also means binding our particular grievances—for better health care, and better schools, and better jobs—to the larger aspirations of all Americans—the white woman struggling to break the glass ceiling, the white man whose been laid off, the immigrant trying to feed his family. And it means taking full responsibility for own lives—by demanding more from our fathers, and spending more time with our children, and reading to them, and teaching them that while they may face challenges and discrimination in their own lives, they must never succumb to despair or cynicism; they must always believe that they can write their own destiny. (Obama, 2008)

The path forward that Obama laid out also requires white Americans to recognize that we do not live in a post-racial era, acknowledging that what ails the African American community does not just exist in the minds of black people; that the legacy of discrimination—and current incidents of discrimination, while less overt than in the past—are real and must be addressed. Not just with words, but with deeds—by investing in our schools and our communities; by enforcing our civil rights laws and ensuring fairness in our criminal justice system; by providing this generation with ladders of opportunity that were unavailable for previous generations. (Obama, 2008)

In keeping with his campaign theme of hope, change, and unity, Obama concluded that effectively closing the racial divide "requires all Americans to realize that your dreams do not have to come at the expense of my dreams; that investing in the health, welfare, and education of black and brown and white children will ultimately help all of America prosper" (Obama, 2008). In short, Obama argued that many black *and* white Americans have reasons to be resentful about their current economic and social situations, but that by acknowledging each others' perspectives *and the present racial inequality that exists today*, we can come together to make a stronger America.

The speech was a resounding political success, and calmed most white voters' fears that Obama might have an "anti-white" agenda. The message that present-day racial discrimination and racism is very real was quickly lost—and Obama did not repeat it. Indeed, when Obama won the presidency a few months later, many commentators declared that his election signaled that we now live in a "post-racial" era.

Obama's overall lack of emphasis on race was a key part of his successful campaign. He was embraced by the majority of white Americans who grew up in an era of colorblindness. In fact, the Obama campaign drew more young people into politics during the 2008 presidential election and led to an increase in voters under the age of 30 (2 percent more than in 2004 and 11 percent more than in 2000) (Kirby and Kawashima-Ginsberg, 2009). Sixty-six percent of voters aged 18–29 voted for Obama, including 54 percent of white voters in that age range (Keeter and Tyson, 2008). Overcoming their initial disbelief that white Americans would actually vote for a black person, African Americans overwhelmingly (96 percent) voted for Obama, and two-thirds of Latino Americans also pulled the lever for Obama (Kuhn, 2008). The campaign script of colorblindness had resonated—with consequences.

For adherents of the colorblind ideology, Obama's election seemed to provide strong evidence that America had moved into a "post-racial" society. Obama, himself, in his euphoria at winning the election, unintentionally aided this view. After hearing news of his victory on election night, Obama declared "It's been a long time coming…but tonight, because of what we did on this date in this election at this defining moment, change has come to America" (Obama, 2008). While Obama did not mean that the "change" was a move into a post-racial society, many of those listening heard that message. Echoing that theme in defeat, McCain noted that both he and Obama "realize [tonight] that we have come a long way from the injustices that once stained our nation's reputation" (Nagourney, 2008).

Pundits took these post-racial messages and ran with them. For example, on election night, newscaster Chris Wallace declared Obama a "post-racial figure." Conversing with the elated Wallace, Republican strategist Karl Rove said that young Americans were, indeed, "colorblind" but that Obama only had the *potential* to be "post-racial." Rove cautioned that Obama's acknowledgement of black racial anger during his "A More Perfect Union" speech indicated that he had not yet earned the "post-racial" title (Wallace and Rove, 2008). This observation was a warning, of sorts, to Obama, that he must avoid racial issues during his presidency or face a potential racial backlash. For most Americans, the message from Obama's victory was clear. A strong majority (even a majority of McCain supporters) said that his election was one of the most important advances (or *the* most important advance) over the last 100 years for black Americans (Gallup, 2008). For many, Obama's election was a sign that the last vestiges of racial injustice had fallen. How can racial inequality still exist in a country where a black man can be elected President? It was finally true, children (boys, at least) of any race can grow up to become President!

How can one explain racial inequality in a President Obama/post-racial era? Culture!

When one script becomes no longer useful (that is, it consists of innate, biological explanations) to explain present-day racism and racial inequality, other scripts can be utilized in their stead—especially in the colorblind era when Americans discuss racial matters without reference to race at all. In order to make sense of racial inequality in a "post-racial" President Obama era, cultural arguments are very useful. If one believes that we live in a society in which race no longer has an impact on what one can achieve, it follows that the racial inequality that still exists must be due to the cultural attributes of black Americans who remain poor. According to the cultural explanation, poor racial minorities keep themselves down by their own actions (or lack thereof). If only poor black parents would take the interest in their children's schooling that Obama's white mother had taken in his education! In any event, Obama's election gave proof that the opportunity for success is there—if only black people will step up and take advantage of it. The image of a black/multiracial President only makes this argument stronger. If Obama could make it, why do we need to help other Americans of color?

Obama's election, however, did not change the facts of racial discrimination in the United States. Although the election of an African American President certainly marks a moment of great individual progress, the points Obama made about the reality of racial discrimination during his March 2008 speech on race were still true in November of 2008 and still ring true today. In fact, today life is even more challenging for most Americans of color than it was in 2008. The Great Recession has hit racial minorities hardest of all. It has also made white Americans less interested in acknowledging and addressing the racial divide.

The Great Recession and race

Today, Obama faces a discontented public looking for a scapegoat. Anti-immigrant and racist rhetoric and laws are increasingly popular (e.g. the Arizona SB 1070 law that makes it a state crime not to carry papers proving legal residency and the vocal racism of some Tea Partiers such as Mark Williams (Kennedy, 2010)). As of July 2010, over half of all Americans support the Arizona immigration law (Condon, 2010). Spurred on by Obama's election, the Great Recession, and its related anti-immigrant sentiment, the number of hate groups in the United States is on the rise (Potok, 2009). In this climate, Obama is looked upon with suspicion by racists and with impatience by most Americans eager for signs of economic recovery.

In a depressed and fragile economy, convincing people that helping other Americans achieve their dreams does "not have to come at the expense" of their dreams is an increasingly tough sell—especially when the scripts at play are ones that stress individualism and not structure. Persuading white Americans in the midst of the Great Recession and fears of overwhelming budget deficits that they should support policies aimed at closing the racial gap does not appear politically feasible. With the official unemployment rate (those actively seeking jobs) hovering close to 10 percent (with almost half of those job-seekers enduring more than six months of unemployment), and fear of huge budget deficits making government stimulus and support for long-term unemployment benefits untenable, most Americans are understandably anxious.

Conservative pundits feed on the public's anxiety (and help create it) by arguing that Obama is more interested in the welfare of racial minorities than righting the American economy (e.g. Baldwin, 2010; Limbaugh, 2009; Beck, 2009). As we note above, Obama has carefully avoided any action that might indicate that he favors racial minorities and he has been quick to accept the resignation of anyone who appears to do so (e.g. Shirley Sherrod, Van Jones). However, the fact that he is black/biracial makes him susceptible to charges of favoring racial minorities.

White American males are facing historically high unemployment levels, due to the recession (Cauchon, 2009). For the first time in U.S. history, more women than men are now employed (Rampell, 2010). However, looking at economic data, instead of the transcripts of political pundits, it becomes obvious that black and Latino Americans have been hurt the most by the Great Recession. As of June 2010, 8.7 percent of white, 15.6 percent of black, and 12.3 percent of Latinos were unemployed (Bureau of Labor Statistics, 2010)—and underemployment statistics are even more dismal. Moreover, the wealth gap between white and black Americans increased fourfold between 1985 and 2007. One-fourth of black families had no assets to turn to when the Great Recession hit at the end of 2007 (Shapiro et al, 2010) and they will have even less as one of the central mechanisms of wealth generation for average Americans is home ownership. The subprime mortgage fiasco of 2000–6 (DiMartino and Duca, 2007) has led to one of the greatest transfers of wealth from the have-nots (largely and disproportionately black and Latino) to the haves (largely white) in the history of the country.

While millions of Americans, of all races, are suffering because of the housing crisis, minorities were hit particularly hard. Black and Latino homeowners were more likely than white people to receive higher priced subprime interest loans (even when controlling for income), leading to many more Latino and black homeowners facing foreclosure (Bocian et al, 2010). As of 2010, among Americans who owned their home in 2006, approximately 17 percent of Latino, 11 percent of black, and 7 percent of non-Latino white homeowners have lost or are likely to lose their home to foreclosure (Bocian et al, 2010).

Meanwhile, additional forms of racial discrimination are only growing stronger. Schools are becoming increasingly re-segregated. Forty percent of Latinos and 39 percent of African American children attend schools in which at least 90 percent of the population is comprised of students of color (Orfield and Lee, 2006; Jonsson and Khadaroo, 2010). Racism in employment is alive and well, with equally qualified minorities only 54 percent as likely as white people to receive a job offer in fine restaurants in New York City (Bendick et al, 2009) and white ex-convicts being more likely to be hired than qualified black people with no criminal records (Schultz and Barnes, 2005; Pager, 2007). Racial hate crimes are also on the rise, with the number of anti-black crimes "jumping" around the 2008 presidential election (LCCR, 2009; FBI, 2009). Clearly, racial discrimination in the U.S. is still a significant problem. However, without a script that reflects this reality, policies and laws aimed at alleviating racism and racial inequality will be nigh impossible.

No action on racial inequality under Obama

We are very unlikely to see President Obama directly address racial inequality. While the fact that he made it to the presidency as a black/ biracial person is inspiring to many racial minorities (and can open up a sense of possibilities once seen as hopelessly closed to them), his racial background, combined with the greatest economic downturn since the Great Depression and the influence of the colorblind ideology, has led to a lack of action on racial issues. In fact, it is possible to argue that Obama's election has helped promote the re-emergence of an emphasis on cultural, rather than structural, factors connected to racial inequality.

While a structural explanation of racial inequality focuses on patterns of discrimination among the major institutions in the U.S. (education, employment, housing, government), cultural explanations point to values and patterns of behavior to explain inequities between racial groups. As we note above, a cultural argument makes much sense in a "colorblind" and "post-racial" era. Obama's inclusion of cultural as well as structural explanations in his limited racial remarks provides the public with a cultural argument on which to seize, while his understandable reluctance to press home the structural argument (systemic racism is alive and well) allows them simply to ignore that key part of the explanation for racial inequality. This tendency to ignore structural arguments in favor of cultural ones is not new in either the public sphere or in the field of sociology (Steinberg, 1997; Wilson, 2009; Winant, 2007), but has reason to gain even greater traction in a post-racial era with a black/biracial President.

Obama has consistently described racial inequality as both a product of systemic racial discrimination and a culture among poor black people that leads to a lack of social mobility. However, following the colorblind racial script, he favors "race-neutral" programs to address racial inequality, believing they are more politically feasible than those targeted to racial minorities. Obama described his strategy on racial policy making this way:

> I can't pass laws that say I'm just helping black folks. I'm the President of the United States. What I can do is make sure that I am passing laws that help all people, particularly those who are most vulnerable and most in need. That in turn is going to help lift up the African American community. (Stolberg, 2010)

He also realizes that he, as a black/biracial person, cannot even mention that the goal of such programs might be to reduce racial inequality, for fear of charges of being pro-black and anti-white.

Ironically, although President Obama's election signaled to many a colorblind, post-racial America, he has been prevented from taking effective action on racial inequality because of his race. His conservative foes have effectively used the threat of portraying him as anti-white to discourage him from acknowledging racial discrimination, while the impact of the colorblind era and the Great Recession have made most Americans focus on racial recovery, rather than racial equality. The result is that racial discrimination may take cover under the facade of a post-racial society that President Obama's election helped create in the minds of many white Americans. That, indeed, would be a very sad legacy of the first black/multiracial President of the United States.

However, this legacy is not solely of Obama's making and he cannot avoid it alone. President Obama is enmeshed in the racial script of colorblindness. It is up to all of us to critique this script and create one that does not ignore the realities of racism and racial inequality. Neither we, nor President Obama, can effectively address what the American public does not acknowledge.

Note

[1] Obama's black racial identity, while fairly common among black/white multiracial people in this cohort, has different meanings for different individuals invoking this identity (Rockquemore et al, 2009), holds different meanings for others within the society (Khanna, 2010) and the link between racial identity and political identity is a complex one (Brunsma and Delgado, 2008)—linked with class, gender, region, and cohort.

References

Baker, B. (2008) '"Extraordinary" Obama Speech a "Gift" for "Confronting Race in America" with "Honesty"', *Newsbusters*, 18 March (http://newsbusters.org/blogs/brent-baker/2008/03/18/extraordinary-obama-speech-gift-thats-confronting-race-america-honesty).

Baldwin, S. (2010) 'Is Obama a Closet Racist?', Western Center for Journalism (www.westernjournalism.com/exclusive-investigative-reports/is-obama-a-closet-racist/).

Beck, G. (2009) 'Fox Host Glen Beck: Obama is a "Racist"', 28 July, HuffingtonPost.com. Viewed 21 July, 2010 (www.huffingtonpost.com/2009/07/28/fox-host-glenn-beck-obama_n_246310.html).

Bendick, M, Rodriguez RE and Jayaraman S. (2009) 'Race–ethnic employment discrimination in upscale restaurants:Evidence from paired comparison testing', February, 2009. Viewed 22 July, 2010 (www.bendickegan.com/pdf/2009/Testing_article_%20Feb_2009.pdf).

Bocian, DG, Li, W and Ernst, KS. (2010) *Foreclosures by Race and Ethnicity: The Demographics of a Crisis,* CRL Research Report, 18 June (www.responsiblelending.org/mortgage-lending/research-analysis/foreclosures-by-race-and-ethnicity.pdf

Bonilla-Silva, E. (2006) *Racism Without Racists* (2nd ed), Lanham, MD: Rowman and Littlefield.

Brunsma, D. (2006) *Mixed Messages: Multiracial Identities in the Colorblind Era*, Boulder, CO: Lynne Rienner.

Brunsma, David L. and Daniel J. Delgado D=J.. (2008) 'Occupying the Third Space: Hybridity and Identity in Multiracial Experience' in Keri E. Iyall Smith and Patricia Leavy (eEds.), *Hybrid Identities: Theoretical and Empirical Examinations,*. Brill.

Bureau of Labor Statistics, July 2010, Current Population Survey, A-15. Employment Status of the Civilian Noninstitutional Population by Race, Hispanic or Latino ethnicity, sex, and age" (www.bls.gov/web/empsit/cpseea15.pdf).

Carr, LG. (1997) *Color-Blind Racism*, Thousand Oaks, CA: Sage.

Cauchon, D. (2009) 'Older white men hurt most by this recession', *USA Today*, 29 July (http://abcnews.go.com/Business/story?id=8207572&page=1).

Cohen, A. (2008) 'Why Obama Chooses "black" Over "Biracial"', January 9, NPR (www.npr.org/templates/story/story.php?storyId=17958438).

CNN. (2008) 'Exit Polls: Obama Wins Big Among Minority, Young Voters', *CNNPolitics.com*, November 4.(www.cnn.com/2008/ POLITICS/11/04/exit.polls/).

Condon S. (2010) Poll: 'Support for Arizona Immigration Law Hits 57%' *CBSNews.com*, July 13 (www.cbsnews.com/8301-503544_162-20010460-503544.html)

DaCosta, KM. (2007) *Making Multiracials: State, Family, and Market in the Redrawing of the Color Line*, Palo Alto, CA: Stanford University Press.

DiMartino, D and Duca, JV. (2007) 'The Rise and Fall of Subprime Mortgages', The Federal Reserve Bank of Dallas 2,11, November (www.dallasfed.org/research/eclett/2007/el0711.html).

FBI. (2009) 'Hate Crime Statistics, 2008' (www.fbi.gov/ucr/hc2008/ index.html).

Gallup. (2008) 'Americans See Obama Election as Race Relations Milestone', November 7 (www.gallup.com/poll/111817/americans-see-obama-election-race-relations-milestone.aspx).

Gingrich, N. (1997) Speech by Speaker of the House, Newt Gingrich, before the Orphan Foundation of America, June 18, Washington, DC (www.multiracial.com/government/gingrich2.html).

Jonsson, P and and Khadaroo, ST. (2010) 'Are American Schools Returning to Segregation?', *The Christian Science Monitor*, June 18 (www.csmonitor.com/USA/Justice/2010/0618/Are-American-schools-returning-to-segregation).

Keeter, Horowitz, SJ and Tyson, A. (2008) 'Young Voters in the 2008 Election', November 12, Pew Research Center for the People and the Press. (http://pewresearch.org/pubs/1031/young-voters-in-the-2008-election).

Kennedy, H. (2010) 'Tea Party Express Leader Mark Williams Kicked Out Over "Colored People" Letter', July 18, www.nydailynews.com/ news/politics/2010/07/18/2010-07-18_tea_party_express_leader_ mark_williams_expelled_over_colored_people_letter.htmll)

Kirby, EH and Kawashima-Ginsberg, K. (2009) 'The Youth Vote in 2008', CIRCLE Fact Sheet, August 17, 2009. Viewed 21 July, 2010.

Khanna, Nikki. 2010. "Country Clubs and Hip-Hop Thugs: Examining the Role of Social Class and Culture in Shaping Racial Identity" in *Multiracial Americans and Social Class: The Influence of Social Class on Racial Identity*, edited by Kathleen Korgen. New York: Routledge. pp. 53-71.

Korgen, KO. (1998) *From black to Biracial*, Westport, CT: Praeger.

Kornacki, S. (2008) 'Obama Gives a Presidential Speech about Race.' *The New York Observer*, March 18 (www.observer.com/2008/obama-gives-presidential-speech-about-race).

Kornblut, AE. (2008) 'Issue of Race Creeps Into Campaign.' *The Washington Post*, October 12.(www.washingtonpost.com/wp-dyn/content/article/2008/10/11/AR2008101102216.html).

Kuhn, DP. (2008) 'Exit Polls: How Obama Won', *Politico.com*, November 5 (www.politico.com/news/stories/1108/15297_Page2.html)

Leadership Conference on Civil Rights (LCCR). (2009) 'Confronting the New Faces of Hate: Hate Crimes in 2009'.Viewed 10 October, 2011 (www.civilrights.org/publications/hatecrimes/).

Limbaugh, R. 2009.'Obama's Entire Economic Program is Reparations', The Rush Limbaugh Show, June 22.Viewed 21 July, 2010 (http://mediamatters.org/mmtv/200907220040).

Nagourney, A. (2008) 'Obama Elected President as Racial Barrier Falls', *New York Times,* November 5.Viewed 19 July, 2010 (www.nytimes.com/2008/11/05/us/politics/05elect.html)

Obama, B. (2008) 'A More Perfect Union' speech (http://blogs.wsj.com/washwire/2008/03/18/text-of-obamas-speech-a-more-perfect-union/).

Obama, B. (2008) '"This Is Your Victory," Says Obama', transcript, viewed October 10 2011 (http://articles.cnn.com/2008-11-04/politics/obama.transcript_1_transcript-answer-sasha-and-malia?_s=PM:POLITICS)

Orfield, G and Lee, C. (2006) 'Racial Transformation and the Changing Nature of Segregation',The Civil Rights Project, January 12 (http://civilrightsproject.ucla.edu/research/k-12-education/integration-and-diversity/racial-transformation-and-the-changing-nature-of-segregation).

Pager, D. (2007) *MARKED: Race, Crime, and Finding Work in an Era of Mass Incarceration,* Chicago: University of Chicago Press.

Potok, M. (2009) 'SPLC's Intelligence Report: Hate Group Numbers Rise Again', Southern Poverty Law Center (SPLC) (www.splcenter.org/blog/2009/02/28/intelligence-report-hate-group-numbers-rise-again/).

Rampell, C. (2010) 'Women Outnumber Men in Workplaces', *New York Times.* February 5 (www.nytimes.com/2010/02/06/business/economy/06women.html?_r=1&fta=y).

Rockquemore, Kerry Ann, Brunsma David L. Brunsma, and Delgado Daniel Delgado. (2009) 'Racing to Theory or Re-theorizing Race: Understanding the Struggle to Build Valid Multiracial Identity Theories' *The Journal of Social Issues,* vol. 65, no. 1, pp. 13-34.

Schultz, S and Barnes, S. (2005) 'Many New York Employers Discriminate Against Minorities, Ex-Offenders', April 1 (www.princeton.edu/main/news/archive/S11/23/70K64/index.xml?section=newsreleases).

Shapiro, TM, Meschede, T and Sullivan, L. (2010) 'The Racial Wealth Gap Increases Fourfold', May 2010, Institute on Assets and Social Policy (IASP),(http://iasp.brandeis.edu/pdfs/Racial-Wealth Gap-Brief.pdf).

Steinberg, S. (2007) *Race Relations: A Critique*, Stanford: Stanford University Press.

Stolberg, SG. (2010) 'For Obama, Nuance on Race Invites Question', *New York Times*, February 8. Viewed 20 July, 2010 (www.nytimes.com/2010/02/09/us/politics/09race.html).

Thernstrom, A. (1987) *Whose Votes Count?: Affirmative Action and Minority Voting Rights*, Cambridge, MA: Harvard University Press.

Thernstrom, S and Thernstrom, A. (1997) *America in black and white*, New York: Simon & Schuster.

Wallace, C and Rove, K. (2008) 'Discuss Obama Victory', November 4. (http://vodpod.com/watch/1137151-chris-wallace-and-karl-rove-discuss-obama-victory).

Wilson, WJ. (2009) *More than Just Race: Being black and Poor in the Inner City*. New York City: W.W. Norton & Company.

Winant, H. (2007) 'The Dark Side of the Force: One Hundred Years of the Sociology of Race' In *Sociology in America: A History* Craig Calhoun (ed) pp. 535-71.

CHAPTER ELEVEN

Barack Obama and the rise to power: Emmett Till revisited

Andrew J. Jolivette

The notion of ideology appears to me to be difficult to make use of, for three reasons. The first is that, like it or not, it always stands in virtual opposition to something else which is supposed to count as truth. Now I believe that the problem does not consist in drawing the line between that which comes under some other category, but in seeing historically how effects of truth are produced within discourses which in themselves are neither true nor false. The second drawback is that the concept of ideology refers, I think necessarily, to something of the order of a subject. Thirdly, ideology stands in a secondary position relative to something which functions as its infrastructure, as its material, economic determinant etc. For these three reasons, I think that this is a notion that cannot be used without circumscription. (Foucault, 1972)

The state of American politics in the age of Obama: striving for a post-racist vs. "post-racial" society

In the social sciences ideology is often viewed as problematic without empirical evidence to support assertions about the social world. While empirical data often supports research findings and new scientific inquiries—it is ideology that often informs behavior in human beings. As the essays in this collection assert—multiracial identity and the construction of mixed race hegemony has profound implications on socioeconomic status, parenting, politics, public policy, the arts, history, and literary analysis. The contributors to this book demonstrate with complex and diverse examples how contemporary American politics in the United States is still deeply affected by race and ethnicity, but these unique essays also provide an understanding of how these discussions play out not just in terms of ideology, but in practice. To grapple with the future of U.S. politics and group relations will require critical engagement with multiraciality in both historic and contemporary contexts.

The implications of the questions raised by this volume are numerous. At stake is the future of U.S. national identity, pluralism, and global competition. How will future generations respond to the significant changes in the U.S. population that occur as a result of interracial marriage, immigration, and the global and transnational transfer of culture? How, as Focault suggests, will ideology be shaped by structural forces including multiracial structures which suggest that our nation should move toward a "post-racial" society? The challenge of understanding race as a social construct—as the contributors to this volume highlight—is the degree to which we as individuals and groups accept race as a stand-alone factor that continues to symbolize and dictate structural inequalities.

> Race must be viewed as a social construction. That is, human interaction rather than natural differentiation must be seen as the source and continued basis for racial categorization. The process by which racial meanings arise has been labeled racial formation. In this formulation, race is not a determinant or residue of some other social phenomenon but rather stands on its own as an amalgamation of competing societal forces. Racial formation includes both the rise of racial groups and their constant reification in social thought. [There are] four important aspects of the social construction of race. First, humans rather than abstract social forces produce races. Second, as human constructs, races constitute an integral part of a whole social fabric that includes gender and class relations [and sexuality—author's note]. Third, the meaning-systems surrounding race change quickly rather than slowly. Finally, races are constructed relationally, against one another, rather than in isolation. (Lopez, 2003)

Multiracial identity, discourse and ideology has certainly shifted conversations, policies, and practices concerning race in a quick rather than a slow fashion. Today as the United States' white population shrinks and the Latino, Asian, and multiracial populations grow there is a strategic attempt to claim both symbolically, literally, and ideologically the bodies of ambiguous ethnic populations. This battle for a new American majority is about claiming multiracial people as being without a race on the one hand and as white in terms of class status on the other. For multiracial people, and immigrant populations who do not fit neatly into white and non-white categories there is a battle to shape the ideology of these groups so that they will align themselves socially, politically, culturally, and economically with white people. Groups such as Latinos, Arab Americans, and Cape Verdeans who are all being inundated by a mixed race hegemonic force that suggests to be a "real American" you must also be "post-racial." In other words these groups are being asked to give up their ethnic and cultural identities to prevent a shift in demographics, ideology, and power in the United States. Not unlike previous historical periods when it was argued that the mixing of races would only be a positive benefit if it included a predominant white identification, degree of mixing, or level of socio-cultural status, today mixed race hegemony suggests that whiteness betters the human condition and thus will advance U.S. society. In this way, mixed race hegemony is being utilized in the age of Obama to suggest that a "post-racial" society is the only way to advance democracy in the twenty-first century. This ideological shift toward mixed race hegemony, though, is a reification of white supremacy which mixed race people themselves must challenge.

> No one acquainted with the indolent, mixed race of California, will ever believe that they will populate, much less, for any length of time govern the country. The law of Nature which curses the mulatto here with a constitution less robust than that of either race from which he sprang, lays a similar penalty upon the mingling of the Indian and white races in California and Mexico. They must fade away; while the mixing of different branches of the Caucasian family in the states will continue to produce a race of men, who will enlarge from period to period the field of their industry and civil domination, until not only the Northern States of Mexico, but the Californias also, will open their glebe to the pressure of its unconquered arm. The old Saxon blood must stride the continent, must command all its northern shores, must here press the grape and the olive, here eat the orange and the fig, and in their own unaided might, erect the altar of civil and religious freedom on the plains of California. (Farnham, 1840)

The salience of Farnham's comments still reveal much about the foundations and current aims of white supremacy and the battle for a new American majority where the mingling of white with non-white will somehow lead not to a *post-racist* (a society free from discrimination and structural inequality on the basis of socially constructed racial categories) society, but to a supposedly "post-racial" nation (where we ignore racial and ethnic difference despite the socially constructed inequalities embedded in a "formerly" race-conscious society). An important and more recent example of how white supremacy functions through symbols and ideologies, and is then translated into practice can be found in the historic case of slain African American teenager, Emmett Till. His death and the circumstances behind it, like the racial tensions surrounding the campaign, election, and first term of President Obama reveal the ongoing significance of white supremacy, privilege, and neoliberal racism.

Fifty-five years ago, on August 28 1955, Chicago teenager Emmett Till was murdered while visiting relatives in Money, Mississippi. Eight years later to the day, Dr. Martin Luther King, Jr. delivered his famous "I Have a Dream" speech in front of the Lincoln Memorial in Washington, D.C., and on August 28 2008, Barack Obama accepted the Democratic Party's nomination for President of the United States. That these three historic events all happened on the same day of the year is not only ironic, but also links the history of civil rights and struggles for racial justice to Barack Obama's presidency.

Not only is the story of Mr. Obama's first term in office unfinished, but, sadly, so too is the murder investigation of Emmett Till. In 2005, 50 years after his violent murder the case was re-opened and his body exhumed for autopsy. On June 20 2007, the U.S. House of Representatives passed H.R. 923, the Emmett Till Unsolved Civil Rights Crime Act of 2007 which allows the Justice Department to investigate unsolved cases from the civil rights era. Many people have forgotten about the Till case and the images of his savagely mutilated body. Till was a Chicago native (another connection to President Obama) who was murdered for "whistling at a white woman" named Carolyn Bryant. That was his "crime"—he dared to break to the unspoken laws of the South and paid for it with his life. Consider the following passage from reporter William Bradford Huie's 1956 interview with Till's killers in *Look* magazine where, after acquittal, they confessed to the murder of the 14-year-old:

> When her husband was away, Carolyn Bryant never slept in
> the store, never stayed there alone after dark. Moreover, in

the Delta, no white woman or group of white women ever travels country roads after dark unattended by a man. This meant that during Roy's absences—particularly since he had no car—there was family inconvenience. Each afternoon, a sister-in-law arrived to stay with Carolyn until closing time. Then, the two women, with their children, waited for a brother-in-law to convoy them to his home. Next morning, the sister-in-law drove Carolyn back. Juanita Milam had driven from her home in Glendora. She had parked in front of the store to the left; and under the front seat of this car was Roy Bryant's pistol, a .38 Colt automatic. Carolyn knew it was there. After 9, Juanita's husband J. W. Milam would arrive in his pickup to shepherd them to his home for the night. About 7:30 p.m., eight young Negroes—seven boys and a girl—in a '46 Ford had stopped outside. They included sons, grandsons and a nephew of Moses (Preacher) Wright, 64, a 'cropper. They were between 13 and 19 years old. Four were natives of the Delta, and others, including the nephew, Emmett (Bobo) Till, were visiting from the Chicago area. Bobo Till was 14 years old: born on July 25, 1941. He was stocky, muscular, weighing about 160, five feet four or five. Preacher later testified: "He looked like a man." (Huie, 1956)

In 1955 the "worst crime" a black man could commit was to have "inappropriate" contact with a white woman. Dating back to slavery there was a fear among white men of black men doing to white women what they had done to African women—violate, rape, and impregnate them with "mongrel" children. That some 55 years after Till's murder the son of a white woman and a black man currently occupies the office of President of the United States is not only a sign of "change" as many neoliberals have embraced, but it is also a reminder that many have not let go of the symbols and ideologies of white supremacy nor the disapproval of many when it comes to interracial mixing. The other parallel between Till and President Obama—besides interracial disapproval—is that Obama represents a twenty-first-century version of Till. He not only physically embodies interracial mixing, but he also challenges the status quo of white power by his ascension to the White House, another symbol of unspoken privilege. That he is the first person of color to hold this office is on the one hand a moment many never dreamed would happen and yet during his campaign in 2008 and since he took office in 2009 he has been metaphorically "lynched" for daring to "take this country away from real Americans" as Till was murdered for attempting to "take a White woman's virtue."

Emmett Till, unfamiliar with the unspoken laws and de facto racism of the southern United States, went into the Bryant family's small store with family and friends unaware that his actions would not only later lead to his own death, but would shock the nation and lead to a national Civil Rights Movement.

> Bobo's party joined a dozen other young Negroes, including two other girls, in front of the store. Bryant had built checkerboards there. Some were playing checkers, others were wrestling and "kiddin' about girls." Bobo bragged about his white girl. He showed the boys a picture of a white girl in his wallet; and to their jeers of disbelief, he boasted of his success with her. "You talkin' mighty big, Bo," one youth said. "There's a pretty little white woman in the store. Since you know how to handle white girls, let's see you go in and get a date with her?" "You ain't chicken, are yuh, Bo?" another youth taunted him. Bobo had to fire or fall back. He entered the store, alone, stopped at the candy case. Carolyn was behind the counter; Bobo in front. He asked for two cents' worth of bubble gum. She handed it to him. He squeezed her hand and said: "How about a date, Baby?" She jerked away and started for Juanita Milam. At the break between counters, Bobo jumped in front of her, perhaps caught her at the waist, and said: "You needn't be afraid o' me, Baby. I been with white girls before." At this point, a cousin ran in, grabbed Bobo and began pulling him out of the store. Carolyn now ran, not for Juanita, but out the front, and got the pistol from the Milam car. Outside, with Bobo being ushered off by his cousins, and with Carolyn getting the gun, Bobo executed the 'wolf whistle' which gave the case its name: "The Wolf-Whistle Murder: A Negro 'Child' or 'Boy' Whistled at Her and They Killed Him" (Huie, 1956)

Carolyn Bryant was 21 years old at the time, not a child like Till, but because of the way in which race and gender has functioned in the United States she was seen as a victim. Her "virtue and purity" had been "tainted" by the touch of a "Negro" child who looked like a "man." The "only" choice for Bryant's husband in order to preserve his dignity as a white man was to take matters into his own hands by defending what was "his' and in so doing he was "defending" the nation from the encroachment of black men (and black people in general) by reminding them of their "place" in U.S. society.

> That was the sum of the facts on which most newspaper readers based an opinion. The Negroes drove away; and Carolyn, shaken, told Juanita. The two women determined to keep the incident from their "men-folks." They didn't tell J. W. Milam when he came to escort them home. By Thursday afternoon, Carolyn Bryant could see the story was getting around. She spent Thursday night at the Milams, where at 4 a.m. (Friday) Roy got back from Texas. Since he had slept little for five nights, he went to bed at the Milams' while Carolyn returned to the store. During Friday afternoon, Roy [Carolyn's husband at the time] reached the store, and shortly thereafter a Negro told him what "the talk" was, and told him that the "Chicago boy" was "visitin' Preacher." Carolyn then told Roy what had happened. Once Roy Bryant knew, in his environment, in the opinion of most white people around him, for him to have done nothing would have marked him for a coward and a fool. (Huie, 1956)

It would only be a matter of time before Bryant and his co-conspirators took action for Till's "crime" against white women. Knowing the de facto laws of the south, Bryant likely assumed any act of retaliation would be seen by the legal system as his "God-given right" and thus he could act without impunity. So, too, have groups angry with President Obama believed that organizing with fully-loaded guns outside the White House is their "God-given" and constitutional right. Imagine, as noted anti-racist scholar, Tim Wise has suggested (2010), that an all-black—or mostly all-black—group had organized themselves with loaded weapons in front of the White House during the Bush or Reagan Presidencies. According to Wise these protests would immediately be called into question, but they are tolerated by white Americans and encouraged by political pundits as examples of "free speech."

> Imagine that black protesters at a large political rally were walking around with signs calling for the lynching of their congressional enemies. Because that's what white conservatives did last year, in reference to Democratic Party leaders in Congress. In other words, imagine that even

one-third of the anger and vitriol currently being hurled at President Obama, by folks who are almost exclusively white, were being aimed, instead, at a white president, by people of color. How many whites viewing the anger, the hatred, the contempt for that white president would then wax eloquent about free speech, and the glories of democracy? And how many would be calling for further crackdowns on thuggish behavior, and investigations into the radical agendas of those same people of color? (Wise, 2010)

Wise's essay is an important reminder that despite calls for a "post-racial" America this can never happen until there is a full recognition of the myriad ways in which white power and privilege continues to function in the United States. Just as a mob gathered 55 years ago to put Bobo Till in "his place" so, too, are Tea Party and Birther groups along with conservative political commentators like Glenn Beck and Rush Limbaugh working to put President Obama in "his place." Even as President of the United States, Mr. Obama is unable to escape the realities of social and institutional racism. His rise to power has been marked by many incidents related to race from the now infamous arrest of noted African American scholar and Harvard University professor, Henry Louis Gates to more recent incidents that led to the resignation of Shirley Sherrod, an African American female and former state Director of Rural Development because of the misinterpretation of comments she had made regarding racial discrimination toward white farmers. The misrepresentation of Ms. Sherrod's comments were due to the release of video footage by conservative commentator Andrew Breitbart on his website which only gave a partial clip of Sherrod speaking about her initial reluctance to help white farmers. The comments suggested that rather than help a white farmer with a loan Sherrod decided to take him to one of "his own" to have them help him.

> You know, the first time I was faced with helping a white farmer save his farm, he took a long time talking but he was trying to show me he was superior to me. I know what he was doing. But he had come to me for help. What he didn't know, while he was taking all that time trying to show me he was superior to me, was I was trying to decide just how much help I was going to give him. I was struggling with the fact that so many black people had lost their farmland. And here I was faced with having to help a white person save their land. So, I didn't give him the full force of what

I could do. I did enough so that when he... I assumed the Department of Agriculture had sent him to me, either that, or the Georgia Department of Agriculture, and he needed to go back and report that I did try to help him. So I took him to a white lawyer that had attended some of the training that we had provided because Chapter 12 bankruptcy had just been enacted for the family farm. So I figured if I take him to one of them, that his own kind would take care of him. That's when it was revealed to me that it's about poor versus those who have, and not so much about white—it *is* about white and black, but it's not, you know, it opened my eyes because I took him to one of his own. (Sherrod, 2010)

It was later revealed after Sherrod's resignation that the full excerpt of her speech was about reconciliation and learning. It wasn't just about race, it was also about class and addressing poverty for all people. In fact, the white couple Sherrod ended up helping, came out, after she was forced to resign, in support of her. Sherrod had become friends with the family and they credited her assistance with saving their family farm. But because race does still matter President Obama's administration has taken a different approach than other Presidents because any action he takes that appears to favor people of color or discriminate against white people would be seen as favoritism when the same has never been true of white Presidents who favor the wealthy who are overwhelmingly white. This double standard speaks to Wise's point about how Americans view the social and political undermining of President Obama.

To ask any of these questions is to answer them. Protest is only seen as fundamentally American when those who have long had the luxury of seeing themselves as prototypically American engage in it. When the dangerous and dark "other" does so, however, it isn't viewed as normal or natural, let alone patriotic. Which is why Rush Limbaugh could say, this past week, that the Tea Parties are the first time since the Civil War that ordinary, common Americans stood up for their rights: a statement that erases the normalcy and "American-ness" of black people in the civil rights struggle, not to mention women in the fight for suffrage and equality, working people in the fight for better working conditions, and LGBT folks as they struggle to be treated as full and equal human beings. And this, my friends, is what white

privilege is all about. The ability to threaten others, to engage
in violent and incendiary rhetoric without consequence,
to be viewed as patriotic and normal no matter what you
do, and never to be feared and despised as people of color
would be, if they tried to get away with half the shit we do,
on a daily basis. (Wise, 2010)

This final statement about patriotism speaks to a fundamental
question raised throughout this book. How have race and interracial
relations affected our nation since the election of Barack Obama? The
field of mixed race studies continues to wrestle with the notion that
any person of color whether racially mixed or not will still be marked
as "other," as non-white, and as un-American. The question that we are
left with is, "Does it matter that President Obama is biracial, particularly
since he identifies as African American?" We still have to ponder the
impact of his mixed heritage on his ability to win the presidency in
2008 and what it may mean for his possible re-election 2012. His rise
to power as a black leader is not unique when we look at the rise in
African American elected officials across the United States. According
to Gwen Ifill, author of *The Breakthrough: Politics and Race in the Age
of Obama*:

> The next African American candidates (and a fair share of
> those already in office) subscribe to a formula driven as
> much by demographics as destiny. When population shifts
> occur—brought about by fair housing laws, affirmative
> action, and landmark school desegregation rulings—political
> power is challenged as well. It happened in Boston, New
> York, Chicago and every other big city reshaped by an
> influx of European immigration. It is happening again now
> in Miami and Los Angeles, in suburban Virginia and rural
> North Carolina, where political calculus is being reshaped
> by Latino immigrants. With African Americans, freighted
> with the legacy of slavery and pushback from white people
> who refuse to feel guilty for the sins of their ancestors, the
> shift has been more scattered and sporadic, but not less
> profound. (Ifill, 2009)

Demographic shifts in the population along with the rise in the
number of multiracial couples and adults of voting age are only a
part of the equation however. There has also been a slow, but steady
ideological shift in the nation that prides itself on being "colorblind"

or "post-racial." What better way to demonstrate that we, as a nation, have moved past race than by electing a mixed race African American man with an immigrant African father and with an Indonesian Muslim stepfather? His story is, after all, as he said during the election, "only possible in the United States." So while works like Ifill's demonstrate that other African American candidates have seen growing success (not to mention Latino and Asian American politicians) with demographic shifts from increased immigration into communities of color, we still must reckon with one thing—would Mr. Obama have won had he not been racially mixed and what does this mean about our nation's hope for a more racially just, democratic society?

The truth is that the answer to this question is just as complicated as the experience of being a racially mixed person in 2011. There are many who still argue that if you are a person of color (especially of African ancestry) with at least one white parent you will inevitably be viewed as black and if you claim otherwise then you are simply "confused." Then there is an entirely different school of thought that suggests that self-identification is always an individual's right. Both sides have some validity to them. Race in the United States has been constructed based on phenotype and other ascribed physical attributes, but these are not always as distinguishable to every observer. Individuals can assert a biracial identification or even a monoracial identity, but this does not mean that their physical features or lived experiences will reflect that self-identification in practice. Biracial writer Shelby Steele suggests that Obama's use of his identity is "disingenuous" because "no one would know he had a white mother unless they saw her."

> Biracial writer Shelby Steele told ABCNews.com that he thinks Obama's use of his background was "disingenuous." He believes the ruminations about mixed heritage show Obama to be not an expert but rather a man confused about his racial identity. "Obama is a black man with a white mother. Being biracial is an impossibility," said Steele, who said that no matter what, when Obama walks down the street he is viewed as a black man. "How could you possibly live as both? If you didn't know his mother was white, you'd say he's black and you wouldn't have a second thought." "He's confused," said Steele of Obama. "Are you really black or are you playing the biracial card?" (Friedman, 2008)

Steele's comments speak to one viewpoint that has tended to dominate American views of mixed race African Americans. If you say you are anything other than black then you must be denying your blackness. But what of the other possibility? Is asserting a "black only" identification as a biracial person manipulating or misappropriating blackness for political and/or social access? In other words, rather than be challenged as not being black enough, is it better to simply to deny one's real lived experiences having being shaped by growing up with at least one white parent? For the children of single parents like President Obama it is also necessary to examine who raised the child. Obama was raised with his maternal side of the family and never spent any substantive time with his African father, so how could his life experience be the same as monoracial African American people who are not raised by white people?

In the same way that Emmett Till's life is a reminder about the differential treatment of white and black (colored) bodies, so, too, is the mixed race subject's body a reminder that race does indeed still matter in contemporary U.S. politics. President Obama for better or worse is the new "poster child" for mixed race politics. Every response to his policies is in and of itself a commentary about the state of race relations in this country. From the war in Afghanistan, to a shrinking economy that is devastating communities of color, to anti-Arab sentiment and immigration reform, President Obama is a symbol of the country's best hopes and worst fears. Can his election, like Till's murder, spark yet another movement for civil rights in this country that will bring us closer to a new American majority? Perhaps the answer to this question can be found in a critical assessment of white bodies today and what critical mixed race pedagogy can do to destabilize white supremacy as an unspoken prerequisite for citizenship and patriotism.

On white bodies and critical mixed race pedagogy

The salience of white bodies as inherently more valuable than the bodies of women, children, and men of color is being deconstructed not only by people of color, but by a growing chorus of anti-racism white privilege scholars. Despite the best of intentions behind this movement there have basically been two responses to efforts to deconstruct white privilege. First, those generally considered to be politically conservative have labeled these attempts to be reverse racist, socialist, and anti-American. Those on the more "liberal' side of things have embraced the tenets of multiculturalism and the need for a white privilege movement, but these same liberals and progressives also tend to embrace a paternalistic approach where white people play the role of "savior" or "protector" for communities of color. Critical mixed race pedagogy would attack both positions as an affront to true social change for all Americans. Critical mixed race pedagogy, as I define it, contains four basic components: 1) social justice; 2) self-determination; 3) cross-ethnic and transnational solidarity; and 4) radical love.

Social justice

As articulated by critical mixed race pedagogy, social justice asserts that all communities regardless of history, socioeconomic circumstance, educational background, health status or national origin require access to the same rights of national and global citizenship as all other bodies. Social justice as defined by critical mixed race pedagogy is about explicitly working to reform laws that privilege certain bodies while marginalizing others. As the beneficiaries of both the Civil Rights Act and the *Loving vs. Virginia* case (which struck down interracial marriage bans) we must, in mixed race communities, look to laws that today prohibit others from having access to their full civil and human rights, not just under United States law, but also under international law.

Self-determination

In critical mixed race pedagogy, self-determination accepts as valid, calls for an interrogation of capitalism as a pillar of oppression in the United States and worldwide. Self-determination in this sense is about a full recognition of the rights and responsibilities of the United States to people of color, Indigenous Nations, queer populations, immigrants, veterans, women, the poor, political prisoners, and children. Critical mixed race pedagogy must include research and activism that is guided by principals that place those with whom we work at the center of our work. We as educators and organizers must be sure that questions about political agendas, about researching social problems, must emerge from the community. As Cree scholar Shawn Wilson (2009) states in *Research is Ceremony*, indigenous research must be guided by specific principals. I have modified some of these principals and applied them to mixed race communities.

Mixed race people, together with other people of color, themselves must approve the research, the research methods, and/or the organizing approach. A knowledge and consideration of community and the diversity and unique nature which each individual brings to the community must be respected. Mixed race research as an act of self-determination must involve a deep listening and hearing with more than the ears. A critical mixed race pedagogy must include a reflective, non-judgmental consideration of what is being said and heard both in community-based research and organizing. In order to include self-determination, critical mixed race pedagogy must incorporate an awareness and connection between logic of the mind and the feelings of the heart. Listening and observing the self as well as in relationship to others is the only way to maintain balance. Finally, there must be an acknowledgement by mixed race educators and organizers that we bring our own subjective identities to the work that we are doing (Wilson, 2009).

Cross-ethnic and transnational solidarity

The third aspect of a critical mixed race pedagogy is cross-ethnic and transnational solidarity. This aspect must focus on linking struggles for justice on a global scale. How are the voices and representations of indigenous peoples, people of color and marginalized groups understood in the context of putting power into the hands of the masses? Critical mixed race studies scholars and organizers must articulate ways of working with multiple groups around the world toward a United Nations Declaration on the rights of oppressed groups. This should include plans of action for dealing with child exploitation, xenophobia, race and religious-based discrimination, a decentralization of borders which exclude those deemed as threats to nationalism. We need international justice exchange and fellowship programs that encourage transnational cooperation and shared leadership. Critical mixed race pedagogies can only form coalitions nationally and transnationally by seeking to connect seemingly divergent political issues into consensus issues that are seen as having an impact on all global citizens and not just on those with the most power or visibility. President Obama is a symbol for a movement, in the same way as is Emmett Till. The President's symbolism, though, is global and transnational and can be the impetus for renewed discussions of peace all around the world. In order to accomplish this Mr. Obama must continue to build a new American majority made up of diverse political ideologies, racial backgrounds, and economic status groups.

Radical love

The fourth and final component of critical mixed race pedagogy is radical love. So what is radical love? A dear friend with whom I spoke about this concept asked me, "Well what is love? Can it be used to say that, if we act in the name of love and with good intentions, we are therefore exempt from the pain we may inflict by saying we had good intentions or that we acted with love?" I would say that we cannot presume to know what is best for our communities in national or transnational contexts. Only these communities can inform the moral and ethical questions that need to be addressed and this includes multiracial populations as well.

Radical love is about being vulnerable. It is about being unafraid to speak out about issues that may not have a direct impact on us on a daily basis. Radical love is about caring enough to admit when we are wrong and to admit to mistakes. Radical love should ask how the work in which we are engaged helps to build respectful relationships between ourselves and others involved in social justice movements. Radical love asks if we are each being responsible in fulfilling our individual roles and obligations to the other participants in the struggle for social justice and human rights. Finally, radical love in critical mixed race studies, means asking ourselves if what we are contributing is giving back to the community and if it is strengthening the relationship of all of those involved in the process. Is what is being shared adding to the growth of the community and is this sharing reciprocal? Is what we are working toward leading to a more peaceful and equitable society?

We—each of us, whether heterosexual, queer, mixed, of color, Muslim, young or elder—can benefit from a world where there is peace. Peace, however, as the saying goes, is more than the absence of violence. Peace is about the active willingness to dare to love without condition. Peace is to be unafraid to speak up when someone is disrespectful towards another person. Peace is when we have economic fairness in housing. Peace is about social justice.

Cornel West has recently said that "justice is what love looks like in public" (West, 2010). I've been seeing this quote all over the place recently and I've been thinking, "justice is what love looks like in public." This sounds good, but what does it mean? Does it mean that we are not afraid to show love in public? Does it mean that justice, like love, could be the most emotionally meaningful thing in the world? Just like in the time prior to 1967 when interracial love couldn't be public, queer love and desire cannot be public, heterosexual love among brothers and men of color, especially among black men is not supposedly acceptable in public. Undocumented children are afraid to talk too much in public about the love of their families for fear of being disappeared by the Immigration and Naturalization Service (INS). So justice is what love looks like in public, but we have to deconstruct what love is and what is allowed in public in this nation and what this nation does to regulate love on public display in other nations. Justice must also be about love in private. It must be about ending domestic violence, about ending child abuse. Love in private and in public must foster safety and empowerment for children of color, for mixed race youth—for all youth.

So I would slightly amend this statement to, "justice is what love looks like in the light." It's easy to love someone in public when it is safe for us to do that. It is easy to love someone in the dark when we cannot see each other. It is, however, in our full vulnerability of the light that we can truly understand if and how much we are willing to love and if this comes without condition. Therefore justice has to be about loving in the light of day. Justice has to look like love in public and in private. Justice is not about being in a movement when it is convenient or it is the thing that other people are doing. It is not about being seen by the public eye.

Justice in a critical mixed race framework is about exposing the erasures that society has created to have us believe that we are born to be enemies. Justice is about speaking up when no one else may see or hear our actions. Today young people are expressing, in their experiences and in their organizing, the reality that we are indeed a nation of multiples. We have to see that change can only come when we see our community as all communities. Justice, social change, and a new American majority that seeks a more equitable society will only come to fruition when we acknowledge that our differences are a source of strength.

Critical mixed race studies should move toward a revolutionary space where justice, new racial representations, and political contestation are central to dismantling ongoing colonialism in the United States and globally. Critical mixed race studies as a pedagogy and emerging paradigm must center social justice, self-determination, cross-ethnic and transnational solidarity, and radical love so that each of us can re-awaken movements both small and large that will reform the societies and spaces that have kept us confined to the margins. We must re-center love as a radical act that defies boundaries. We must re-center love as a radical act that brings people together not to erase ethnic identity (or to become "post-racial") but to strengthen it. In this way critical mixed race studies can build a true cultural and political revolution and a unique new American majority.

Revolution

There was something sleeping within me and there you
were to awaken it
There was this silence unexposed that you were able to
break
Shattering a million fragmented pieces into a new whole
When I had forgotten who I was
You were there to restore
What was hidden deep within

There was something sleeping within me and there you
were to awaken it
You reminded me of what it means to laugh
You reminded me of what it means to be free and true

There was this silence unexposed that you were able to
break
In your smile, in your unhidden, expression filled face
You reminded me of the power of the wind

The power of the wind to create breath
The power of the wind to allow life to breathe in its full
and complete joy
Revealing each day new experiences as yet unknown

Revolution isn't a place
Revolution isn't a person

Revolution is the Fruit of Desire

It's about community
It's about connections
Multiple spaces and relationships

Revolution is now awake
It is strong,
It is free,
It is alive within me…Revolution

Wrapping your inner most beauty all around me
And yet even with the absence of your touch

Of your lips against my skin
It is just a reminder of the revolution within

There was something sleeping within me and there you
were to awaken it

Quietly, gently without cause...
You allowed me...to be me
Us to be us...unmasked

And that is the fire that burns...

The fire that bore
Our Revolution

A Revolution Born...
From a Thousand Silent and Miraculous Gazes

From words of freedom
From hearts open to all possibilities
From intimacies re-imagined

From a Thousand Silent and Miraculous Gazes
A seed was planted for our own

(Andrew J. Jolivette; previously unpublished)

Conclusion and implications

Critical mixed race pedagogy and mixed race hegemony as outlined
throughout this work will serve as important theoretical frameworks for
future discussions of race relations in the United States. Multiraciality
as it has been asserted by the contributors to this book plays a vital role
in the creation of power structures, the ongoing construction of racial
projects and economic inequality. That a biracial and self-identified
African American was elected to the presidency of the United States
should signal a shift in the power structures that perpetuate inequality,
but in reality Mr. Obama's election is about a shift in ideology and the
use of race and mixed race to re-embed old scripts which organize
individual and group relations within an oppressive system based on
the exploitation of those with the least amount of power.

At stake in the first term and upcoming re-election campaign of Mr. Obama are the foundations of either a new system of racial politics and public policy or the re-imagining of old systems and policies that will maintain the status quo for those with the most power and privilege. There are at least five fundamental implications of this book and each relates to the outcome of 2012 campaign for President. First, history will be made once again if Mr. Obama is re-elected because this time around his message of hope, change, and pluralism will have to be based on more practical policy decisions that he has actually made while President. He will have to not only symbolically refer to his mixed heritage, but he must demonstrate that his policies have reached across different groups and political ideologies to construct a new American majority. Rhetoric alone will not suffice in his bid for re-election. Second, because Mr. Obama used (see Miletsky, Chapter Eight) his biracial heritage strategically in the first campaign to suggest that he could be "post-racial," he must now demonstrate to both white people and people of color (especially African Americans and Latino people) that he has shifted perceptions of racial discourse in a positive direction. If U.S. citizens do not believe that attitudes about racial equality have changed (even if in perception and ideology only) then Mr. Obama's chances of re-election are likely to be slim.

Third, the economic situation in the country is worse than it has been since the Great Depression. If white people and people of color do not see their economic conditions as linked then there will likely be a repeat of previous historical moments when certain groups were blamed for our economic trouble. If class and racial inequalities are not carefully discussed in the 2012 campaign, President Obama will very probably lose the support of independent and young voters. Fourth, over the last three years we have witnessed an enormous cultural change in this country by electing a person of color to the White House. This has brought both positive and negative change. If President Obama is re-elected there is sure to be a continuation of racial progress (albeit limited) in one way or another because of his background and presidential legacy. If he is not re-elected it may signal that the nation is not truly ready to continue on this road of cultural change and that the battle for a new American majority will have to be put on hold as citizens align themselves with different political camps. Finally, the global significance of Mr. Obama's election should not be forgotten. That the world, not just the U.S., celebrated his victory is revealing. Here too, Mr. Obama's mixed heritage played a vital role in global perceptions (see Chapter Six) where he was virtually claimed by every nation from Kenya—the place of his father's birth, to Obama Japan, to

Indonesia, and Ireland. His re-election on a global scale will have the potential to develop a new paradigm for dealing with the most pressing social problems facing society. How he approaches these issues will all be affected by his own lived experience as a biracial man of African, Native American, and European descent.

This book has examined the ways in which President Obama's biracial identity functioned during his bid for the White House as well as during his first three years in office. The United States is at an important cross-road—where the American majority, certainly once dominated by a white racial hierarchy, is now potentially beginning to shift. This shift, though, is not simply because a person of color was elected to the highest office in the country, some say in the world. This shift is also about Mr. Obama's ability to build a critical mass coalition of supporters which was also a first in U.S. history. Today the climate of the country is shifting. Time and the 2012 re-election campaign will tell if we are inching any closer to a new American majority.

References

Farnham, TJ. (1840) *Life, Adventures and Travel in California,* cited from 'The Social Construction of Race: Some Observations on Illusion, Fabrication, and Choice' by Ian F. Haney Lopez *Harvard Civil Rights-Civil Liberties Law Review* 1 1994.

Foucault, M. (1972) *Power/Knowledge: Selected Interviews and Other Writings, 1972-1977,* New York: Pantheon Books.

Friedman, E. (2008) 'Is Being Biracial an Advantage for Obama', from ABC News (http://abcnews.go.com/Politics/Vote2008/Story?id=4490194&page=1).

Huie, WB. (1956) 'The Shocking Story of Approved Killing in Mississippi', *Look* 20 (24 January 1956), pp. 46-50, cited from Devery Anderson "Emmett Till Murder," (www.emmetttillmurder.com/).

Ifill, G. (2009) *The Breakthrough: Politics and Race in the Age of Obama,* Norwell, MA: Anchor Press.

Lopez, Haney IF. (2003) 'The Social Construction of Race: Some Observations on Illusion, Fabrication, and Choice', in *Mixed Race America and the Law* Kevin R. Johnson (ed), New York: New York University Press. Originally Published by *Harvard Civil Rights-Civil Liberties Law Review* 1, 1994.

Sherrod, S. (2010) 'Shirley Sherrod Resigns from USDA over Race Remark Furor', posted by David S. Morgan, *CBS News* (www.cbsnews.com/8301-503544_162-20011026-503544.html).

West, C. (2010) 'Interview with Tavis Smiley' (www.pbs.org/wnet/tavissmiley/interviews/princeton-professor-dr-cornel-west-2/).

Wilson, S. (2008) *Research is Ceremony: Indigenous Research Methods*, Toronto: Fernwood Publishing.

Wise, T. (2010) 'Imagine if the Tea Party Was Black' (www.examiner.com/civil-rights-in-washington-dc/tim-wise-imagine-if-the-tea-party-was-black).

Index

Page numbers followed by 'n' refer to information in a note.

Ireland and Obama's flexible
racialization 113-25
bloodline criteria for citizenship
121-2
Irish Americans and Obama's Irish
roots 118-19, 120, 124
Islam
anti-Muslim responses 20-2, 61-2
Muslim experience as positive asset
106

J

Jackson, Reverend Jesse 35, 146, 157,
193
Jeter, Mildred 37
Jim Crow laws and segregation 32, 36,
86-7, 88
John Birch Society 91
Johnson, James Weldon 149
Johnson, Lyndon 42
Johnston, M.P. 32-3
Jones, Van 198
Joyner, James 179-80
justice
and radical love 219-20
see also social justice

K

Kearney, Falmouth (great, great
grandfather) 118, 122
Kennedy, Edward 12
Kennedy, Robert 15
Khanna, Nikki 152-3
Kich, George 117, 123
kin-aesthetics and mixed race people
129-39
Kina, Laura 132
King, Dr. Martin Luther, Jr. 34, 81,
193, 208
Koch, Charles G. 91
Koch, David H. 91
Koch, Fred 91
Korgen, Kathleen 152, 207
Kwan, SanSan 66

L

Latina/o group

and mixed race identity 149
and return of segregation in schools
198-9
and unemployment levels 198
law enforcement and skin color 39,
46, 160-1
Lee, General Robert E. 42
Lewinsky, Monica 10-11
Li-lan and kin-aesthetics 129-39
identity in work 135-7
and self-identification as Asian
American 133-4
Limbaugh, Rush 42, 90-1, 212, 213
liminality 14-15, 36, 76, 123, 148,
159, 163
Lippman, Walter 64
Lipsitz, G. 32
literature
mixed race autobiographies 65-6,
75-6, 138, 149
and Obama's search for identity 70
Livingston, R.W. 39
Locke, Alain 64
Logan, Enid 115-16
Logan, Rayford 81
Lopez, Haney I.F. 206
love: radical love 218-20
Loving vs. Virginia 36-7, 152, 192, 217
Lowe, Lisa 134

M

McBride, James 65
McCain, John 43, 44, 61, 196
McClain, Carol 153
Mackin, James 61
Madison, James 42
'Magic Negro' 90
Malcolm X 70, 149
'Marginal Man' thesis 5
marginalization and mixed race
identity
isolation and need to connect 137,
138-9
and movement across spaces 14-15,
135, 163
Obama on assumptions about 151
Obama's appeal for 'new majority'
16-17, 20, 218
power and 'either/or' binary 14-15,
32, 91
Marshall, Thurgood 40

white supremacy and racial purity
ideology 32, 86-7, 144, 207-8
white racism 47, 91, 192-3, 212-13
see also blackness; skin color and
politics of inclusion
Wilder, L. Douglas 40
Williams, Mark 43, 197
Williams, Vanessa 41
Wilson, Joe 22-3, 46-7
Wilson, Shawn 217
Winant, Howard 3-4, 40
Wise, Tim 155, 211-12, 213-14
women *see* interracial intimacy and
marriage; mothers
Women for Obama networks 100
Works Progress Administration
(WPA) slave narratives 176-7
Wright, Reverend Jeremiah 14, 18-
19, 33, 146, 194
and kin-aesthetics and self-
identification 132, 134, 137
Obama's understanding and
explanation of sermons 34, 35,
62-3
and Republican election campaign
61-2
Wright, Moses (Preacher) 209

Y

Yun Gee 132

Z

Zeleny, Jeff 62-3
Zogby International 43